T0193870

DEMOCRACY
AND
ISLAM

DEMOCRACY AND ISLAM

TWO SYSTEMS OF GOVERNANCE

Bill KHAN

DEMOCRACY AND ISLAM
TWO SYSTEMS OF GOVERNANCE

iUniverse books may be ordered through booksellers or by contacting:

iUniverse
1663 Liberty Drive
Bloomington, IN 47403
www.iuniverse.com
1-800-Authors (1-800-288-4677)

ISBN: 978-1-5320-6954-3 (sc)
ISBN: 978-1-5320-6955-0 (e)

Print information available on the last page.

iUniverse rev. date: 02/22/2019

CONTENTS

INTRODUCTION

Samuel Huntington (1993) in his book "The Clash of Civilizations" put forward a hypothesis that human beings are divided along cultural lines defined by their civilization, the major contemporary civilizations being: Western, Islamic, Chinese, Japanese, Hindu. These are cultural blocks each with its own distinct set of values and these civilizations will split along cultural fault lines. In his subsequent book, "The Clash of Civilization and Remaking of World Order, (1996), Huntington discusses the origins of these civilizations, the causes and dynamics of cultural fault line wars and the question of "universal civilization", which is defined as the cultural coming together of humanity and the increasing acceptance of common values and beliefs. The most important distinctions among people, he maintains are not ideological, political or economic. They are cultural. People define themselves in terms of ancestry, religion, language, history, values, customs and institutions. They identify themselves with cultural groups: tribes, ethnic groups, religious communities, nations, and at the broadest level, civilizations. He maintains that a civilization-based world order would be based on societies sharing cultural affinities and cooperating with each other. Huntington concludes that nation states remain the principal actors in world affairs. Avoidance of a global war of civilizations depends on the world leaders accepting and cooperating to maintain the multicivilizational character of global politics. In his book "World Order" Henry Kissinger (2014) reveals his analysis of the ultimate challenge of the twenty first century: how to build a shared international order in a world of divergent historical perspectives, violent conflict, proliferating technology and ideological extremism. There is no consensus among the major actors about the rules and limits guiding this process, or its ultimate destination. The result is mounting tension. Kissinger explains the four systems of historic world order: the European system based on the Westphalian model of sovereign states with equal status within the system, the Chinese system based on traditional ideas of the Middle Kingdom as a great regional power, the Islamic system based on the idea of an *ummah* (community) founded on the religious supremacism of political Islam, and the democratic idealism of the United States. Kissinger argues for a balance of power as the outcome of to-day's struggling framework for international order. For international order to take hold and last, Kissinger argues, it must relate "power to legitimacy". Kissinger maintains that cultural (preferring this word to civilizations) aspects shape societies' world view but that culture "is not an impermeable barrier to a wider model of order" Hence Kissinger recognises the need to engage with civilizations rather than assert the inevitability of their clashing. Indeed, international problems are increasingly discussed by nongovernmental organisations, businesses and individual citizens. Hence foreign policy is impacted upon by people and not only by governments. Kissinger notes "that any system of world order, to be sustainable, must be accepted as just, not only by leaders, but also by citizens."

This book analyses two systems of governance: The European Model of democracy and Islam, and provides readers with an opportunity to assess Huntington's hypotheis and Kissinger's thesis as influencing the evolution of World Order. The reader is empowered to analyse the drivers in the evolution of World Order. Here are some questions which enable the reader to reach one's own conclusions regarding the future of World Order.

To what extent are national leaders of world powers likely to support Kissinger's vision of cultural change to seek out a way to international peace and cooperation? To what extent will a desire for a diverse and open society, devotion to human rights and democratic values act as drivers to build world peace and cooperation? To what extent will governments engage peoples and societies, the sources of legitimacy, to secure a balance of power that underpins international order? To what extent will individuals, civil societies, NGOs contribute momentum towards a balance of power in World Order? How will population growth and migration impact on the evolution of a universal civilization? To what extent could the compelling power of governments and individuals change the path of international relations in view of the power of transnational corporations?

1

Islam Differs from Democracy in Fundamental Aspects of Governance and Individual Rights

The Clash of Civilizations is a hypothesis that people's cultural and religious identities will be the primary source of conflict in the post-Cold War world. It was proposed by political scientist Samuel P. Huntington in a 1992 lecture at the American Enterprise Institute, which was then developed in a 1993 Foreign Affairs article titled "The Clash of Civilizations?" Huntington addresses a number of issues. However, his core argument is that conflict would occur because of cultural differences, rather than ideology or economics. The hypothesis is that Nation states will remain the most powerful actors in world politics in the near future and the clash of civilizations will dominate global politics. The fault lines between civilizations will be the battle lines of the future. The people of different civilizations have different views on the relations between God and man, the individual and the group, the citizen and the state, parents and children, husband and wife, as well as differing views of the relative importance of rights and responsibilities, liberty and authority, equality and hierarchy. These

1

differences are the product of centuries. They are more fundamental than differences among political ideologies and political regimes.

In his subsequent book, "The Clash of Civilizations and the Remaking of World Order," Samuel Huntington (1996) concludes that clashes between civilizations are the greatest threat to world peace. Hence an international order based on civilizations is the best safeguard against war. *Huntington argues that international cross civilization cooperation is a way of restoring peace. "World Order" by Henry Kissinger* followed in 2014. Four specific conceptions of "order" are identified by Kissinger: The European system based on its Westphalian model of sovereign states with equal status within the system; an Islamic system based on the idea of an *ummah* (community); a Chinese system based on the traditional ideas of the Middle Kingdom as a regional power and the American order. In this chapter the fundamental aspects of governance in Islam and Democracy are reviewed.

The Caliphate. The definition of a caliphate is the rule of land by an Islamic political leader. The word "caliph" comes from the Arabic Khalifa, meaning "successor." A "caliphate" is "government under a caliph." Caliphate governance is based on Islamic law (Sharia). Muslim society is regulated through Sharia.

Muslim countries use Sharia (Islamic Law) as Country law. The classic Sharia law text is based on the Classic Manual of Islamic Sacred Law, "The Reliance of the Traveller" written by Ahmad ibn Naqib al-Misri (died 1368 AD) (Amana publishers). It covers the political control of non-Muslims, prayer, jihad, inheritance, punishments and land use, legalities and theology. While the original document dates to the 14th Century it has been updated and has the approval of the Fiqh Council of North America and the authorative Al-Azhar Islamic Research Academy in Egypt. Sharia Law focuses primarily on the religious practice of Islam and includes sections on Trade, Inheritance, Marriage, Divorce and Justice which fall under civil law in a democracy.

Sharia is based on the sources: The Quran (the total collection of laws, deemed to be unchangeable, derived from direct quotes from Allah given to Muhammed and enshrined in 7th Century text is regarded as the eternal, literal word of Allah and Muhammed who is regarded as the last prophet. The Sunnah is a collection of writings documenting the traditions or known practices of the Prophet Muhammad, many of which have been recorded in the volumes of Hadith literature. These include many things that he said, did, or agreed to how he performed ablutions, how he prayed. The judgments he passed so that they were used for reference in future legal rulings. Many issues concerning personal conduct, community and family relations, political matters, etc. were addressed during the time of the Prophet, decided by him, and recorded. The Hadith contains the collection of sayings of Muhammad himself and narrations of the Companions about Muhammed. There are several versions of the Hadith, but the most commonly used is by Sahih Bukhari and Sahih Muslim, (Sahih meaning authorative). Many claim later additions (Kamguian 2001). Islam is 14% words of Allah (ie the Quran) and 86% words of Muhammed (ie The Sunna). The Sunna compliments the Quran and is essential for its proper understanding and to clarify where the Quran is silent. Other sources are the consensus (ijma) of the scholars of the orthodox community and the method of reasoning of Islamic Jurists by analogy on precedent cases (qiyas). Islamic scholars define "community" in different ways, depending on the situation: for example, ijma al-ummah is a consensus of the entire community, while ijma al-aimmah is a consensus by religious authorities.

There are also biographies (Sira, the most authoritative version is by Ibn Ishaq), the works of al-Ṭabari and others and accounts of the Maghazi (battles). Each law in Sharia is based on a reference to the Quran or to the Sunna. The overall norm is: The Quran does not allow freedom of individuals to have an opinion: "When Allah and His Messenger have decreed a matter, they (the believers) should not have any option in their decision. And whoever disobeys Allah and His Messenger, he has indeed strayed into a plain error" Quran 33:36. Sharia is divine and unchangeable. Islamic Law is regarded as expressions of God's command that must be obeyed absolutely, without doubts, without questions and without qualifications. However, some interpretation of the Quran and Sunna are needed and this is the task of the Fiqh. They founded schools of interpretation, four of which survive till to-day:

1. Malik ibn Abbas (d. 795), one of the last survivors of the Prophet in Mecca. His work (Muttawa) has been adopted by Muslims in Africa except Lower Egypt, Zanzibar and S. Africa.
2. Abu Hanifa (d. 767) in Iraq, is followed by Muslims in India and Turkey.
3. Al-Shafi (d. 820) whose work is taught in Iraq and Egypt, in Indonesia, Lower Egypt, Malaysia and Yemen.
4. Ahmand ibn Hanbal (d. 855) born in Bagdad. His works are followed by the Wahhabis in Saudi Arabia

The "Doctors of Law" (the *ulama*), have the power to deduce from the Quran and Traditions, authorative solutions (Kamguian 2001). By the beginning of 900 A.D., Islamic law became rigidly and inflexibly fixed because, to quote Schacht 1964, "the point had been reached when the scholars of all schools felt that all essential questions had been thoroughly discussed and finally settled, and a consensus gradually established itself to the effect that from that time onwards no one might be deemed to have the necessary qualifications for independent reasoning in law, and that all future activity would have to be confined to the explanation, application, and, at most, interpretation of the doctrine as it had been laid down once and for all." This closing of the gate of independent reasoning, in effect, meant the unquestioning acceptance of the doctrines of established schools and authorities. Islamic law "became increasingly rigid and set in its final mould." This is a major factor why there has been so little intellectual progress in Muslim societies, why critical thought has not developed. Throughout Islamic history, but especially in recent times, the *ulama* have actively hindered attempts to introduce the idea of human rights, freedom, individualism and liberal democracy. The Sharia Law reflects the social and economic conditions of the time of the early Abbasids. Sharia law is the basis for political, religious and cultural life of all Muslims to-day. When a Muslim wears a headscarf, that is in obedience to Sharia.

When hospitals treat Muslim women in special ways, that is obeying Sharia. When textbooks in democratic countries have to be vetted by Muslim organisations before they are used in schools, that is obeying Sharia. There is a need to understand Sharia: What it says and how it affects citizens living in democratic countries.

The Nature of Islamic Law.

1. The Quran and Sunna are regarded as expressions of God's commands. This means that commands are valid because they exist and not because of any rational basis. Moreover, commands are obeyed because this is required at Law not because there is a spiritual basis.

   Example: The Quran explicitly prohibits the taking of interest and Schacht explains: commercial life requires the giving and taking of interest. Hence devices were developed to circumvent the Quran. One device consists of giving real property as a security, allowing the creditor to benefit from it (ie get interest). Another device consists of a double sale. The prospective debtor sells to the creditor a slave for cash and immediately buys back the slave for a greater amount of cash.

2. All human acts are assessed on concepts based on what is obligatory, forbidden, reprehensible or recommended.
3. Islamic Law has a basis for material considerations but does not impose rules on the concerned parties such as fairness, justice, truth.
4. Since Sharia Law rests on the Muslim, all policy and administration of an Islamic State also rest with the Muslim. Such a state intentionally discriminates between Muslims and non-Muslims and in such a state a non-Muslim is not allowed to hold any political, social or business position above the Muslim.

Islam is based on five core concepts.

1. 1.Islam has a religious and cultural basis. Islamic doctrine is based on principles dealing with religion, politics, submission, kafirs and dualism. The Quran is what Mohammed said that the angel Gabriel said that Allah said. The Quran repeatedly says that all of the world should imitate Mohammed in every way. All commands come from Allah. Islam is a theocracy. The Quran does not allow individuals to be free to express an opinion, "When Allah and His Messenger have decreed a matter, they (the believers) should not have any option in their decision. And whoever disobeys Allah and His Messenger, he has indeed strayed into a plain error" Quran 33:36. According to verse 4:80 of the Quran, "Those who obey the Messenger obey Allah." Muhammed links his authority to Allah. Obeying Allah and obeying Muhammed were key instructions to his followers. Religious Islam is based on five requirements: testifying that there is no deity but Allah and that Muhammad is the Messenger of Allah, performing the prayers, paying the zakah, making the pilgrimage to the Kaba, and fasting in Ramadan. The Fatiha (first chapter) (Quran 1:1-7) is Islam's most common prayer, recited 5 times a day, "In the name of God, the Almighty, the Most Merciful. Praise be to God, the Lord of the worlds. The Almighty. The Most Merciful. Possessor of the Day of Judgement. You alone we serve and You alone we seek, not those who have incurred they wrought, nor the misguided." The Wahabis (Saudi) added "such as Jews and Christians."

2. Islamic Political ideology is founded on a concept of supremacy through the Prophet's hadith: *"al-islam ya`lu wa la yu`la"* (a hadith narrated by al-Rawyani, al-Daraqutni, al-Bayhaqi, and al-Diya from Aidh ibn Amr) "Islam dominates and is not dominated." Islam is a political ideology using principles from the book of Allah which exclude all other religions. It is written in Arabic which is hence called a "sacred" language. Quran 9:33 "It is He who has sent His Messenger (Muhammed) with

guidance and the religion of truth (Islam) to make it superior over all religions even though the Mushrikun (disbelievers) hate it" SAHIH INTERNATIONAL,SAHIH AL-BUKHARI, VOL 6, BOOK 65, NO 4557. Quran 3:110 "You are the best nation produced (as an example) for mankind. You enjoin what is right and forbid what is wrong and believe in Allah. If only the People of the Scripture had believed, it would have been better for them. Among them are believers, but most of them are defiantly disobedient." SAHIH INTERNATIONAL 5:56 "And whoever is an ally of Allah and His Messenger and those who have believed - indeed, the party of Allah - they will be the predominant." Bukhari (52:65). The Prophet said, "He who fights that Allah's Word, Islam, should be superior, fights in Allah's Cause," a reference to Jihad. Islam seeks supremacy over all governments: Saifur Rahman (2006), The Sealed Nectar p.227-228, "Embrace Islam. If you two accept Islam, you will remain in command of your country; but if your refuse my Call, you've got to remember that all of your possessions are perishable. My horsemen will appropriate your land, and my Prophethood will assume preponderance over your kingship." One of several letters from Muhammad to rulers of other countries. Indeed, Islam destroyed the Sassanid, Roman and Byzantine Empires as it conquered its way through the Middle East, Asia and North Africa. Quran 18:26, "He maketh none to share in His government." Political Islam promises the land of unbelievers (pagans, Jews, Christians) to Muslims: "And He made you heirs to their land and their dwellings and their property, and (to) a land which you have not yet trodden, and Allah has power over all things" 33:27; Bukhari 53:392.

3. The Quran is devoted to the division between those who believe Mohammed (Muslims), and those who do not, the kafirs (Kafir, singular; Kuffar (plural). Islam divides the world into two factions: The first, dar al-Islam, is the "realm of submission," the world where Sharia governs; the second, dar al-Harb (the realm of war), is the non-Islamic world. This division of the

7

Quran means that there are two points of view of the Quran, the view of the Muslim and the view of the kafir. Political Islam is the doctrine that relates to the unbeliever, the kafir. Islam's relationship to the kafir cannot be religious since a Muslim is strictly forbidden to have any religious interaction with them. Kafirs must submit to Islam in all politics and public life. Every aspect of kafir civilization must submit to political Islam. The success of Islam comes primarily from its politics. In thirteen years as a spiritual leader in Mecca, Mohammed converted 150 people to his religion, mostly from his family. When he became a political leader and warrior in Medina, Islam exploded in growth, and Mohammed became king of Arabia in ten years by killing all the pagan, Jewish and Christian communities.

Islamic supremacy. The fundamental belief is that Islam is superior to every other nation, culture, faith, government and society and that it is ordained by Allah to conquer and dominate them through Jihad.

The kafir is someone who rejects Allah and who does not believe in Muhammed as the final messenger of Allah. It refers to infidels, pagans, non-believers, non-Muslims. Not only does the Quran advocate religious superiority over the kafir (unbeliever), ie the kafirs go to Hell whereas Muslims go to Paradise, but its doctrine also demands that Muslims dominate the kafir in all politics and culture. Islam has a complete doctrine of how to treat the kafir. The Koran has 61% of its text devoted to the kafir. The Sira has about 75% of its text devoted to the kafir and jihad. The religion of Islam is what is required for a Muslim to avoid Hell and enter Paradise. A kafir is not only a non-Muslim, but also a person who falls under a different moral code from the Muslim. The political system determines how they are defined and treated. Non-believers have several names.

Christians and Jews are called People of the Book or infidels. Other religious names for non-Muslims are atheist, polytheist, and pagan. But the Quran uses one word that includes all of the religious names. That name is kafir, an Arabic word. Kafir is usually translated as unbeliever. However the word "unbeliever" is a neutral word. The Quran defines the kafir by how it speaks of them and treats them. Kafirs can be robbed, murdered, tortured, enslaved, crucified. A Muslim cannot be killed for killing a kafir.

4. Another fundamental core concept is Submission. Islam means submission and Muslim means one who has submitted. Submission is political, as well as religious. Islam demands that non-Muslims (kafirs) submit in every aspect of public life. Every part of kafir culture is an offense to Allah. Hence, Islamic law unambiguously splits the world into two perpetually warring halves: the Islamic world versus the non-Islamic, and holds that it is God's will for the former to subsume the latter.

5. Dualism. Political Islam has two different ways to treat kafirs demonstrating dualistic ethics. Kafirs can be abused in the worst ways or they can be treated like a good neighbour. As an example, here is a verse from the Koran. Quran: 109:2 "I do not worship what you worship, and you do not worship what I worship. I will never worship what you worship, and you will never worship what I worship. You to your religion, me to my religion". This sounds very tolerant, but this verse was abrogated by a later verse: Quran: 9:5 "When the sacred months are passed, kill the kafirs wherever you find them. Take them as captives, besiege them, and lie in wait for them with every kind of ambush. If they submit to Islam, observe prayer, and pay the poor tax, then let them go their way. Allah is gracious and merciful." This is total intolerance. This contradiction occurs several times in the Quran. The solution to contradiction is called abrogation of the former verse where the later verse "is

9

better than the earlier verse". The logic here is very important. Since Allah is perfect and the Quran is the exact words of Allah, then both contradictory verses are true, but the later verse is better or stronger. This leads to dualistic logic where two contradictory facts can both be true.

What is Democracy? The word democracy is a composite of two words: `demos`, meaning the masses or people, and `kratia` meaning to rule. Democracy is a form of government in which power is invested in the people and exercised directly by them or by their elected agents through a free electoral system.

Democracy implies that the people must take responsibility for choosing rulers and representatives for the maintenance of their own `rights` against the possible encroachment of government which the citizen has sanctioned to act for him in public matters. The system is a rule of law where all citizens, including those in leadership, are equally subject to laws of a country. Citizens are allowed active participation in all political and civil processes. The principle demands that elected public officials conduct business in line with the needs and demands of the people. The officials are subject to elections at intervals prescribed by law and cannot extend their stay in public office without procedural authorization from the electorate.

In a democracy there is separation of state and church powers, ie democracy is secular. Michael Crozier, Samuel P. Huntington, Joji Watanuki (1975), IN: "The Crisis of Democracy" believe that democratic systems are viable provided that the public truly understands the nature of democracy system and particularly if they are sensitive to the subtle interrelation between responsibility and liberty. In Europe the European Commission for Democracy through Law, better known as the Venice Commission as it meets in Venice, is the Council of Europe's advisory body on constitutional matters. The role of the Venice Commission is to provide legal advice to its member states and, in particular, to help states wishing to bring their legal and institutional structures into line with European standards and international experience in the fields of democracy, human rights and the rule of law. It also helps to ensure the dissemination and consolidation of a common constitutional heritage, playing a unique role in conflict management, and provides "emergency constitutional aid" to states in transition. The "Rule of Law" Checklist (2016) of the Council of Europe provides guidance in the European Union.

In a democracy there is a separation of powers. The framers of the European and the U.S. Constitution built a system that divides power between the three branches of government: legislative, executive and judicial, and included various limits and controls on the powers of each branch, with all these bodies subject to the rule of law. A system of checks and balances in government was developed to ensure that no one branch of government would become too powerful. Checks and balances operate throughout a democratic government, as each branch exercises certain powers that can be checked by the powers given to the other two branches. "There are two principles implied in the concept of the rule of law, one is that government is to be conducted according to law. The other principle is that the Law is sovereign and supreme, and is to be obeyed by all authorities of the State. These principles are enshrined in the Constitution, and all power of the State is subject to law. The rule of law is the pillar of a democratic state.

The democratic political system framework consists of the executive (government), the legislative (parliament), and the judicial. There is a separation of powers between the executive, the legislature and the jury and this separation of powers must be clear and real. Checks and balances prevent the accumulation of power in any of the three branches. Transparency and accountability underpin the functions of these three areas. The President, Parliament, Cabinet, the Judiciary and the Ombudsman should have an institutional position that is strong enough to provide sufficient checks and balances. Power should not be concentrated in the Prime Minister. When the Prime Minister has effective control over all levers of government, checks and balances are weak.

The president should have sufficient power to act as a check and balance. The separation of power between Prime Minister and President must be real. Hence attainment to this position cannot be by appointment by the Prime Minister but potentially by election by a qualified majority. The independence of the Judiciary must be guaranteed which means they cannot be appointed by the Prime Minister.

The Attorney General cannot serve as the government 's lawyer providing advice to government when he also has the duty to prosecute members of the government.

The Police Commissioner must be independent in order to investigate wrongdoing effectively. This means that the appointment of police commissioner should be through an independent evaluating selection committee.

The media and civil society should have the freedom of a strong voice. Civil Society has the right to hold government accountable.

In the US the system is more complex than in Europe. The executive branch in the US, through the Federal agencies, has responsibility for day-to-day enforcement and administration of Federal laws. These Federal departments and agencies have missions and responsibilities that vary widely, from environmental protection to protecting the Nation's borders. The President in the executive branch can veto a law, but the legislative branch can override that veto with enough votes. The legislative branch makes laws, but the judicial branch can declare those laws unconstitutional. The legislative branch has the power to approve Presidential nominations, control the budget, and can impeach the President and remove him or her from office. The executive branch can declare Executive Orders, which are like proclamations that carry the force of law, but the judicial branch can declare those acts unconstitutional. The judicial branch interprets laws, but the President nominates the Supreme Court justices, court of appeals judges, and district court judges who make the evaluations. The judicial branch interprets laws, but the Senate in the legislative branch confirms the President's nominations for judicial positions, and Congress can impeach any of those judges and remove them from office.

Overall, the system has functioned as it was intended both in the US and in Europe, ensuring that the three branches of governance are in balance. The real test lies in whether the persons chosen to lead those institutions are fully committed to the values of integrity, honesty, objectivity and strength of character to uphold those same values, especially when challenged by those who appointed them in the first place. It is critical in a democracy that all the country's citizens, without exception and without any shadow of doubt, should have the firm belief that there existed within the state the necessary checks and balances to ensure the supremacy of law. Writing in the early part of the fifth century, St Augustine asked rhetorically, *'Remota iustitia, quid sunt regna nisi magna latrocinia?'* – 'If you remove justice, what would States be but big bands of thieves?' (De Civ. Dei IV, 4).

Democracies may be either direct or indirect. In a direct democracy, the people vote directly on public policy through referendums. In a direct democracy, any and all citizens may act directly to enact public policy without the intermediary step of an elected official. In an indirect democracy, also called a representative democracy, and a republic, the will of the people is enacted by elected officials. Free elections, the involvement of the public in all aspects of civic life, upholding human rights and the equal application of law to all citizens are cornerstones of democratic societies. The power of elected representatives in indirect democracies is normally checked by a constitution.

Today, all Western-style democracies (except Switzerland which has Direct Democracy), are forms of an indirect democracy. In a democracy, the people possess the ultimate power, while a dictatorship is a government in which the ruler possesses all the power. In a democracy, freedom of thought, speech and press, the right to argue, the freedom to present another side of an argument are fundamental rights. Trade, inheritance, marriage (suitable partners, legal rights, custody), divorce and justice fall under Civil Law in a democracy.

When the word of God determines the ultimate code of conduct, Democratic Governance and Human Rights have no place. Hence alternatives are not possible. Democracy therefore works only within and between democratic nations. When a Democratic country harbours within it a non-democratic system of governance (a state within a state), Democracy sows the seeds of its own destruction. "Western ideas of individualism, liberalism, constitutionalism, human rights, equality, liberty, the rule of law, democracy, free markets, the separation of church and state have little relevance to Islamic cultures" said Samuel P. Huntington, in "The Clash of Civilizations?" (1993). Hence cultural differences are the underlying causes of fault lines between cultures (Huntington 1996).

The Islamic view of Democracy is enshrined in Quran 18:26, "He maketh none to share in His government." Allah shares his government with no one. http://www.tafsirq.com/en/2-al-baqara/verse-98. Democracy is heresy.

Shaykh Muhammed Saslih Al-Munajjid, IN: Concept of Democracy, 2015, https://islamqa. info/en/98134, maintains that: "Democracy is a system that gives the power of legislation to the people or to those who represent them (such as members of Parliament). Based on that, in democracy, legislative authority is given to someone other than Allah, rather it is given to the people and their deputies, and what matters is not their consensus but the majority. Thus what the majority agree upon becomes laws that are binding on the nation. What all Muslims must do, rulers and ruled alike, is adhere to the laws of Allah." He goes on to explain: "Allah has told us in His Book that legislative authority belongs to Him alone, and that He is the wisest of those who issue rulings and judgements." "He has forbidden the association of anyone with Him in His authority, and no one is better than Him in ruling", and quotes: "So the judgement is only with Allah, the Most High, the Most Great" Sahih International 40:12. "The command (or the judgement) is for none but Allah. He has commanded that you worship none but Him (i.e. His Monotheism), that is the (true) straight religion, but most men know not" Yoosuf 12:40. "Is not Allah the Best of judges?" Sahih International 95:8. "Say: 'Allah knows best how long they stayed. With Him is (the knowledge of) the unseen of the heavens and the earth. How clearly He sees, and hears (everything)! They have no Walee (Helper, Protector) other than Him, and He makes none to share in His Decision and His Rule' al-Kahf 18:26. "Do they then seek the judgement of (the Days of) Ignorance? But who is better in judgement than Allah for a people who have firm Faith?" Sahih International 5:50. Byoren Kessler (1920) IN: http://www.jpost.com/International/

Democracy-and-political-Islam-cant coexist, March 18, 2011, explains that Democracy and Islam cannot co-exist.

The Doctors of Law interpret the application of the words of Allah and His Prophet. It is only in certain narrowly defined limits, fixed by God Himself that one can use a kind of reasoning known as qiyas, reasoning by analogy. The decisions of the learned having the force of law rest on the infallibility of the community (the Ummah), an infallibility that God Himself conferred through Muhammed on his community (Bousquet, Hurgronje, Schacht, quoted by Kamguian 2001). Hurgronje (a major Islamic scholar) argued that Islamic Law "aimed at controlling the religious, social and political life of mankind in all its aspects, the life of its followers without qualification and the life of those who follow tolerated religions to prevent their impact on Islam." Several philosophers and scholars have provided insights. Bertrand Russell (1920) regarded the Totalitarian nature of Islam in "The Practice and Theory of Bolshevism" where he argued that Bolshevism is to be reckoned with Mohammedanism rather than Christianity, p5,114-115. Albert Speer (Hitler's Minister of War) (1969), IN: Inside the Third Reich: Memoirs, p115 related that Hitler decried that Europe was Christian "Why did it (Europe) have to have Christianity with its meekness and flabbiness?" Carl Jung (psychology analyst), "We do not know whether Hitler is going to found a new Islam. He is like Muhammed. Other scholars, intellectuals and writers are G.H. Bousquet, Schacht, Monnerot, Manfred Halpern (Totalitarianism and Fascism. Islam seeks to alter the social order of the whole world and rebuild in conformity to its own ideals), Maxime Rodinson (archaic fascism defined as totalitarianism brutally enforcing the moral and social order), Voltaire and William Montgomery Watt. Ibn Warraq (2003), writes, "Orientalism taught an entire generation of Arabs the art of self-pity, encouraged the Islamic fundamentalist generation of the 1980s and bludgeoned into silence any criticism of Islam."

The tenets of Sharia Law (relevant verses in brackets):

1. While all legislative powers are vested in Parliament (Congress in the US), in Sharia Law the source of legal rulings is Allah (w42.3; w50.4).
2. The Powers of Parliament (Congress in the US) include levying taxes, to make laws, to declare war. In Sharia Law it is obligatory to obey the commands and interdictions of the caliph even if he is unjust because the purpose of his authority is Islamic Unity. (025.5)
3. In a democracy (Europe, US) no religious test is required as a qualification to any public office. In Sharia Law, a caliph must be a Muslim, male, of the Quraysh tribe, etc. (025.0).
4. In a democracy, Government officers are removed if found guilty of bribery or other high crimes. In Sharia Law there is no provision for removal of the Caliphate.
5. The Constitution and Laws of a democratic country (Europe and the US) are the supreme law of the land and judges are bound by them. In Sharia Law the source of legal rulings is Allah a1.1.
6. Parliament (Congress in the US) shall make no law regarding religion or abridging freedom of speech. In Sharia Law non-Muslims are obliged to comply with Islamic rules that pertain to safety, indemnity of life and property, are forbidden to display wine or pork, their religion or display feast days and funerals, are forbidden to build new churches and may not enter a mosque without permission. Non-Muslims are denied legal protection if the non-Muslim commits adultery with a married woman, leads a Muslim away from Islam, kills a Muslim, says anything derogatory about Allah, the Prophet or Islam (o11.5 to 0.11.10).
7. The US Constitution (amendment 2) states that: the right of people to keep and bear arms shall not be infringed. Europe does not allow citizens to keep arms. Sharia Law requires that someone buying weapons be of a people who are not at war

with Muslims. (k1.2(f)). Sins include selling weapons to non-Muslims. (w52.1 (192).

8. US Constitution Amendments 4-8 prohibit unreasonable searches, excessive fines, cruel treatment. Amendment 4 provides for equal protection of the laws for all citizens. In Sharia Law: no testimony may be made by people who have low jobs as street sweeper and bath attendant or non-Muslims (o24.2-3). Testimony regarding fornication or sodomy requires four male eye witnesses to the act. (o24.9).; a woman's testimony is worth half that of a man. (o24.10). There is no provision for a jury trial under Sharia Law. Cruel and unusual punishments under Sharia include: stoning for adultery (o12.2); 40 lashes with hands, or whip for drunkenness (o16.3;3) severing right hand for theft over 36 dollars and left foot for a repeat (o14.1); death for apostacy (o8.2). Indemnity (compensation) for accidentally killing a male Muslim is 100 camels or 4,235 grams of gold. A woman receives half of that. For killing a Jew or Christian it is one third of the indemnity paid for a Muslim man; for killing a Zoroastrian it is one fifteenth of that of a Muslim; Jews and Christians are subject to a poll tax not less than 1 dinar (144 dollars) per adult male per year. (o11.4). This is a penalty for remaining in their religion instead of embracing the "religion of truth" (o9.8); a husband may beat a rebellious wife for not allowing immediate sexual intercourse when he asks for it, if she can physically endure it; answering him coldly; being averse when previously she was kind (m5.1; m10.12). The only limitation is that he may not break her bones, wound her or cause bleeding. The concept is beating her "into subjugation."

9. Slavery and involuntary servitude are abolished by US Amendment 13; Sharia Law retains slavery (k32.0; w13.1).

10. European and US Constitution allow the manufacture, sale and transport of alcoholic beverages. Sharia makes it unlawful to sell grapes to someone who will make wine from them (k4.9). "Allah cursed whoever drinks wine, gives it to others to drink, presses

it, transports it, receives it, eats its price." Sins include drinking wine or other toxicant and serving it (O16.6; w52).

The Principles on which Democracy is based are: individual freedoms and civil liberties; Rule of Law; sovereignty resting upon the people; equality of all citizens before the law; vertical and horizontal accountability for government officials; transparency of the ruling systems to the demands of the citizens; equality of opportunity for citizens. This approach emphasises civil liberties, human rights and freedoms, instead of over-reliance on elections and formal institutions of states. These, not the sword, not guns, shape the state. Ibn Warraq IN: http://www.westminster-institute.org/articles/the-superiority-of-western-values-in-eight-minutes/ argues for the superiority of western values in providing liberty.

Governance. Governance in Europe is based on Democratic Principles and The Universal Declaration of Human Rights of 1948. Democracy includes voting and respect for election results, but it also requires the protection of liberties and freedoms, respect for legal entitlements, and the guaranteeing of free discussion and uncensored distribution of news. Western society is governed by a democratically elected parliament; society is regulated by legislation (made by parliament) and by an independent judiciary.

In contrast to Democracy, a Caliphate uses the revealed words of God to govern, ie a Caliphate is a theocracy. Islamic Law is created through revelation (Schacht 1982 p. 4). Islamic Law, as we know it had acquired its essential features by AD 750, early Abbasid dynasty (Schacht 1982 p. 49) and was further consolidated by schools of scholars of that time (Schacht 1950). Reliance of the Traveller, compiled by Ahmad ibn Niqib al-Misri (d. 1368), is the Classical Manual of Islamic Sacred Law (Umdat Al-Salik) or Sharia which literally means "well-worn camel path to the watering place" and has been termed the "Sacred path." It provides Muslims with religious and political guidelines. It is derived from commands in the Quran (19%) and the example of Muhammed (85%). This "classic manual of Islamic Sacred Law" was translated into English by Nuh Ha Mim Keller in 1991.

While European Law is Human and Changing, Caliphate Law is unchangeable because the Islamic concept of law maintains that the Quran is an expression of the divine will as revealed to Prophet Muhammed. Hence Islam does not consider Western concepts such as Human Rights. At the core of Western Democracy is freedom of expression, an independent and free media and Human Rights. Critical thinking has no place in Islam. While one of the fundamental principles of Democracy is the separation of church and state, this is denied in a Caliphate. Secular jurisprudence of Western societies distinguishes between criminal and civil law. Unlike secular jurisprudence of Western societies that distinguishes between criminal and civil law, the Sharia does not address criminal law. The idea of Criminal guilt does not exist in Sharia. There is no general concept of penal law in Islamic Law (Schacht 1982, p. 187). Schacht explains: "In what we would call penal law, Islamic law distinguishes between the rights of God and the rights relevant to humans and only the rights of God entail a penal sanction in the proper meaning of the term. At the centre of penal law, the idea of a claim on the part of god predominates, just as if it were a claim on the part of a human plaintiff." The rights or claims of God (Hadd) cover acts forbidden by the Quran (crimes against religion/Hadd crimes also called Hudud crimes), have the character of a penal law, of a law which imposes penal sanctions on the guilty. These include unlawful intercourse (zina), drinking wine, some forms of theft, highway robbery are Hadd crimes. No pardon or amicable settlement is possible (Schacht 1982, p. 206,176), are punished by public death by stoning, crucifixion or sword, flogging, cutting off hands or feet (Schacht 1982, pg 178). The other division of penal law is private vengeance (relating to humans/ Hakk Adami raised by the person concerned), existing as "redress of torts" which existed among the tribes of pre-Islamic Arabia. Whatever damage has been caused, it is regarded as a private matter (Schacht 1982, p.207). There is no fixed penalty for causing damage to a person or one's property, but only the exact reparation of the damage caused. Islamic law prescribes a retaliatory punishment analogous to the crime (qisas) or monetary compensation (diya), and for other crimes the form of punishment is left to the judge's discretion (tazir). Example: exact equality for loss of a hand, foot or tooth; loss of seeing power of an eye with a red hot needle. Murder is not a Hadd crime. Quran verse 2:178 establishes a law of retaliation (qisas) for murder: equal recompense must be given for the life of the victim which can take the form of blood money (diyah). Payment for killing a woman is half of that to be paid for killing a man. The payment for killing a Jew or a Christian is one third of that paid for killing a male Muslim (Spencer, 2009; Ahmed ibn Naqib al-Misiri, 2001). The Iranian Sufi Sheikh Sultan Hussein Tababeh, one of the founders of the legal codes explains that if a Muslim male commits adultery, his punishment is 100 lashes, shaving his head and one year banishment but a non-Muslim male who commits adultery with a Muslim woman is executed because this is regarded as sacrilege. Abortion without the father's consent involves payment of 500 dirham. Special measures include killing a male apostate and beating a woman apostate every three days (Schacht 1982 p.186-187). The notion of an individual, a moral person who is capable of taking rational decisions and accepting moral responsibility for one's free acts is fundamental in a Democracy but lacking in a Caliphate where ethics is based on obeying orders. Of course, there is the notion of an individual who has legal obligations, but not in the sense of an individual who may freely set the goals and contents of his life and decide what meaning one wants to give to one's life. In a Caliphate, it is God and theocratic Rule which set limits as to the possible agenda of one's life. Western legislation does not address matters considered an individual's private matters. In contrast, a Caliphate covers both religious and non-religious aspects of life. Democracy functions by critical thinking, discussion and rational thought. Critical thinking, critical analysis and the right to ask questions of all institutions by the people, is a cornerstone of Democratic governance, a basis on which Democracy functions. Governance in a Caliphate is based on the words of god and is unchanging. Unlike Western society, Sharia imposes laws on all aspects of life. It is a system of morals, religious observance, ethics, and politics that covers both religious and non-religious aspects of life for Muslims. It imposes laws on several aspects of life such as food, diet, medicine, education, as well as personal matters such as marriage, sexual conduct and dress, diet, fasting and prayer, agricultural contracts, lodging of slaves. These are considered an individual`s private matters where Western legislation will not intrude.

The Declaration of Human Rights. At the core of Western Democracy is The Universal Declaration of Human Rights. The Universal Declaration on Human Rights (UDHR) was proclaimed at UNESCO in 1981.

Since Loche`s development of human rights, three points are claimed by advocates of human rights: "(1) These rights are fundamental, (2) these rights cannot be relinquished, transferred or forfeited (ie they cannot be alienated from anyone by anything or anyone, since (3) they are rights that human beings have simply because they are human beings and independent from any varying social circumstances or degrees of merit." Men and women are seen as an autonomous individual, endowed by nature with certain inalienable fundamental rights that could be invoked against a government and should be safeguarded by it. Human rights are henceforth seen as elementary preconditions for an existence worthy of human dignity.

Iran declared that the UDHR could not be implemented by Muslims. In the year 1990 the Organisation of the Islamic Conference (which included 45 Muslim countries) passed the Cairo Declaration on Human Rights in Islam (CDHRI). With this, Muslim countries came to a political consensus on certain issues of doctrinal matters. In the Cairo Declaration the rights of women and of freedom of religion have glaring limitation. The Cairo declaration prohibits the *forced* conversion to Islam. Yet death for apostacy thwarts the freedom to change one`s religion. The prohibition of missionaries in practice thwarts the provision of choice and hence freedom of conscience.

Article 10 of the CDHRI states:

Islam is the religion of true unspoilt nature. It is prohibited to exercise any form of pressure on man or to exploit his poverty or ignorance in order to force him to change his religion to another religion or to atheism. This is in keeping with: Q2:257, "There must not be any coercion in matters of faith". This means that there should not be any compulsion or constraints in the matters of belief or *disbelief.*

Article 24 of the CDHRI states that it is "subject to the Islamic sharia." Article 25 confirms that sharia "is the only source of reference for the explanation or clarification of this Declaration. Sharia has supremacy over the Universal Declaration of Human Rights. This was supported by the then High Commissioner for Human Rights, Mrs Mary Robinson who wrote "We have agreed that for the purpose of this seminar, Islam is understood in terms of Sharia (Quran and Hadith). The Geneva based international Commission of Journalists (ICJ) strongly criticized the CDHRI at the OIC Summit Meeting of Heads of State and government in Dakar on 9 December 1991. The secretary general declared in a joint statement to the UNCHR for the ICJ and for the Paris-based International Federation for Human Rights (Feb. 1992): 1) It gravely threatens the inter-cultural consensus on which the international human rights instruments are based; 2) It introduces, in the name of the defence of human rights, an intolerable discrimination against both non-Muslims and women; 3) It reveals a deliberately restrictive character in regard to certain fundamental rights and freedoms, to the point that certain essential provisions are below the legal standard in effect in a number of Muslim countries; 4) It confirms under cover of the "Islamic Sharia (Law)" the legitimacy of practices, such as corporal punishment, that attack the integrity and dignity of the human being, (Reference: David G. Littman, National Review, 2003).

The United Nations Human Rights Council. This Council investigates allegations of breaches of human rights in UN member states and addresses important thematic human rights issues such as freedom of association and assembly, freedom of expression, freedom of belief and religion, Womens' rights, LGBT rights and the rights of ethnic minorities. Now Muslim countries that are members of the UN are signatories of the Cairo Declaration of Human Rights in Islam 1990 (CDHRI) NOT the Universal Declaration of Human Rights (UDHR) 1948.

Ibn Warraq, 2003, p.185, in support of Bernard Lewis, maintains that there is no difference between Islam and Islamic fundamentalism and that Islam is incompatible with democracy. Ibn Warraq, 2003 concludes that Islam will never achieve democracy and human rights if it applies Sharia and as long as there is no separation of church and state.

The Declaration of Human Rights (agreed to be the foundation of international Human Rights law), are: Article 1"All human beings are born free and equal in dignity and rights. They are endowed with reason and conscience and should act towards one another in a spirit of brotherhood." This article negates Bukhari (52:65): The Prophet said, "He who fights that Allah's Word, Islam, should be superior, fights in Allah's Cause". Muhammad's words are the basis for offensive Jihad - spreading Islam by force. Islam establishes a hierarchy of relative worth rather than a Law of Equality as found in a democracy. The tenets of this hierarchy are clearly set. (1) The Quran makes it clear that Islam is not about universal brotherhood, but about the brotherhood of believers: "The believers are but a single Brotherhood (49:10); Not all men are equal in Islamic Law. Slaves are not equal to free men (16:75-76). Muslim believers are not equal to non-Muslims. "Are those who know equal to those who know not" (39:09). "Is the blind equal to the one who sees? Or darkness equal to light?" (13:16). A believing slave is superior to an unbeliever (2:221) when selecting a wife. "Ye are the best of peoples, evolved for mankind, enjoining what is right, forbidding what is wrong and believing in Allah. If only the People of the Book (Christians and Jews) had faith, it were best for them: among them are some who have faith, but most of them are perverted transgressors" (3:110). Even Allah chooses to whom to show mercy. Verses 11:118-199 say that Allah does not bestow mercy on everyone, and chooses not to guide some people "And Allah is the direction of the way, and some (roads) go not straight, And had he willed he would have led you all right" (16:9). "Those who reject our signs, we shall cast unto the fire…" (4:56).

Article 2 "Everyone is entitled to all rights and freedoms set forth in this Declaration without distinction of any kind, such as race, colour, sex, language, religion, political or other opinions, national or social origin, property, birth or other status. No distinction shall be made on the basis of the political, jurisdictional or international status of the country or territory to which a person belongs." This negates the Islamic principle of supremacy over all religions and of Muslims over all others. Article 3 "Everyone has the right to life, liberty and security of person" This includes atheists and gay persons. It negates the privileges that Islam gives to husbands and rapists over the use of women's bodies. Article 4 "No one shall be held in slavery or servitude; slavery and the slave trade shall be prohibited in all their forms" Slavery is recognised in the Quran. The legal position of slaves is discussed in Schacht 1982, p.127 and Ibn Warraq, 2003, p.196. Sharia permits slavery. Moreover, Muslims are allowed to force sex with any of their female slaves (Quran 4:3). They are allowed to take possession of married women if they are slaves (Quran 4:28). Article 5 "No one shall be subjected to torture or to cruel, inhuman or degrading treatment or punishment." This includes amputations, crucifixion, stoning to death, floggings, cutting off hands and feet, wife beatings/physical violence of women and girls (marital rape, rape, assault for imagined infidelity, child brides, honour killing, female genital mutilation). Degrading treatment includes: putting women in a position of servitude towards their husband (such as: beating the wife; instilling fear in a wife). Article 6 "Everyone has the right to recognition everywhere as a person before the law." This means that a person can make choices and be held legally responsible for these. This concept is lacking in Islam because a Muslim must obey Sharia as is and not alter to suit choices. Articles 7, 8, 9, 10, 11 deal with the rights of an accused person. This includes recognition as a person before the law, with access to equal protection, access to a fair hearing by an independent tribunal, the right to be presumed innocent until proven guilty, the right to an effective remedy by competent national tribunals and protection against arbitrary arrest or exile. These only have a subordinate role in Islam. A Muslim can put his hand on the Quran and lie in favour of Islam and this is not a sin. Revenge for a killing and payment of blood money as recompense to the family of the victim (a form of tort) are excluded by these articles. The concept of criminal guilt is lacking in Islam. This Article requires that witnesses are bound by a code of ethics requiring truth (which excludes Taqiyya). This article requires that there is no discrimination on the basis of religion or female sex regarding the right to be a witness such as the Islamic condition that the testimony of a woman in a court of law is worth half that of a man.

The Islamic legal procedure does not have the tools to provide an impartial and fair trial. This goes against Articles 7, 8, 9, 10, 11 which deal with the rights of an accused person to a fair trial. It is a Democratic Right that an accused person has a fair trial. Sharia does not recognise trial by jury, discovery of evidence or legal representation. The legal procedure, under Islam cannot be regarded as impartial or fair, for in the matter of witnesses all sorts of injustices emerge. Non - Muslims living in Muslim countries have inferior status under Islamic law, they may not testify against a Muslim. For example, a Muslim may rob a non -Muslim in his home with impunity if there are no witnesses except the non-Muslim himself. The evidence of Muslim women is admitted only very exceptionally and then only from twice the number required of men. Revenge for a killing is officially sanctioned (though money as recompense is also possible). This is against Human rights. Article 12 states that no one shall be subjected to arbitrary interference with privacy, home or attacks on honour. Article 13 recognises the right to freedom of movement and residence. Article 14 provides that everyone has the right to seek and enjoy asylum from protection. Article 15 states that everyone has the right to a nationality. Article 16 deals with the rights of marriage of men and women, giving women equal rights to marry whom they wish or not to marry at all. This means that a woman is not put under an imposition to marry the man chosen for her by her parents or guardian. In Islam, women who marry a man other than the one chosen by her family or guardian are killed even if their marriage is legal and even if she is pregnant and wishes to reconcile with her family. She is killed by her father, brothers and uncles. This Article requires that a woman does not have a divorce position that is less advantageous than a man on the basis of female gender. In Islam the children are given to the husband and rights of divorce are not equal. Lack of equality for women includes: women are not free to marry whom they wish, the rights of divorce are not equal. They cannot marry a non-Muslim. Article 17 provides a right to own property. Article 18

"Everyone has the right to freedom of thought, conscience and religion. This right includes freedom to change one's religion or belief, and freedom, either alone or in community with others and in public or private, to manifest one's religion or belief in teaching, practice, worship and observance" and Article 19 "Everyone has the right to freedom of opinion and expression. In Islam for those changing to another religion (apostasy) or to none at all, the punishment is death. Moving away from Islam incurs losing one's rights, marriage declared null and void, children are taken away to be brought up by believers, forfeiting rights of inheritance. In Saudi Arabia, following a tradition of Muhammed who said "Two religions cannot exist in the country of Arabia," non-Muslims are forbidden to practice their religion, build churches, possess Bibles etc. Article 19 "Everyone has the right to freedom of opinion and expression. This right includes freedom to hold opinion without interference and to seek, receive and impart information and ideas through any media and regardless of frontiers". A Muslim may not convert to another religion. This would be apostasy which is punishable by death. Those who convert to Christianity and choose to stay in the Muslim country do so at great personal danger. The convert has most of his rights denied him. Identity papers are often refused him, so that he has difficulties leaving his country. His marriage is declared null and void, his children are taken away from him to be brought up by Muslims and he forfeits his rights of inheritance. Often the family will take matters into their own hands and simply assassinate the apostate. The family are, of course, not punished. The rights enshrined in articles 18 and 19 include: the right of (i) access to knowledge and dissipation of knowledge (ii) openly practicing one's chosen religion. Pluralism, the tolerance of opinion follows from this Article. Article 20 provides the right to peaceful assembly. Article 21 refers to a right to participate in government directly or through chosen representatives and periodic and genuine elections. Article 22 refers to the right to social security. Article 23 refers to the right to work. Article 23. "Everyone has the right to work, to free choice of employment, to just and favourable conditions of work and to protection against unemployment." This Article requires that women are free to choose their type of work and to have the freedom of working outside the home. Under Islamic Law women are not free to choose their work. Many Islamic sects forbid women from working outside their home. Women are excluded from several positions: head of state, head of armed forces, imam, judge. Orthodox Islam and many Islamic sects forbid women from working outside the home. Non - Muslims are not free to choose their work in Muslim countries, or rather certain posts are not permitted them. The relevant verses are "Allah does not give the disbelievers triumph over the believers" Quran 4:141. "Force and power belong to God and to His Prophet and to believers Quran 63:8. A recent example from Saudi Arabia makes the point. A group of Muslims working in a company owned by a Muslim were shocked when the Muslim owner appointed a new manager, who was a Christian. The Muslims demanded a religious ruling asking whether it was permissible under Islam to have a Christian in authority over them. A Sheikh Mannaa K. Al Qubtan at the Islamic Law College of Riyadh declared that it was intolerable under Islam that a non - Muslim should wield authority over Muslims. He pointed to two verses from the Koran to back up his argument, Sura 4:141 "Allah will not give the disbelievers triumph over the believers" and Sura 63:8 "Force and power belong to God, and to His Prophet, and to believers."

Article 24 refers to the right to rest and leisure. Article 25 refers to the right to an adequate standard of living. Article 26 refers to the right to an education. Article 27 refers to the right to participate in cultural life. Article 28 refers to social and international order. Article 29 states that everyone has duties to the community.

Schacht 1964, 1982, p. 130-132 explains the basis of Islamic Law towards unbelievers demonstrating inequality on the basis of religion through treatment of unbelievers as inferior citizens, which includes: denial of fair treatment at work; payment of a fixed poll-tax (jizya) and land tax (kharaj); prohibited from openly performing their worship or their distinctive customs, including drinking wine and eating pork; must not build new churches, synagogues, hermitages; are excluded from the specific privileges of believers: "The unbeliever cannot be a witness against a believer, he cannot be the guardian of his child who is a believer. A believer can marry an unbeliever but the children must be believers".

Blasphemy. In a Democracy there is no equivalent of blasphemy law as in Islam which addresses blasphemy towards God and religious persons and is punishable by death. Conversion to Christianity is regarded as blasphemy and the person is killed. Blasphemy towards God and the Prophet are punishable by death. In practice, blasphemy has become a tool for Muslim governments to silence opposition, or for individuals to settle personal scores in disputes. The commonest are disputes over water, property and jobs. Mobs play a significant role in enforcing blasphemy charges.

Equal Opportunity. Articles 23 and 26 collectively address Equal Opportunity. Article 26 deals with the right of education to full development of the human personality. This means that women have a right to an education to their full development and no fields of learning are denied to women. Islamic countries either deny women an education or bar them from some fields of learning. Women have full citizenship. These Articles recognise women as full, equal human beings, who deserve the same rights and freedoms as men and exclude polygamy. Women are not put under the obligation that the only option in life is to marry, obey their husbands, and stay out of public life altogether, because such attitudes do not permit a woman to develop as an individual in her own right, acquire an education or get a job. Islam has a clear message: "Men are in charge of women by (right of) what Allah has given one over the other and what they spend (for maintenance) from their wealth. So righteous women are devoutly obedient, guarding in (the husband's) absence what Allah would have them guard. But those (wives) from whom you fear arrogance, advise them, forsake them in bed, and (finally), strike them, Quran 2.228. But if they obey you (once more), seek no means against them. Indeed, Allah is ever Exalted and Grand" Sahih International 4:34;

Separation of church and state is Fundamental in Democracy: Secularism. This is denied in Islam. Defences of liberalism have been made by many scholars. Muhammed Ali (1769-1849) in Egypt was the first secularist in the Arab world. Prince Sabaheddin (d 1948) in Egypt advocated individualism and federalism. In Egypt, Ahmad al Sayyid (1872-1963) argued for a separation of powers. Zakariya, an Egyptian teaching at the University of Kuwait argues for rationalization, critical spirit and intellectual independence as universal values.

Contempt for human reason and the denial of critical thinking. Human reason and critical thinking are fundamental in a Democracy and necessary for scientific discovery, business and industrial progress. Islam continuously manifests hostility towards human reason, rationality, critical discussion without which democracy, scientific and moral progress are not possible. Islam does not accept the concept of cause and effect which is fundamental to scientific method. Hence a Muslim is not in a position to undertake scientific research because Scientific Method is based on investigating Cause and Effect.

Threats to governments are clear. Saifur Rahman, The Sealed Nectar p.227-228, "Embrace Islam. If you accept Islam, you will remain in command of your country; but if your refuse my Call, you've got to remember that all of your possessions are perishable. My horsemen will appropriate your land, and my Prophethood will assume preponderance over your kingship." One of several letters from Muhammad to rulers of other countries. The significance is that the recipients were not making war or threatening Muslims. Their subsequent defeat and subjugation by Muhammad's armies was justified on the basis of their unbelief. Similarly, "It has been narrated by Umar b. Al-Kittib that he heard the Messanger say: "I will expel the Jews and Christians from the Arabian Peninsula and will not leave any but Muslim" Sahih Muslim Book 019, Hadith No 4366. Muhammed accomplished this goal through genocide. Muslims are required to go to war with non-Muslims to conquer them and add their territory to the "House of Islam." Q.2:191, 9:5, 9:29. Q.9:5 and 9:29 are interpreted that the Quran permits genocide of non-Muslims. Muslims have been given a mandate to spread Islam world wide "until all chaos ends, and all religion belongs to Allah."

The Charter of Human Rights prohibits living off booty. Several verses clearly encourage booty. Narrated ibn Umar that the Prophet said, "My livelihood is under the shade of my spear, and he who disobeys my orders will be humiliated by paying Jizya." Sahih Bukhari vol iv p.104 "Under the shades of my spear" means "from war booty;" Narrated Jabir bin Abdullah "Allah`s Apostle said, "Booty has been made legal for me" Sahih Bukhari 4:53:351; Quran 8:68-69 "So enjoy what ye took in war/booty, spoils are lawful and good: but fear Allah, for Allah is Oft-forgiving, Most Mercyful" "The Apostle distributed the booty between his relatives, his wives and other men and women" Ishaq 522; "Allah made booty lawful and good. He used it to incite Muslims for unity of purpose. So enjoy what you have captured" Ishaq:327. "Allah saw what was in their hearts (what they coveted) so he rewarded them with victory and with as much spoil as they could take. Allah promised that they would soon capture a great deal of booty" Ishaq: 503; "We ask thee for the booty of this town and its people. Forward in the name of Allah" He used to say this of every town he raided Ishaq:510. "If people are obstinate, and refuse to surrender, know that Allah is your Supporter. And know that one fifth of all the booty you take belongs to Allah, and to the Messenger, and for the near relatives (of the Messenger)" Quran 8:40. "Allah addressed the believers and said, "In Allah`s Apostle you have a fine example for anyone who hopes to be in the place where Allah is" Ishaq 467. "Allah made booty lawful and good. He used it to incite the Muslims to unity of purpose. So enjoy what you have captured" Ishaq 237.

However, it was not only in raids that booty taking was encouraged. Individual assassinations rewarded the murderer. "I went up to a man and struck off his hand. He fell and I killed him while he was down. But I was too occupied with fighting to pay and more attention to him. So one of the Meccan Muslims passed by and stripped him. Then when the fighting was over and we had finished with the enemy, the Apostle said that anyone who had killed a foe could have his spoil. I told the Apostle that I had killed a man who was worth stripping but had been to busy killing others at the time to notice who had spoiled him. Abu Bakr said "To Allah`s lions who fight for his religion go the spoils that come from their prey. Return the booty to the man who killed him." The Apostle confirmed Abu Bakr`s words. So I was given the property of the man whom I had killed. I sold it and bought a small palm grove with the money. It was the first property I ever owned" Ishaq 571. Booty also came from raiding the trade caravans that plied the road from Mecca to Syria and back. "Abu Jandal, Suhal's son joined Abu Basir. Nearly seventy Muslim men gathered around and they harassed the Quraysh. Whenever they heard of a Meccan caravan setting out for Syria, they intercepted it and killed everyone they could get hold of. They tore the caravan to pieces and took the goods, Ishaq 508, Al-Tabari vol 8 p.91; As well as raiding caravans, whole communities were destroyed and their land and wealth captured as spoil. "Allah's Apostle besieged the Jewish community of Khazbar until they could not hold out any longer. Finally, fearing they would perish, they asked Muhammed to spare their lives and banish then instead. He did and took all their property" Ishaq 515; Al Tabari vol 8 p.128; "The messenger divided the wealth, wives and children of the Banu Qurayza Jews among the Muslims" Al Tabari vol 8 p.38; All the Jewish communities in Arabia suffered this destruction.

Impact of Islamic Colonialism on Human Rights. In a short time Islam conquered and established an empire from the Indus to the Atlantic in the West. Narrated Abu Huraira, "The Prophet said: "Khosrau will be ruined, and there will be no Khosrau after him, and Caesar will be ruined and there will be no Caesar after him, and you will spend their treasures in Allah's Cause. War is deceit" Sahih Bukhari 4:52, 268, 269; While European colonialism is regarded with disdain and Europeans are expected to feel ashamed, Muslims brag about their conquests. Yet the Arab conquests were achieved with extraordinary cultural costs. After the initial invasion by the Bedouin Muslim tribes, Syria's Christian communities realized this was not just a raid by desert nomads. In 634 AD Damascus fell to the Arab invaders with ensuing slaughter of Syria's Christians, burning churches, convents, monasteries, huge tracts of land expropriated and settled by the Muslim conquerors. The Byzantine civilization in Syria was at an end. The Hellenic and Christian cultures, the magnificent monasteries were further destroyed by Turkish invasions of 1060s and 1070s. Many fled, were captured, massacred and enslaved. In these modern times there has been kidnapping of Greek Orthodox and Syrian Orthodox

Archbishops of Aleppo, kidnapping of nuns in Maaloula, burning churches and rockets fired at Armenian schools in Damascus continue. The Iranian Zoroastrian religion has been obliterated. The Shah who had westernisation in mind was deposed and replaced by Ayatolla Komeini. Christianity in biblically historic lands as Iraq, Syria, and Turkey will disappear by 2030. The French invaded Algeria, but so did the Arabs and the Turks before them. In Algeria, the teaching of French ended because it was seen as a colonial language, yet Arabic is an imposed language. Arabic imperialism imposed Arabic language and Islamic culture, destroying the local language and culture throughout the Middle East and Asia. Berber language and culture in North Africa existed since 7000 BC, a rich culture of united tribes under Masinissa (202 BC) with its own language, script and history. The Berbers slowly converted to Islam not from religious conviction but for material selfinterest. Berber belongs to the Afro-asiatic (Semito-Hamitic) family of languages, with some 300 dialects. Kateb Yacine (1929-1989) rejected Arab and Islam imperialism in Algeria. He described the Algerian Arab-Islamism as an Algeria against itself. He wanted Algeria to be called by its name: Tamezgha and Berber not Arabic spoken. The Algerian language and poetry are suppressed and the Algerians are forced to learn Arabic. The Berber Spring occurred in 1980 when the Berbers rioted in favour of their language. In 1994 Berbers commemorated this with marches.

The present-day Muslims in India are the descendants of Hindu Converts; in Iran of Zoroastrians; in Syria of Christians; in Afganistan of Budhists; Millions in 57 countries have been forced to adopt a religion and culture that originated thousands of miles away in Arabia, to read a book in a language they do not understand. These people have lost their ethnicity and language that existed before they were colonized by islamization. The Arabs destroyed the culture and history of the conquered peoples. In contrast, the British in India gave back to all Indians their own culture such as intellectual works, architectural monuments including saving the Taj Mahal from ruin. The Arabs are the most successful colonial imperialists of all time since to be conquered by them and then be like them is still the way to be saved.

Impact of Sharia on Western Societies. Sharia Law emerged in 7th century Arabia. The political significance of Sharia for western democracies is profound. Western political institutions have no place under Sharia. Democratic elections and representative government are replaced by theocratic rule, ie sheikhs and imams issue fatwas (religious rulings) based solely on the religious 7th century texts. Muslims promoting Sharia in the West have sought, as a first step, the application of Sharia to family law. For countries with large Muslim minorities (France, parts of Scandinavia) autonomous Islamic communities have evolved where police and civil officials are (forcibly) excluded and Sharia is enforced within the community itself. This means that Sharia and Muslims become a state within a state.

In our Western Societies we appreciate our liberal constitutions, independent judiciary, independent and free media. Democracy offers us freedom, independence and Human Rights. Scientific research in all spheres of human endeavours has provided the knowledge that advanced our standards of living (Ibn Warraq, 2012).

Democracy has its limits: At its limits, Democracy sows the seeds of its own destruction.

Democracy works when a nation deals with another democratic country. Democracy sows the seeds of its own destruction when it harbours and supports elements which are contrary to the Charter of Human Rights, thus creating a state within a state. Islamists maintain that the terrorism they direct against the West is merely reciprocal treatment for decades of Western and Israeli oppression. Yet in writings directed to their fellow Muslims, this spirit is presented, not as a reaction to military or political provocation but as a product of religious obligation. The fact remains: Right and Wrong in Islam have little to do with universal standards but only with what Islam itself teaches, much of which is contrary to Western norms.

The Clash of Civilizations. In the original essay, Huntington's hypothesis is that: The conflicts of the future will occur along the cultural fault lines separating civilizations. The hypothesis predicts that people's cultural and religious identities will be the primary source of conflict in the post-Cold War world. Differences among civilizations are not only real; they are basic. Civilizations are differentiated from each other by history, language, culture, tradition and, most important, religion. The conflicts of the future will occur along the cultural fault lines separating civilizations. This points to major cultural fault lines between the two world cultures: Islam and Democracy. On Migration towards the EU, Huntington predicted that European societies will have great difficulties in integrating Muslim immigration and it remains uncertain if Muslim immigrants and their children want be integrated. Regarding Turkey, Huntington predicted that it will try to move from Islamic civilization to Western civilization since Mustafa Kemal Atatürk, but will probably fail and remain torn or return to an Islamic civilization under the Islamic leader Recep Tayyip Erdogan.

2

Contemporary Scenarios
in the Middle East

After the conquest of Arabia, Islam spread throughout the Middle East through conquest, slaughter and subjugation. The turmoil continues till to-day. Iman Rasool quoting Quran 3:26, "O Allah, Possessor of the Kingdom, You give the kingdom to whom You will and You take the Kingdom from whom You will and You endue with honour whom You will and You humiliate whom You will. In your hand is the Good. You are able to do all things." Referring to the conquests of Christian Byzantium and Zoroastrian Persia, he says the lesson has not been learnt. The Quran promises: "See they not, that We gradually reduce the land (in their control) from its outlying borders? Is it then they who will win?" Quran 21:44. So, who is winning in the Middle East wars?

Democratization of the Middle East

Democratization is the progressive political changes moving in the direction of democracy. What are the prospects for democratization in the Middle East? To what extent will the event in Tunisia, when a 26-year old Tunisian vendor light himself on fire influence other nations in the region? What regional differences impact on the likelihood and direction of progression towards democratisation? Differences in the nature of regimes, the degree of exposure to western civilization, poverty, oppression, the level of education of citizens, the strength of civic institutions including the strength of women's voices, culture and history are some of the forces that individually or collectively drive political change. The three dictatorship types, monarchy, civilian and military have different approaches to democratization as a result of their individual goals. Monarchic and civilian dictators seek to retain the power indefinitely through heredity rule in the case of monarchs or through oppression in the case of civilian dictators. A military dictatorship seizes power to act as a caretaker government to replace what they consider a flawed civilian government. Military dictatorships are more likely to transition to democracy. The transition is slow and may experience reversals. Democracy protests tend to lead to democratization. A study found that a quarter of all cases of democracy protests between 1989-2011 lead to democratization (Brancati 2016). Threat of civil conflict encourages regimes to make democratic concessions. Death of a dictator rarely ushers in democracy, rather the regime persists after the autocrat's death. An emerging trend is that high economic freedom increases the Gross Domestic Product/capita. A high GDP/capita also increases political freedom but political freedom did not increase GDP/capita.

Samuel P. Huntington in "The Third Waves." sees the Middle East passing through the three waves of Democratization. In the 15th Century it was part of the Ottoman Empire. In the 19th Century, when the empire finally collapsed towards the First World War, the Western armies moved in. However ethnic divisions complicate democratization. Edward Said identifies as orientalist 'the intrinsic incompatibility between democratic values and Islam and states that the Middle East lacks the prerequisites of democratisation (Posusney and Angrist 2005). Is the Middle East then locked into authoritarianism through its resilience?

Authoritarianism is challenged by a trigger that sets socio-economic changes. This may give rise to the formation of political parties and revision of constitutions, to militias or a return to authoritarianism. If political parties and a constitution form, citizens may still not be able to access their rights and freedoms equally, due to social, economic and cultural barriers. Constitutions may contain special guarantees for privileged groups.

The trigger for change in the Middle East was the event when a 26-year-old Tunisian vendor light himself on fire. This triggered the spread of popular Arab uprisings in Tunisia, Egypt, Libya and Yemen in 2011. Two dictators were overthrown: Ben Ali in Tunisia and Mubarak in Egypt. Protests in Tunisia, Egypt, Syria and in 2018 in Iran have focused on ending dictatorship and corruption, improving basic rights and material living standards. The factors which influence the evolving political scenario include the weakness of civil society and opposition political parties as these are persistently manipulated by the state. The autocratic Arab regimes have been adept to manipulating electoral processes through building patron client relationships and co-opting opposition. Opposition political parties, NGOs and trade unions are delegitimized and hence barely credible. The Arab world has a strong array of coercive institutions with strong capacity to repress democratic initiatives originating from society. There is strong dependence on representative militaries. Transitions have also begun much later, in an era of globalized capitalism. The current situation seems to be leading to the destruction of the state and hence no regime at all (Libya) or a transition to a hybrid regime (Tunisia, Egypt), rather than to a democracy or a reversal to a traditional Islamic State (Iran). Libya under Gaddafi and the Arabian Peninsula demonstrate the most restrictive rules of civil society actors. During his 42year tenure in office no political parties or civil society organisations were allowed to form. To-day there is no central authority. Only militias.

Regime change in the Arab world is emerging through new information and communication technologies (ICT), thus activists can bypass their repressive authoritarian regimes, thus enhancing the possibility of demonstrations as in Egypt and Tunisia, and promoting democratization through a "neighbourhood effect."

The Arab world does not have viable and attractive regional organisations capable of ensuring the existence of a secure community imposing political conditionality and rewarding conformity. The League of Arab States (formed in Cairo in 1945 including 22-member countries: Algeria, Bahrain, Comoros, Djibouti, Egypt, United Arab Emirates, Iraq, Jordan, Kuwait, Lebanon, Libya, Mauritania, Morocco, Palestine, Qatar, Syria (suspended), Oman, Saudi Arabia, Somalia, Sudan, Tunisia and Yemen) and the Gulf Cooperation Council (six Middle Eastern countries: Saudi Arabia, Kuwait, the United Arab Emirates, Qatar, Bahrain, and Oman) do not have political unity to intervene in order to protect democracy. They are interested in protecting their own sovereign states. They ignored the uprising of Egyptian and Tunisian citizens. The Gulf Cooperation Council supported authoritarianism in the region through direct military intervention in Bahrain and Yemen and through financial aid to Egypt.

Contemporary Iran.

The Pahlavi dynasty was the last ruling house of the Imperial State of Iran from 1925 until 1979, when the 2,500 years of continuous Persian monarchy was overthrown and abolished as a result of the Iranian Revolution. The dynasty was founded by Reza Shah Pahlavi in 1925 whose reign lasted until 1941 when he was forced to abdicate by the Allies after the Anglo-Soviet invasion of Iran. He was succeeded by his son, Mohammad Reza Pahlavi (1941 to 1979), the last Shah of Iran. In 1935, Reza Shah renamed Persia as the Imperial State of Iran. He maintained a pro-Western foreign policy and fostered economic development in Iran. Reza Shah was a force for modernisation despite his despotic rule. Construction of railways and the institutionalisation of educational systems were some of his achievements, while his controversial decree banning all Islamic veils, which was forcibly implemented, antagonised people in the Muslim-majority nation. Faced with growing public discontent and popular rebellion throughout 1978 he resigned in January 1979. This gave rise to a series of events that quickly led to the end of the state and the beginning of the Islamic Republic of Iran on 11 February 1979, officially ending the 2,500-year-old Persian monarchy.

Islamic Republic of Iran. Ayatollah Khomeini became the supreme religious leader of the Islamic Republic of Iran in 1979, following many years of resistance to Shah Pahlavi. Following his appointment as Ayatollah, Khomeini worked to remove the Shah from power for his associations with the West, continuing his Islamic pursuits till his death. The December 1979 constitution, and its 1989 amendment, define the political, economic, and social order of the Islamic Republic of Iran, declaring that Shia Islam of the Twelver school of thought as Iran's official religion. Iran has an elected president, a parliament, an "Assembly of Experts" (which elects the Supreme Leader), and local councils. According to the constitution all candidates running for these positions must be vetted by the Guardian Council before being elected. The Iranian presidential election (2013) saw Hasan Rouhani (Moderation and Development Party) as president. Ali Khamenei is the current Supreme Leader (elected by the assembly of experts).

The situation of women and girls changed in conformity with Sharia. Women were forced to wear veils. Marriage to little girls became legal. Before the Islamist party of the Ayatollah Khomeini came to power in 1979, the legal age of marriage was 18 for girls and 20 for boys. After the mullahs' party imposed Sharia law in Iran as the official unquestionable law of the land, the authorities immediately changed the age of legal marriage to 9 for girls and 13 for boys. After 40 years, the Sharia-based law has not changed. According to official Iranian statistics, 180,000 child marriages take place there each year. In addition, in 2013 in Iran, a law was passed that allows men to marry their adopted daughters. According to the latest statistics, confirmed by the Managing Director and Member of the Board of Directors of the Association for the Protection of the Rights of Children, Farshid Yazdani, 24 percent of all marriages in Iran are child marriages. As well as physical and sexual abuse these little girls encounter emotional abuse. Under Sharia law, these young girls must completely comply with their husbands wishes. The husbands have the right to divorce their wives at any time, but the wives do not have such a law. "At eight years old my parents sat me down for a serious talk," said Noushin, during the interview. "I can still remember the tremble in my mother's voice. She told me that in two days I would be part of an Islamic religious blessing. My father insisted that I behave, and not cause a scene. I was confused, but I trusted them, that they were telling me the truth. I trusted them right up to the moment that the wedding ring went onto my finger and I became the bride of a 43-year old man." Noushin said the wedding was "a nightmare I could not wake up from. I understood that I was married, but I did not understand what that meant." She said was forced to have sexual intercourse before she reached puberty. "Each day was filled with new confusion, and new horrors," she said, as she tried to become accustomed to the role she was forced to endure. "I thought the move into my husband's house was a punishment by my parents because I had not listened when they told me to stop playing a week before. I hoped to be taken back to my parents the next day. But it soon became clear that this was not a temporary punishment, it would last a lifetime."

In 2016, the relationship between the regime of Ayatollah Ali Khamenei and the Obama administration seemed to have reached a euphoric level. Many exorbitant concessions were made by the United States to the Islamic Republic. The argument for these concessions was that such policies of appeasement would inspire Iran to change its malignant behaviour, and that the freedoms that resulted would trickle down to the Iranian people. People began to think it would be safe to travel to Iran again. As tourism began to increase, however, it soon became clear that there was still rampant danger. People started becoming the new hostages of Iran.

Serial kidnapping and hostage taking is a major source of income. Iran took two hostages, an innocent British mother, Nazanin Zaghari-Ratcliffe who travelled with her baby to Iran to visit her family on Norowz, the Iranian New Year in 2016. At the Khomeini Airport. She was surrounded by The Islamic Revolutionary Guard Corps (IRGC) and arrested. They confiscated both her and her daughter's passports. Baby Gabriella does not have an Iranian nationality; she was born in Britain. As is true in many Iranian court cases authorities are not required to, and did not offer, any reason to detain or arrest anyone. Nazanin was faced with the confusion of why she had even been arrested in the first place. Ambiguous and vague charges surfaced. Although the authorities never presented any evidence, Zaghari-Ratcliffe was accused of "plotting to topple the Iranian government." With no ability to defend herself, and no requirement for actual proof that such a crime had occurred, she was sent to prison. With no fair and due process in the Sharia court, she has been consistently denied access to her lawyer. The Iranian regime has even refused to allow the British authorities to have access to her. The Sharia court then sentenced her to five years in prison. Currently the treatment of Nazanin Zaghari-Ratcliffe, who has exceeded 1,000 days in prison as of January 2019, amounts to torture. From what information her family has been able to gather, her situation as a prisoner in Iran is dire, and she has said she will go on a hunger strike.

The entire situation looks like another instance of Iranian serial kidnapping and hostage taking, starting with the Iran hostage crisis of 1979-81, in which 52 American citizens and diplomats were held for 444 days. When President Ronald Reagan expected not to look kindly upon the situation, was elected, the hostages were immediately released. The Iranians proceeded to kidnap more Americans, five of whom were released by then-President Barack Obama for an illegal ransom of $1.7 billion. Former FBI agent Robert Levinson, about whom a "proof-of-life" video from 2010 was released in 2012, is still missing. In 2007, Iranians seized five Britons from a government ministry building in Baghdad in May 2007, apparently to stop Iran's diversion of $18 billion to Iraq from being exposed. Only Peter Moore, made it out of Iran alive," according to the Guardian. In 2018, Iran kidnapped 58 members of a Qatari royal falcon-hunting party. The government may have paid $1 billion for their release.

Iran aims to become the major power in the Middle East, thus continuing the Islamic tradition of Jihad. Iran pursues military strategies, funds Hezbollha and Hamas terrorist activities and reaches out to all Arabs and Muslims to recruit their youth for terrorist activities.

The nuclear agreement, known as the Joint Comprehensive Plan of Action Agreement (JCPOA), effective, as of October 18, 2015, is supported by Resolution 2231 which stipulates that Iran should not undertake any ballistic missile activity "until the date eight years after the JCPOA Adoption Day or until the date on which the IAEA submits a report confirming the Broader Conclusion, whichever is earlier."

In contrast to the Joint Comprehensive Plan of Action Agreement (JCPOA), Iranian President Hassan Rouhani boasted: We will have a new ballistic missile test in the near future that will be a thorn in the eyes of our enemies. Iranian Defence Minister Hossein Dehqan said that there will be no limit for the range and amount of missiles that Iran will develop. The range of existing Iranian ballistic missiles has grown from 500 miles to over 1,250 miles which can reach Eastern Europe and as far as Israel. Iran's state-owned Fars News Agency in Dec 6, 2016 confirmed an increase in production (of ballistic missiles) and that The Islamic Revolution Guards Corps (IRGC) fired 2 home-made 'Qadr H' ballistic missiles from the Eastern Alborz Mountains at a target in Iran's South Eastern Makran seashore some 1400km away. Qadr is a 2000km range liquid fuel and ballistic missile that can reach Israel.

Iran has repeatedly test-fired, long-range ballistic missiles and laser-guided surface-to-surface missiles. For example, on March 2016, Iran tested a new ballistic missile, capable of carrying multiple warheads. More recently, Iran fired a test missile with an accuracy within 25 feet, which is characterized as zero error, according to Brig. Gen. Ali Abdollahi, the Iranian military's deputy chief of staff, and Iran's semi-official Tasnim news agency. According to a report obtained by the Associated Press, the launches are `destabilizing and provocative` and the Shahab-3 medium-range ballistic missile and Qiam-1 short-range ballistic missile fired by Iran are `inherently capable of delivering nuclear weapons`.

In addition to violating the nuclear agreement, provoking and threatening other nations, and destabilizing the region, Iran is breaching two UN Security Council Resolutions. Security Council resolution 2231 (section 3 of Annex B) "calls upon Iran not to undertake any activity related to ballistic missiles designed to be capable of delivering nuclear weapons, including launches using such ballistic missile technology." The second United Nations Security Council resolution, 1929, states: "Iran shall not undertake any activity related to ballistic missiles capable of delivering nuclear weapons, including launches using ballistic missile technology, and that States shall take all necessary measures to prevent the transfer of technology or technical assistance to Iran related to such activities."

Iran has the largest ballistic missile arsenal in the Middle East. It is also the most diversified one. No country, other than Iran, has acquired long-range ballistic missiles before obtaining nuclear weapons. However, the world's expert on Iran ballistic missiles, Uzi Rubin, revealed on July 15 that Iran has five new missile capabilities that can strike the middle of Europe, including Berlin; they can target with GPS accuracy military facilities in Saudi Arabia; they can launch missiles from underground secret tunnels and caves without warning; they have missiles that are ready to fire 24/7; and they have developed other accurate missiles whose mission is to strike targets throughout Gulf region. The Associated Press revealed that a side agreement under the Joint Comprehensive Plan of Action (JCPOA) nuclear deal actually allows Iran to break out of the agreement in year 11, not 15, at which point Iran will not even be six months away from having sufficient nuclear fuel to arm a nuclear warhead, and Iran will be able to install nuclear centrifuges five times more efficient than the ones they have today. Moreover, German intelligence reports that Iran has, a few dozen times since the July 2015 nuclear agreement, sought to purchase nuclear ballistic missile technology, a violation of previous UN resolutions. Iran is also increasingly provoking other countries in the region, and has made it clear that the ballistic missiles are aimed at targeting other nations. Brig. Gen. Amir Ali Hajizadeh, said previously to FARS news agency that "Iran has built missiles that can hit targets at 2,000 km. They are designed to hit Israel at such a distance." Iran also exports these missiles to its proxies across the region.

The relations between the European Union and Iran have been declining sharply. Europeans and Iran are at odds on a range of issues: Iran's ballistic missile program, attacks and plots against Iranian dissidents in Europe and slow progress towards relieving the effects of US sanctions. Several European countries have alleged that Iran's security services have plotted to assassinate dissidents in Europe. The European Union identifies the problem with undertaking discussions with Iran as: "The main difficulty with Iran is that there are many Irans."

Russia has increased its military support to the Assad regime with the transfer of three S-300PM-2 missile batteries whose radar and communication technologies are more sophisticated than those deployed to Syria previously. On February 7 2018 Russian fighters advanced towards an oil refinery in Dier al-Zor., a province held by Kurdish forces and the US led coalition which responded with heavy air strikes. The Deir al-Zor battle on 7 February 2018 was the first direct confrontation between the US and Russia since the collapse of the Soviet Union, as reported by Reuters. Russia used secret private military contractors in Syria to carry out this mission.

Russian's delivery of advanced air defence systems to Syria has emboldened Iran to ramp up its shipments of weaponry to Hezbolla. In his speech to the UN General assembly, Prime Minister Netanyahu showed three sites in the Lebanese capital where Hezbolla at the request of Iran have built underground missile manufacturing facilities that can reach Israel anywhere. Hezbolla has an arsenal of more than 100,000 rockets and missiles many housed in residential areas to protect them from attack.

Iran funds terrorists: Hamas in Gaza and the Lebanese Shiite Hezbolla. Rouhani is clear in confirming of Iran's openly declared goal of destroying Israel in keeping with Khamenei's prediction of Israel's destruction in 2040. Iran supplies the means to anyone who shares the Islamic Republic's objective of eliminating Israel. Hezbollah has been receiving billions of dollars from the Iranians in order to prepare for the next war against Israel. Hamas and Islamic Jihad in the Gaza Strip have been receiving political, financial and military aid from Iran in order to continue their attacks on Israel. With Iranian support the Lebanese Shiite terrorist organization, Hezbollah has been aiming tens of thousands of rockets and missiles at Israel. Iran has reportedly delivered GPS components to Hezbolla in Lebanon that will allow them to transform rudimentary projectiles into precision-guided missiles. With the support of the Iranian military and financial backing, Hamas,

Islamic Jihad and other terrorist groups fired more than 500 projectiles at Israel in 24 hours in November 2018 (Gatestone Institute).

The decision to fund the families of Palestinian terrorists was announced during a conference of The World Forum for Proximity of Islamic Schools of Thought, a forum established in 1990 by order of Khamenei for the reconciliation of different Islamic schools and branches. The man who announced the decision was Mohsen Araki, the leader of the forum. Iran, he said, has decided to "adopt" the families of the Palestinians killed on the Gaza-Israel border. When the Iranians talk about "adopting" someone, they mean that Tehran will look after the families of those who targeted Jews and provide them with everything they need, including money, healthcare and education. The Iranian money promised to the families is meant to encourage all Arabs and Muslims to send their children to launch rocket attacks on Israel and throw stones and firebombs at Israeli soldiers.

Iran care nothing for the Palestinians. Iran seeks to be the main power driver in the Middle East. Iran aims to obliterate Israel and the US. The expansion of Iranian influence to the Middle East in general and the Palestinian arena in particular began during the Obama administration, which turned a blind eye to Iran's aggressive intentions, and later embarked on a policy of appeasement toward its mullahs. Under the Obama administration, the Iranians must have felt they had a pass to do whatever they wanted. That is evidently why, today, they are sitting not only in the Gaza Strip and Lebanon, but also in Syria, Yemen, Libya and Iraq.

Contemporary Pakistan.

The Constitution. Wikipedia (the free Encyclopedia) describes the Constitution of Pakistan: The Constitution of Pakistan establishes Islam as the state religion, and provides all its citizens with the right to profess, practice and propagate their religion subject to law, public order, and morality. The Constitution also states that all laws are to conform with the injunctions of Islam as laid down in the Quran and Sunnah. The constitution limits the political rights of Pakistan's non-Muslims, and only Muslims are allowed to become the President or the Prime Minister. Moreover, only Muslims are allowed to serve as judges in the Federal Sharia Court, which has the power to strike down any law deemed un-Islamic, though its judgments can be overruled by the Supreme Court of Pakistan. Extract from the Constitution: On the constitution of the Islamic Republic of Pakistan. Preamble of the 1973 "Whereas sovereignty over the entire Universe belongs to Almighty Allah alone and the authority to be exercised by the people of Pakistan within the limits prescribed by Him is a sacred trust; And whereas it is the will of the people of Pakistan to establish an order; Wherein the Muslims shall be enabled to order their lives in the individual and collective spheres in accordance with the teachings and requirements of Islam as set out in the Holy Quran and Sunnah; Wherein the principles of democracy, freedom, equality, tolerance and social justice, *as enunciated by Islam,* shall be fully observed;

Article 1 of the 1973 Constitution: The Islamic State and territories. (1) Pakistan shall be a Federal Republic to be known as the Islamic Republic of Pakistan, hereinafter referred to as Pakistan. *Article 2 of the 1973 Constitution: Islam to be State religion;* Article 2 of the Constitution states: `Islam shall be the state religion of Pakistan`. Article 2-A stipulates: *`wherein the principles of democracy, freedom, equality, tolerance and social justice, as enunciated by Islam, shall be fully observed.`*

Article 31; Government role to promote Islamic way of life: Article 31deals with the particular steps which "shall be taken" to enable the Muslims of Pakistan to conduct themselves in what the heading of Article 31 describes, "Islamic way of life." It is only through such like provisions of the Constitution the Article 2 can be given an operative shape.

Article 41 of the 1973 Constitution: The President. *A person shall not be qualified for election as President unless he is a Muslim* of not less than forty-five years of age and is qualified to be elected as member of the National Assembly. The Third Schedule to the constitution, which contains the text of the oath to be taken by the president before entering upon the said office, specifically provides, in relevant part, *that the candidate shall affirm that he is a Muslim and believes in the Oneness of*

Allah, the Holy Quran, and that the Prophet Muhammad was the last of the prophets of Allah. Thus, the constitution clearly discriminates and excludes any member of the minority community of Pakistan from holding the office of the president of Pakistan.

Article 91; the Prime Minister must be a Muslim. The original language of the 1973 Constitution was substituted by P.O. No. 14 of 1985, providing that, "after the election of Speaker and Deputy Speaker, the National Assembly shall, to the exclusion of any other business, proceed to elect without debate one of its *Muslim* members to be the Prime Minister."

Article 91 of the 1973 Constitution: The Cabinet. (1) There shall be a Cabinet of Ministers, with the Prime Minister at its head, to aid and advise the President in the exercise of his functions. (2) (3) After the election of the Speaker and the Deputy Speaker, the National Assembly shall, to the exclusion of any other business, proceed to elect without debate one of its *Muslim* members to be the Prime Minister. By virtue of Article 91, the National Assembly of Pakistan is restricted to electing only one of its *Muslim* members as the prime minister of Pakistan. The Third Schedule to the Constitution, which contains the text of the oath to be taken by the prime minister before entering upon the said office, specifically provides, in relevant part, that the *candidate shall affirm that he is a Muslim and believes in the Oneness of Allah, the Holy Quran and that the Prophet Muhammad was the last of the prophets of Allah.*

Thus the Constitution is, in express terms, discriminatory and excludes any member of the minority community of Pakistan from holding the office of prime minister of Pakistan. It is clear from a bare reading of Articles 41 and 91 and the relevant oaths of office contained in the Third Schedule to the constitution that members of the minority communities have been denied the right to hold the high constitutional offices of the president and prime minister of Pakistan.

Articles 62 and 63: Articles 62 and 63 were added to the constitution by Zia and were later protected through the eighth amendment to the constitution (P.O No.14 of 1985). Apart from other qualifications to being a member of the parliament a candidate has to be "of good character *and not commonly known as one who violates Islamic injunctions.*"

He or she must have *adequate knowledge of Islamic teachings and must be a practicing Muslim* who "abstains from major sins." He/she should be "sagacious, righteous and non- profligate and honest and amin."

Article 203C of the 1973 Constitution: The Federal Sharia Court. *All judges of the Federal Shariat Court as provided in Article 203C are to be Muslims.* (1) The Court shall consist of not more than eight *Muslim* [Judges] including the [Chief Justice] to be appointed by the President.

Article 203E of the 1973 Constitution: A party to any proceedings before the Court under clause (1) of Article 203D may be represented by a legal practitioner who is a *Muslim* and has been enrolled as an advocate of a High Court for a period of not less than five years or as an advocate of the Supreme Court or by a juris consult selected by the party from out of a panel of juris consults maintained by the Court for the purpose.

Article 203E Sub Article (4). Expressly provides *that the legal practitioner representing a petitioner in the Federal Sharit Court must be a Muslim.*

Article 227 of the 1973 Constitution: Provisions relating to the Holy Quran and Sunnah. *All existing laws shall be brought in conformity with the Injunctions of Islam as laid down in the Holy Quran and Sunnah,* in this Part referred to as the Injunctions of Islam, and no law shall be enacted which is repugnant to such Injunctions. Any legislative or executive authority cannot enact a law or promulgate any Ordinance or Order in view of Article 227 of the Constitution which clearly prohibits the enactment of law which is repugnant to the Injunctions of Islam as laid down in the Holy Qur'an and Sunnah.

Article 228- the Council of Islamic Ideology. Article 228 established the Council of Islamic Ideology in an institutionalized role to oversee the legislation. Article 203 (A–J) additional powers of the Sharia Court. Article 203 (A–J) enjoys additional powers similar to those of the Council. Under Article 203–D, the Sharia Court can declare any law defunct if it is assumed to be against Islamic injunctions.

Under Article 260(3) (a) of the Constitution, a person belonging to the Ahmadi group is not a Muslim. A number of decisions have emphasized that according to the constitutional amendment, Ahmadis cannot claim the rights or follow the law that are specially determined for Muslims.

The Constitution of Pakistan, by declaring Islam as the national religion, ignores the several other religions which existed in Pakistan before it was overrun and seized by Muslims. Islam replaced indigenous beliefs and customs.

Treatment of minorities. Children are instructed at an early age that Christians, Jews and Hindus are the worst creatures and enemies of Islam, so one must grow up and fight against them. Hate is so deep rooted that a non-Muslim cannot drink a glass of water from a public place or even eat in a restaurant because they think that non-Muslims are unclean untouchables and a curse on earth. People can be killed for touching a glass of water from a public place. Non-Muslim women and girls are raped and forcibly converted. This is considered a religious obligation to please "Allah". Muslims burn the homes of non-Muslims, their places of worship, their holy books, burn their women and children and there is no law or punishment to prevent this criminal behaviour or to make non-Muslims safe. There is no one who speaks for them. According to Islamic doctrines, the value of a non-Muslim is that of filth that needs to be cleaned from the earth. A non-Muslim has to face and accept discrimination, lack of religious freedom, and physical and psychological torture as part of daily life.

Muhammed set the standard. Muslim clerics and Supreme Court judges often say on national TV, that Pakistan was made by "Muslims and is only for Muslims" and there is no place for non-Muslims. This echoes the statement of Muhammed, that "Arabia is only for Muslim."

Blasphemy Laws in Pakistan are strong instruments for discrimination against Christians and Jews. Blasphemy laws are abused to settle issues, such as personal grudges, even for extremely minor disputes, such as money or even children quarrelling. The general public does not wait for the legal process; they murder people on the spot. They burn them alive, they destroy their houses and places of worship, not just the accused person but also, collectively, other members of the community. Even if a case of 'blasphemy' is not proven against Christians, they can still be killed by an angry mob or while in police custody. In the 71 years since the creation of Pakistan, there have been no cases of someone being punished for killing, burning or raping a non-Muslim man, woman or child, or for burning their places of worship, their homes or their holy books (A.Z. Mohammed). Pakistan is suffering from the severest religious extremism. This situation was recently corroborated by reports from the Centre, from Open Doors USA and from the Gatestone Institute.

Discrimination in court. Justice is not available to non-Muslims. According to Islamic law, a non-Muslim cannot appear in court as a witness against a Muslim, because his testimony or claim is considered unreliable and biased. A non-Muslim cannot take a case against a Muslim to the Federal Sharia Court. If there is a case against a non-Muslim and he wants to hire a non-Muslim lawyer as counsel, it is not permitted. Only a Muslim lawyer can be present in court, and it is compulsory that the judge must also be Muslim. Even if a case of blasphemy is not proven against Christians, they still can be murdered by an angry mob or while in police custody. Non-Muslims can also easily be sentenced to death by a court: even a single claim by a Muslim against a non-Muslim is enough to `prove` him guilty. Non-Muslims are killed in public in broad daylight.

No rights in Pakistan. To speak for your own rights or someone else's is taking on a suicidal risk. You could face charges of blasphemy, be murdered in cold blood, or `disappeared`. Salmaan Taseer, the Governor of Punjab Province, criticized the abuse of Pakistan's blasphemy laws. For this, he was murdered by his own bodyguard in 2011. Rashid Rehman was a lawyer who agreed to take on a blasphemy case. He was gunned down by two men who walked into his office posing as clients.

Discrimination in holding public positions is extreme. It is compulsory for every public officer to take an oath that he is Muslim before being appointed. Only low paid jobs are available for non-Muslims. Newspapers advertise that only non-Muslims may apply for such jobs. Government failure to provide security and safety to religious minorities is a strong reason for religious minorities, especially Christians and Hindus to flee from Pakistan.

Fundamentalists are supported. Usually a country's authorities are supposed to support and help persecuted people. In Pakistan, instead, the institutions of government provide funds only to fundamentalists and other segments of the population engaged in persecuting non-Muslims. These taskmasters see themselves as soldiers of "Allah."

Cases. The case of Asia Bibi, actual name Aaslya Noreen. Rita Panahi, commented on Bibi`s case in Australia's *Herald Sun*. When Bibi, working in the field on a scorching day, was asked to bring water from a well, she committed the alleged blasphemy of drinking some of the water from the cup. "Another female farmhand, who already had a feud with Bibi, claimed she had "soiled" the utensil and the water supply with her unclean, Christian hands. Bibi was accused of "defiling the water." "For once," Bibi recounted, in her memoir, *Blasphemy: Sentenced to Death Over A Cup of Water (2013),* "I decided to defend myself and hold my head high. I said, `I think Jesus would have a different viewpoint to Mohammad.` The woman replied, "How do you dare to question the Prophet, dirty animal?" "Soon a mob confronted Bibi and her family before the police arrived." Many accused of blasphemy in Pakistan are not so fortunate and are killed before they are formally charged." Nisar has also refused to let Asia Bibi, a Christian mother of five, who has been on death row for ten years for "blasphemy," have an early hearing for the final appeal of her death sentence, after a trial that has been called "unfair." "The Maulvis (clerics) want her dead. They have announced a prize of Rs 10,000 to Rs 500,000 (£60 to £3,200) for anyone who kills Asia. They have even declared that if the court acquits her they will ensure the death sentence stands."

Cases reported by A.Z. Mohammed (2017). In September 2017, two Christian boys employed as cleaners in a hospital in Pakistan were arrested because they swept some bits of paper on which were written some Quran verses and burnt them. The police arrested them for blasphemy. The case is described of a Christian man charged with blasphemy and sentenced to death in 2017 because he wrote a poem insulting Muhammed and sent it to a Muslim friend on WhatsApp. Other young men were also sentenced to death for posts on Facebook. Writes Ibrahim (2018), a Muslim man charged Stephen, a Christian youth of 16 years with blasphemy against Islam because he stole from a bazar. He beat the boy and then told the imam that he burnt the Quran. The imam tracked the boy and attacked him again. The police were called by passerbys and instead of protecting the boy the police put him in prison on blasphemy charges. A mob of 300 gathered at the prison demanding a public lynching of Stephen.

The education system in Pakistan gives rise to disputes (Ibrahim 2018). The senate approved a bill requiring the compulsory teaching of the Quran to all primary and secondary school students, including non-Muslims. It is not explained how the Quran teachings of death and insults towards Jews, Christians and others will be presented so as not to engender hated towards the non-Muslim students and non-Muslims in the Pakistani society. Nosheen Ali, in a scholarly paper (Outrageous State, Sectarianized Citizens: Deconstructing the 'Textbook Controversy' in the Northern Areas, Pakistan) examines the 'textbook controversy' (2000-2005) that arose when the Pakistan state introduced new, overtly Sunni textbooks in the Northern Areas and the response of the local Shia population who began to agitate for a more balanced curriculum. The Shia made it clear that their efforts were directed towards freedom of religious belief which had been promised to every citizen in the constitution and not only to Sunni, although the author also refers to a gradually Sunni-ized Pakistan State. Government action included orchestrating riots in which at least 12 Shia dominated villages were attacked, bodies burnt, Shia mosques torched, crops and animals destroyed. Scholars view the textbook controversy as a "divide and conquer strategy." The conflict reached an acute stage during 2004-2005, as violent confrontations took place between Shia and Sunni communities, and a constant curfew paralyzed daily life in Gilgit for eleven months. It generated the collective mobilization and protest of the Shia community against the state for five years, and at the same time, intensified Shia-Sunni sectarian hostility in Gilgit. Non-Sunni were singled out and killed and the imam of the central Shia mosque was gunned down. The matter was partly resolved in April 2005, when an agreement was reached to withdraw some of the controversial textbooks. However it turned out that Shia were not passing exams for government jobs and they had to revert to using the original text books.

Despite anti-slavery laws in Pakistan, bonded labour is destroying many Christian lives because the Bonded Labour Abolition Act 1992 is not enforced. A Christian man sold himself into slavery to a Muslim family for two years to buy a house for his family. He was abused and prevented from going to church. When the contract ended he asked for his freedom but was he was abused with: "You filthy Chura (worthless thing). Your life is ours. You will clean our excrement every day" He was beaten and retained. Finally they poisoned him. Indaryas Ghulam, 38 was among 42 Christians accused of lynching two Muslims in a 2005 Church attack. The police offered him freedom in exchange for becoming a Muslim. He refused and was tortured and killed.

Pakistan Prime Minister Abbasi addressing the UN General Assembly (2017) refused to speak out against Pakistan's blasphemy law, its abusive application to death sentences and mob rule. Governor Salmaan Taseer, a vocal critic of blasphemy laws was murdered by his security guard. At the same time terrorists are gaining votes for the National Assembly. Although the Muslim League is not a recognised party, it got elected and a new Islamist Party also gained votes. The US had assisted Pakistan with 33 billion dollars in aid over the last 15 years. President Donald Trump has accused Pakistan of giving safe haven to agents of chaos, violence and terror and said that the time has come for Pakistan to demonstrate its commitment to civilization, order and peace. Notwithstanding this, the Taliban and the Haqqani network continue to find sanctuary in Pakistan. Madarasa Haqania, is the birthplace of the Taliban and terrorism in the region. Known also as the "University of Jihad," its students are the leaders of the groups who were involved in bomb attacks on churches. Their murderers are praised as heroes, not only by the general public but also by politicians and judges, who salute them with honour.

Ethnic Cleansing. According to the 2017 consensus, the population of the Islamic Republic of Pakistan is 207.74 million. The country is divided into an overwhelmingly Muslim majority of 96.28%; and the remaining 3.72% are Christian, Bahais, Buddhists, Hindus, Ahmadis,

Jains, Kalasha, Parsis and Sikhs, who are identified as non-Muslim minority Pakistanis. At the time of the partition of India in 1947, they were 23% of Pakistan's population. But instead of their numbers increasing, they have decreased to the current 3.72%. If the Muslim population has grown, why have non-Muslim minorities not grown also? This 23% represents millions of people; how have they vanished? According to the same census, from 1998 to 2017, Pakistan's overall population grew by 57%. Presumably, non-Muslim minorities should have increased at the same rate. Instead, their numbers have fallen drastically. The Hindu population, which, according to the 1951 census, was 12.9%, is now only 1.6%. The fate of minorities in Pakistan is clear. Nosheen Ali (2008) draws attention to the suppression of Shia in Northern Pakistan. In Pakistan the Pakistani citizen is assumed to be a Sunni Muslim, yet in Northern Pakistan there is a preponderance of Shia, thus raising fundamental issues pertaining to religion, nation and citizenship.

Contemporary Turkey.

Double Strategy. Turkish President Recep Tayyip Erdogan has played a double Strategy: Looking at membership of the European Union and aspirations to revive the Ottoman Turkish Rule for a united Ummah. Erdogan's response to the alleged coup of 2016 is far from what is expected of a State aspiring towards democracy. Looking at EU membership is now distant. Up until 2018, Over 50,000 have been jailed so far over Gulen links, yet Gulen, who has lived in self-imposed exile in the United States since 1999, has denied involvement and condemned the coup of 2016 when rogue soldiers commandeered tanks and warplanes to attack parliament, killing more than 240 people. Detention warrants have been issued for 120 suspects from the military. Police began simultaneous raids in 43 provinces to capture the suspects, 58 of whom were believed to be users of the outlawed ByLock messaging app. Turkey banned ByLock following the attempted putsch, saying followers of the Muslim cleric Fethullah Gulen used it communicate on the night of the coup, More than 50,000 people have been jailed pending trial over alleged links to Gulen, while 150,000 people have been sacked or suspended from jobs in the military, public and private sectors. The government dismisses rights groups' concerns about the crackdown, saying only such a purge could neutralise the threat represented by Gulen's network, which it says infiltrated institutions such as the judiciary, army and schools. Gulen taught a Hanafi version of Islam, deriving from Sunni Muslim scholar Nursi's teachings. Gulen has stated that he believes in science, interfaith dialogue with the People of the Book, and multi-party democracy. The growth of the Gulen movement sparked opposition from both Kemalists, who perceived the movement as threatening to undermine secularism, and from more radical Islamists who viewed the movement as "accommodating" and "pro-American".

Persecution in Turkey. History records several cases of persecution in Turkey. Turkey still denies the genocide of 1.5 million Armanians in 1915 and the expropriation of their land. Persecution of the Alevis in Turkey, including threats and arbitrary arrests have made the Alevis victims of Islamic supremacism for centuries, both in the Ottoman Empire and in the Republic of Turkey, just as the Christian, Jewish and Yazidi communities in Turkey. Turkey's membership in NATO since 1952, its negotiations for full membership to the EU since 2005 and its many military, economic and diplomatis agreements with the West have not reduced persecution of religious minorities. The Alevis are a religious minority in Turkey with a distict faith, phiolosophy and culture that holds secularism and humanism. The population is about 25%. The Alevis have been subject to massacres and pogroms in Turkey (1921 Kocgiri massacre; 1937-38 Tunceli massacres; 1938 Erzincan Zini massacre; 1978 Malatya massacre; 1978 Sivas Massacre; 1978 Maras massacre; 1980 Corum Massacre; 1993 Sivas massacre, 1998 Gazi Istanbul massacre). Photos of the massacred have been on display in Germany. The Alevis are constrained to hide their identity. Their tomb shrines have been plundered and burnt.

Child abuse. Another issue that thwarts EU membership for Turkey is child abuse. The Quran does not mention a specific minimum age. But most Muslims believe that their prophet, Mohammad, married

Aisha when the girl was six years old and had sex with her when she was nine years old. In Turkey marriage under the age of 17 is illegal. Children aged 16 can marry subject to a court ruling. But in practice, thousands of children marry, mostly after cases of rape their families' consent. According to official statistics, a total of 482,908 children were married off by their families in the past decade. In 2015 alone, 18,033 female children gave birth, including 244 girls under15. The number of recorded child abuse cases rose from 5,730 in 2005 to 16,957 in 2015. When a child girl gives birth, hospital authorities are obliged to notify law enforcement for legal proceedings, with prison sentences of up to 16 years. Earlier in 2016, the head of a department of the Supreme Court of Appeals revealed that nearly 3,000 marriages were registered between female victims of sexual abuse, including rape, and their assailants. Speaking to a parliamentary commission, the senior judge testified that children between the ages of five and 18 could be subjected to sexual abuse in the country, and that girls between the ages of 12 and 15 were more easily tricked by abusers. He mentioned a particular case in which three men kidnapped and raped a girl, then one of them married her and the sentences for all three were lifted following the drafting of a bill by the Islamist party that would also release about 3,000 men who married children, including men who raped them. In contrast, in 2011a prominent cleric and member of Saudi Arabia's highest religious council, issued a *fatwa* asserting that there is no minimum age for marriage, and that girls can be married "even if they are in the cradle." A report in the Turkish Daily News in 2008 by the Human Rights Directorate in Turkey reported that in Istanbul alone there was one honour killing every week and 1000 during the previous five years. Metropolitan cities were the location of many of these due to growing Kurdish immigration to these cities from the East.

Uniting the Ottoman Ummah is also distant, being fraught with contradictory situations. Arabs do not wish to revisit their Ottoman colonial past inspite of Erdogan's many efforts. Courses in Arabic were added to its curriculum and the state broadcaster, TRT, launched an Arabic television channel. The number of imam (religious) school students, under Erdogan's rule, has risen sharply to 1.3 million from

60,000 when he first came to power in 2002. However, history records how treacherous Arab tribes stabbed their Ottoman ancestors in the back during the First World War, and how Arabs collaborated with non-Muslim Western powers against Muslim Ottoman Turks.

International Relations. In order to be attractive to his Arab neighbours, Erdogan pursued a systematic policy against Israel and presented himself as a champion Muslim leader of the "Palestinian cause" to recognize Eastern Jerusalem as the capital city of the Palestinian state. Yet this met with Iran renouncing Turkey's efforts because, according to the regime, the entire city of Jerusalem, not just eastern Jerusalem, should have been recognized as the Palestinian capital. In January 2018 Erdogen visited the Pope in the Vatican to discuss Jerusalem, returning the visit of the Pope to Turkey in 2014.The Vatican statement said that talks included "the status of Jerusalem, highlighting the need to promote peace and stability in the region (The Middle East) through dialogue and negotiation with respect to human rights and international law. The Pope presented Erdogen with a bronze medallion showing an angel embracing the northern and southern hemispheres while overcoming the opposition of a dragon. "This is the angel of peace who strangles the demon of war" said the Pope.

The relationship with the Sunni is highly unstable. For the Sunni Saudis, the Turks were allies only if they could be of use in fighting Shiite Iran or its proxies, such as the Iraqi government or the Syrian regime. As Turkey, together with Qatar, kept on championing and giving logistical support to Hamas, an Iranian satellite, Saudi Arabia and Egypt distanced themselves from the Palestinian cause and consequently from Turkey.

Both the Saudi kingdom and Egypt's al-Sisi regime have viewed Hamas, an Iranian satellite, with hostility, whereas Turkey gave it logistical and ideological support. Another reason for the change in Saudi Arabia's position toward Turkey is Saudi Arabia's newfound alliance with Egypt's President el-Sisi. El-Sisi replaced the Muslim Brotherhood president, Mohamed Morsi, in Egypt, while Turkey and Qatar, have effectively been the embodiments of the Muslim Brotherhood in the region. Turkey does not even have full diplomatic relations with the most populous Sunni Arab nation, Egypt.

History is also against Erdogan. United Arab Emirates (UAE) Foreign Minister Sheikh Abdullah bin Zayed Al Nahayan tweeted that Turkish troops looted Medina a century ago. In response, Erdogan himself lashed out: "Some impertinent man sinks low and goes as far as accusing our ancestors of thievery." Finally, Anwar Gargash, UAE's Minister of State for Foreign Affairs, said there was a need for Arab countries to rally around the "Arab axis" of Saudi Arabia and Egypt. Gargash also said that "the Arab world would not be led by Turkey".

Another area of instability arises from the Turkish-Kurds relationship. The country's Kurdish population stands at about 15 million. Kurds have been repressed since the founding of the Turkish Republic 90 years ago. The Kurds are one of the peoples of the Mesopotamian plains and the highlands in what are now south-eastern Turkey, north-eastern Syria, northern Iraq, north-western Iran and south-western Armenia. They adhere to a number of different religions and creeds, although the majority are Sunni Muslims.

The reconciliation of the Turkish state with the Kurds living in Turkey has been destabilized. Turkey is determined to prevent the establishment of a Kurdish state across the border in Syria and has used military force in the past. On attacking the Kurds in Syria in 2018, Erdogan said "We know that without security in Syria, there cannot be security in Turkey." Turkish forces tried to cross the border into Syria, near the villages of Kordu and Balya. Turkish airstrikes pounded the Kurdish-held region of Afrin in northern Syria. Erdogan told a news outlet that the Syrian government was informed of the operation in advance, but the Syrian government, speaking through the state-run news agency SANA, said it wasn't notified. Russia says it will back the Syrian government diplomatically and support a demand at the United Nations for Turkey to stop its military operation. It appears that Erdogan himself destabilizes the country by oppressing the Kurds.

Erdogan has interests in the Greek Islands. Although Turkey knows that legally and historically the islands are Greek, Turkish authorities want to occupy them as they did in Anatolia from 1914 to 1923. Turkey's ruling party and its opposition have threatened to invade the Aegean. The 1924 Treaty of Lausanne, the 1932 Turkish Italian agreements and the 1947 Paris Treaty recognised the islands of the Aegean as Greek Territory. Turkey destroyed all remnants of Greek culture that existed in Asia Minor, a Greek land prior to the 11th century Turkish invasion. There are fewer than 2,000 Greeks left in Turkey to-day. Turkey brutally invaded Cyprus in 1974. SoTurkey may brutally invade Greece.

Contemporary Syria

Bashir al-Assad succeeded his father as President and established an authoritarian government as the Ba'ath Party in 2000. Bashar Al-Assad was sworn in for his third seven-year term on July 16, 2014, although Friends of Syria denounced the election, alleging beforehand that it would be rigged and adverse to the premise behind the Geneva 11 talks. The group also questioned the veracity of an election given it would be run in the middle of a civil war and only within government areas "thereby meaning that millions of Syrians were unable to vote as a result of the war either due to being in areas outside government control or due to being displaced." The Gulf Cooperation Council, the European Union and the United States dismissed the election as illegitimate. Hundreds of thousands of refugees who did not leave Syria officially via border posts were excluded from voting. Syrian expatriates were not allowed to vote in many countries.

A surge of interest in political reform took place after Bashar al-Assad was elected President. Human Rights activists and other civil-society advocates, as well as some parliamentarians, became more outspoken during a period referred to as the 'Damascus Spring' (July 2000-February 2011), calling for change on the streets by peaceful protests addressing high unemployment, corruption, lack of political freedom and state repression. The party claims to be socialist (advocating state ownership of the means of industrial production and the redistribution of agricultural land) but in practice it is a mixed economy, composed of large state enterprises and small private businesses. Until the Syrian uprising the president had broad and unchecked decree authority under a long-standing state of emergency. The end of this emergency was a key demand of the uprising, and decrees are now subject to approval by the People's Council, the country 's legislature. The new Syrian constitution in 2012 introduced a multi-party system based on the principle of political pluralism without guaranteed leadership of any political party. The Ba'ath Party emphasises socialism and secular Pan-Arabism. Despite the Ba'ath Party's doctrine on building national rather than ethnic identity, the issues of ethnic, religious and regional allegiances still remain important in Syria.

Several actors. In February 2011, Syria was declared by the Red Cross to be in a state of civil war. This has escalated into a complex conflict that fractionated the population, largely but not entirely along sectarian religious and ethnic grounds. The government resorted to increasingly violent crackdowns, prompting a growing number of armed opposition groups. The Free Syrian Arab army is loyal to Bashar al-Assad and has been backed by militias trained by Iran. Islamist and Jihadist groups as Ahrar al-Sham and al-Nusra front were formed in 2011 and 2012 respectively. Rebel forces were secular, aiming to bring down Assad and establish themselves as controlling power. The Kurds (mainly the YPG) want independence. ISIS conquered large swathes of Syria aiming to form an Islamic Caliphate in the conquered parts of Syria. The anti ISIS coalition consisted of Israel, NATO, Jordan, UAE, Saudi and the US, in a joint effort to defeat ISIS. Turkish airstrikes attacked the Kurds in Syria because Turkey sees the Kurds as a threat as their leaders have long sought an independent state in the region. Turkey is a NATO member, yet attacks the Kurds. While the population regard those who took Rakka from ISIS as heroes, Turkey says these Syrian Kurds are terrorists. Qatar, Saudi and Turkey increased support to Islamist groups who started to adopt a more religious image to attract Gulf funding, pitching the country's Sunni majority against Bashar's Shia Alawite sect. Bashar's alliances with Hezbollha and other Shia militias hardened Sunni Jihadists. ISIS set up the al-Nusra front and merged, forming a caliphate encompassing areas of Syria and Iraq. Defeating ISIS became the priority in Iraq and Syria for Western powers.

Chemical weapons. When Bashar started using chemical weapons in Ghouta agricultural belt, in 2012 Obama declared the US would punish Bashar if he crossed the Red line but accepted that Russia removes the chemical weapons but this emboldened Bashar, Russia and Iran as it appeared to legitimize the use on non-chemical weapons. The use of chemical weapons by Bashar was a significant issue. Human rights experts investigated reports of alleged chlorine bomb attacks on civilians in two Syrian towns, Douma in Eastern Ghouta and Saraqeb in Idlib. The UN's Commission of inquiry on Syria said, "We call on the United Nations and Arab Muslim countries to come see what the Syrian regime is doing in our towns and homes. The Syrian regime claim to kill terrorists but they are killing innocent people, women and children, in cold blood. They are not killing Nusra fighters or ISIS or any other militant group, but they are killing civilians." UNICEF describes the situation as a "war on children." The UN estimated that five million people had fled Syria to neighbouring countries: Lebanon, Jordan and Turkey. A further 6.3 million were internally displaced. 10% of Syrian refugees sought safety in Europe sowing political divisions as countries argue over sharing the burden. 85% of Syrians live in poverty. The warring parties have compounded the problems by refusing humanitarian aid agencies access to the 4.9 million Syrians in besieged areas.

Complex scenario. The emerging scenario in Syria is complex, involving a number of actors. In September 2015 Vladimir Putin deployed Russian troops in Syria which tipped the balance in Bashar's favour. Moscow targeted not only ISIS and al-Nusra but moderate groups including those receiving US support. Rebel-held Aleppo fell in December 2016. Shia Iran is spent billions a year to bolster Alawite Bashar with weapons since Syria is a transit point for Iranian weapons shipments to Lebanese Shia Hezbollah which has sent thousands of fighters to his assistance. Sunni Saudi Arabia has sought to counterbalance its rival, Iran which has been a major provider of military and financial assistance to the rebels with Islamist ideologies.

Turkey sought to contain the Kurdish Popular Front (YPG) militia that is battling ISIS as part of the US-backed Syrian Democratic

Forces (SDF) alliance. Airstrikes by Turkish and Russian planes heavily bombarded Syrian cities such as Afrin City which contains Kurdish families, shattering whole streets, wounding huge numbers and overwhelming hospitals. Pro government fighters entered Kurdish held Afrin to fend off a Turkish assault. Turkish president Erdogan said Russia had stepped in to block the deployment of progovernment forces in Afrin where Ankara is seeking to destroy the Kurdish YPG militia. Human Rights Watch has accused Syrian forces of using barrel bombs to carry out indiscriminate attacks on populated areas in defiance of the rules of war and a UN Security Council resolution.

In the ongoing war, it is civilians who suffer. February 7, 2018, CNN reported that Russian airstrikes hit rebel-controlled Idlib, which had been targeted by Russian-backed Syrian forces. Syrian government air strikes rained on three towns in rebel-held Eastern Ghouta, near Damascus. The rebel-held Eastern Ghouta area had been surrounded by Syrian government forces for more than four years. The siege intensified in May 2017 after government forces conducted a large-scale offensive in the area. According to Syrian activists, conditions in the siege in Eastern Ghouta were the worst they had been in four years and continue to deteriorate, with hundreds of thousands of people suffering a lack of food and medical supplies. The situation worsened since most makeshift tunnels used to smuggle food and other essential materials from Damascus were found and blocked by Syrian regime forces. On February 9, 2018, Reuters reported that France wanted the air strikes in Syria to end and called for the opening of humanitarian corridors as soon as possible, further stating that civilians were the targets, in Idlib and in the east of Damascus. The Syrian civil war, entering its eighth year, had killed hundreds of thousands of people and driven more than 11 million from their homes, while drawing in regional countries and global powers. The UN including Russia voted for a 3-day cease fire but the following day Bashar and Russia bombed Damascus.

Russia in Syria. Russia has clear interests for continuing its presence in Syria. Through the Syrian harbours it has access to the Mediterranean and the African Coast. Russia has already established a strong presence in Cyprus and a Russian axis has been reported in Italy.

Russia now provides missiles which support Syrian strategies against Israel. By promoting a war against Israel, Russia can consolidate its presence in Syria. In late September, Russia announced it would give the Syrian regime the S-300 system in the wake of Syrian air defences mistakenly shooting down a Russian Il-20. The Syrians had used an S-200 to hit the Russian plane, mistaking it for an Israeli warplane during an Israeli raid in Latakia. In October 2018, Russia announced they had completed the delivery of the S-300. 49 units of "equipment, including radars, control vehicles and four launchers," were sent, according to Defence Minister Sergei Shoigu. New electronic warfare systems were also sent to Syria, including systems designed to control a "near zone" 50 km. from the system and a far zone "200 km." away that would guard against Israeli attacks. However, in the past Syrian air defence projectiles have strayed toward Israel. In March 2017 an S-200 reportedly was fired and intercepted over the Jordan valley by an Arrow missile. An F-16 returning from an air strike was pursued by an S-200 missile in February and crashed in northern Israel. A Syrian missile heading for Israel was targeted by Israeli air defence on December 26, 2018.

Minorities in Syria. The treatment of non-Muslims is a major issue in Syria. In late January, a delegation of prominent clerics from Syria's Christian communities visiting Washington, D.C. testified the horrific attacks by anti-Assad rebels against innocent Christian non-combatants. They claimed that both the so-called moderate Free Syrian Army and extremist Islamic factions were guilty of repeated human rights violations against Christians. For Syria's Christians, the outcome of the civil war has existential ramifications. Today's Syrian Christian community continues to face the atrocities of Syria's ongoing civil war. Those who have elected to stay, risk forced conversion, death or *dhimmitude*. After the conquest of Syria's al-Rakaa province by the extremist ISIS, the Christian residents were told to convert to Islam, face the sword, or agree to become *dhimmi*. Reportedly, those Christians who opted for *dhimmi* status agreed to the following conditions: pay the twice annual *jizya* (poll tax), worship quietly inside their churches, display no outward signs of their Christian faith, not improve or expand upon their existing sites of worship, and not criticize the Islamic faith. This is the historical profile of *dhimmitude* since the time of Muhammad. Even fighters of the more moderate Free Syrian Army (FSA) have reportedly committed atrocities against Christians.

Syria has a history of murder and suppression. After the initial invasion in 633 A.D. by Bedouin Muslim Arabs, Syria's Christian communities realized that this was not just another raid by desert nomads. After a month-long siege, on September 19, 634 A.D., Damascus capitulated to the Arabian invaders. Eventually, most of the Levant Christianity was replaced by Islam and local languages replaced with Arabic. The era of Christianity's Eastern Byzantine civilization in Syria came to an end. The impact of Arab invasion was the slaughter of Syria's Christian faithful, the burning of churches, convents, and monasteries, the rape and enslavement of non-combatant innocents, seizure of huge tracts of private land by the Muslim conquerors. The Christian populations of Aleppo and Antioch were nearly extinguished. During the anti-Christian pogrom in Aleppo's Christian quarter in 1850, their dhimmi (protected) status entirely ended. Whenever fanatical imams deemed it appropriate, they would stir up their Muslim faithful into a mob. Moreover, the political leadership responsible for maintaining Islam's contract with the dhimmi proved to be ineffective and willfully passive in the face of mob fanaticism. Neither could Syria's Christians count on moderate Muslim factions for refuge. They disappeared once the radicals went on the rampage. Pockets of Aleppo-based Christians, however managed to survive the Mongols, Tamerlane and several Muslim pogroms.

If Assad fell, the future of Christians in Syria would be unclear, considering that radical Sunni groups kill their fellow Muslim Shias and even moderate Sunni rebel soldiers as well. The stark choice between extinction and exile might explain why many of Syria's Christians support the Assad regime. Many Christians may also remain loyal to the regime out of fear, especially with the increased influence of extremist Sunni Muslim factions in the opposition. One high-profile crime by Chechen foreign fighters allied with al-Nusra was the kidnapping of the Greek Orthodox and Syrian Orthodox Archbishops of Aleppo.

The fate of these two clerics remains unknown. Another crime was the kidnapping of 13 nuns from their convent in Maaloula in 2013. More than forty churches have been burned, rockets fired at an Armenian high school in Damascus killing four students, and several men beheaded because they were Christian. Half a million Christians have been driven from their homes and another 300,000 have fled Syria altogether.

The fate of Syria's Christian population may be similar to those of Iraq. Only a quarter of Iraq's 2003 population of one million Christians remains in the country to-day. Agenzia Fides (Faith Agency), an international Christian aid foundation, accuses the rebels in Syria of having engaged in massive 'ethnic cleansing' of Christians. If the Syrian government does collapse, safe alternatives for Syria's Christian minority are extremely limited. They could either flee the country or migrate to a possible smaller Alawite-ruled Syrian entity. If Syria's civil war continues, it is even more likely that the country's Christian minority will join the hundreds of thousands of their brethren, mostly Iraqi Christians, who have also abandoned their homeland. This migration is likely to be the safest alternative despite Vatican appeals for the region's Christians to remain in their home countries. It appears that the only safe place for a Christian in the Mideast is Israel, populated mainly by Jews who themselves were forced to flee Islamic intolerance in the same lands from which Christians now feel impelled to flee.

Contemporary Egypt.

In Egypt civil society organisations and opposition parties were allowed but controlled by the Mubarak regime. Religious based organisations and business organisations were tolerated but not prodemocracy organisations such as human rights and protest organisations. Under Mohammed Morsi, the first Islamist president and leader of the Muslim Brotherhood, no opposition parties were formed. The Islamist backed Constitution of 2012 placed greater restrictions on individual freedoms and gave unprecedented powers to religious institutions (the Azhar Grand Sheikh and the Coptic Orthodox Church). Young Muslim Brotherhood members see Egypt not as something to be reformed but as an enemy that has to be overhauled and purged. The military ousted Mubarak and Morsi. The military is authoritarian in nature and has dominated political life since 1952. Today headed by president al-Sisi, the Constitution granted unrestrained powers to the military, ensuring an authoritarian reversal rather than a democratization process. The army controls such companies as Tourism, Food and Cement. There is no dominant political party, parliament is composed of fragmented and weak pro regime parties and some independents. US aid to Egypt is more than 30 billion dollars over 20 years yet Sisi has persecuted political opponents, independent NGOs and peaceful protesters rather than use the money to combat terrorists.

Egypt has strong animosity for and restrictions on churches. In one incident over one thousand Muslims surrounded and demanded the instant and permanent closure of a church. The authorities complied including by evicting the church's two priests and a few congregants who were holed up inside the church and then shuttered it to triumphant cries of "Allahu Akbar" from the mob. In a statement discussing this incident, the local bishop of the Coptic Christian Church (Abba Makarius) said, "This is not the first time a place used for worship by Copts in Minya is closed. The common factor among all closures, however, is that they were done to appease fundamentalists and extremists to the detriment of the Copts. It appears to indicate that extremists now hold the upper hand and appeasing them is the easy way out of problems." Closing of Churches is a very regular occurrence in Egypt. Once local Muslims get wind that a church might be recognized in their neighbourhood or that a home is being used as a church, they form into large mobs, typically after Friday prayers, when the imam riles them, riot, attack, and sometimes kill Christians, and torch their homes and/or church in question, always to cries of triumphant Islamic slogans. Then to diffuse the situation, and perhaps show their own Islamic piety, local authorities, some of whom aid or cover for the mob, promptly shut down the church on the claim that it poses a "security concern" for the village. According to a report just published on January 15, 2019, "Egyptian authorities have closed four churches within the last four and a half weeks. No formal procedures against the attackers of these churches have begun. Instead, in the village of Manshiyet, the police arrested the church's priests and transported them to the station in a car used for carrying animals and garbage."

A separate report published on August 29, 2018 tells of another eight churches that were closed in one Egyptian province alone, Luxor, all of them "following attacks by Muslim villagers protesting against the churches being legally recognized."

Responding to one of these closures, Gamil Ayad, a local Coptic lawyer, voiced typical Christian sentiment: "We haven't heard that a mosque was closed down, or that prayer was stopped in it because it was unlicensed. Is that justice? Where is the equality? Where is the religious freedom? Where is the law? Where are the state institutions?"

Discussing the closure of another church under identical circumstances, another Christian explained that "There are about 4,000 Christians in our village and we have no place to worship now. The nearest church is 15km (nine miles) away. It is difficult to go and pray in that church, especially for the old, the sick people and kids."

He too continued by asking the same questions on the minds of millions of Christians in Egypt: "Where are our rights? There are seven mosques in our village and Muslims can pray in any place freely, but we are prevented from practicing our religious rites in a simple place. Is that justice? We are oppressed in our country and there are no rights for us.

"There is, of course, a reason for that. Contrary to popular belief in the West, the persecution of Christians in Muslim nations is hardly limited to a few "extremists"; it is often sponsored by the authorities themselves. After ranking Egypt as the 17th worst nation in the world where Christians experience "very high persecution," the World Watch List (2018) found that "officials at any level from local to national" are "strongly responsible" for the "oppression" of Egypt's Christians. "Government officials," the report adds, "also act as drivers of persecution through their failure to address the rights of Christians and also through their discriminatory acts which violate the fundamental rights of Christians." As for the newly constructed Nativity of Christ, which is being described as Sisi's "gift" to Christians even though it was entirely financed by private (Coptic) donations, one report sheds light on its true significance: "While the new cathedral was welcomed by many, President al-Sisi was also criticized for building a new church in a location where Christians do not live, while other churches languish and close because of heavy restrictions enforced by his government." As one Christian decried "We could build the biggest cathedral in the desert! Now do we close the churches which are in poor places, where the poor and weak people need to pray. The hate has become more direct and clear towards Christians."

The education system is not yet ready to promote tolerance. Al-Azhar University seemed to have a two-faced taqiyyah (dissimulation) attitude regarding tolerance towards Christians and Islamic moderation, according to a report by The Middle East Media Research Institute, "Two Faces of Egypt's Al-Azhar: Promoting Goodwill, Tolerance Towards Christians in Informational Holiday Campaign, but refusing to do the same in its School Curricula." Al-Azhar officials removed the proposed content encouraging tolerance and acceptance of Christians from school curricula, and the official who proposed the curriculum reform was fired. Non-cooperation with the Egyptian President Abdel Fattah el-SISI by Al-Azhar's leaders may have its roots in their Islamic faith and the fear of losing all power and the ability to use taqiyyah when needed.

Egypt to-day has no role of significance in the Middle East. Overall, to Egyptians, the word democracy has a meaning relating to its outcome. The Muslim Brotherhood was elected because it bought votes from the poor (bread and social justice), not because it was fit to lead. It was elected and then removed. A leader of the Salafist Party said that "there are fundamental differences between democracy and Sharia and Egypt must follow its own path according to Sharia Law."

Contemporary Israel

The conflict between Muslims on the one hand and Jews, Christians and pagans on the other started in Mecca because the Jews did not want to give up their Torah, the Christians did not want to give up their Christianity and the pagans did not want to give up their idols to take up Muhammed's teaching. Born in Mecca in 570 AD, of a Jewish mother and a pagan father (Abdullah, meaning servant (abd) of Allah (ullah)) Muhammed contemplated spirituality. After he migrated to Medina in 622 AD his spiritual teachings gave way to wars (political islam) with good returns for the Bedouins who followed him as companions. Chapter eight, Surat l-Anfal (Spoils of War), Quran 8:69, Sahih International "So consume what you have taken of war booty (as being) lawful and good, and fear Allah. Indeed, Allah is Forgiving and Merciful." Quran 8:41 Sahih International "And know that anything you obtain of war booty, then indeed, for Allah is one fifth of it and for the Messenger and for (his) near relatives and the orphans, the needy, and the (stranded) traveller."

Muhammed called for a continual offensive against the Jews, till the end of time. Quran 7:167 "And (remember) when your lord declared that, He would certainly keep on sending against them (the Jews), till the Day of resurrection, those who would afflict them with a humiliating torment. Verily, your Lord in quick in retribution (for disobedience) and certainly He is oft-forgiving and most merciful (for the obedients)."

Medina was the Jewish business hub of Arabia, at the centre of the caravan trade routes to Syria and beyond. There were thriving Jewish communities developing agriculture, animal husbandry, water collection and metallurgy. Some tribes exist to-day under different names. Subjugating and enticing the Bedouins (desert farmers) into wars, it took Muhammed and his followers 10 years to wipe out all the communities "leaving Arabia only for Muslim" as Muhammed planned. After this Muhammed had his sights further afield. His letters to Heracleus, Emperor of Byzantium, Chosroes Emperor of Persia, the Negus of Ethiopia, Muqawqis the ruler of Egypt, Harith Gassani the governor of Syria and Munzir ibn Sawa the ruler of Bahrain invited them to submit to Islam with veiled threats. Bahrain Jews were singled out: "Therefore you may also forgive the people of Bahrain whoever want to continue with their Jewish faith, should be made to pay the Jizia." Muhammed's Letter to Oman: "Peace be upon him who follows true guidance; thereafter I invite both of you to the Call of Islam. Embrace Islam. Allah has sent me as a Prophet to all His creatures in order that I may instil fear of Allah in the hearts of His disobedient creatures so that there may be left no excuse for those who deny Allah. If you two accept Islam, you will remain in command of your country; but if you refuse my Call, you've got to remember that all your possessions are perishable. My horsemen will appropriate your land, and my Prophethood will assume preponderance over your kingship." So Oman has no option by to convert to Islam.

Contemporary scenario. To-day, the Jews are fighting for their homeland, Israel, the Christians are almost wiped out of the Middle East and pagan communities wiped or are reduced to very small isolated communities (The Kalash of Chitra, Pakistan; the Zoroastrians of Iraq; The Druce in the Golan Heights, Israel; Samaritans in Israel; Yazidi in Iraq; Mandaeans in Iraq). Ploys to bring Islam to Jerusalem relate to two claims (1) the political that asks Jerusalem to be the capital of both Israel and the nascent Palestine and (2) emphasis on the holiness of Temple Mount to both Judaism and Islam.

Basic facts: The role that Jerusalem has in the Hebrew holy works is well known. There are varying opinions on the holiness of Jerusalem, specifically Temple Mount to Islam. Jerusalem is not mentioned in the Quran and did not occupy any special role in Islam until recent political exigencies transformed Jerusalem into Islam's third holy site. Jerusalem's role as "The Third Holiest Site in Islam" in mainstream Islamic writings does not precede the 1930s. It was created by the Grand Mufti, Haj Amin al Husseini. The Mufti knew that nationalist slogans alone would not succeed in uniting the masses against arriving Jewish refugees. He therefore turned the struggle into a religious conflict. He addressed the masses clearly, calling for a holy war. His battle cry was simple and comprehensive: "Down with the Infidels!" Haj Amin has worked vigorously to raise Jerusalem's status as an Islamic holy centre. He renovated the mosques on the Temple Mount, while conducting an unceasing campaign regarding the imminent Jewish "threat" to Moslem holy sites. Pictures of Temple Mount taken around 1875 are shown on CMEP & Israeli & Global News, (kahl1@gate.net) demonstrate ruins.

The Islamic claim to Jerusalem is false

Al Aqsa mosque is not the "furthest mosque" referred to by Muhammed in his dream night journey to the "furthest mosque" because Al-Aqsa mosque in Jerusalem was built about 100 years after Muhammed died. So, Muhammed went to another "furthest Mosque" not to the one in Jerusalem. Hence Muhammed 's ascension to heaven in the dream night journey occurred somewhere else and not on the site of the Dome of the Rock. Muhammed's wife, Aisha confirms that it was a dream. Al-Hasan reported: One of Abu Bakr's family told me that Aisha, the Prophet's wife used to say: "The apostle's body remained where it was but God removed his spirit by night" (Ibn Ishaq, p183). In the days of Muhammed Jerusalem was a Christian City within the Byzantine Empire. Jerusalem was captured by Khalif Omar in 638, six years after Mohammed's death. Throughout all this time there were only churches in Jerusalem, and a church stood on the Temple Mount, called the Church of Saint Mary of Justinian, built in the Byzantine architectural style.

The Dome of the Rock,was built in 691-692 by the Umayyad Caliph Khalif Abd El Malik (680-705 AD) and The Aksa Mosque was built 20 years after the Dome of the Rock. The name "Omar Mosque" is therefore false. Abd Al-Malik (685-705 AD) had Damascus as his capital not Jerusalem, not Mecca, not Medina. He was secular, focused on military and financial development to give Arabs an identity, and not focused on religion.

In or around 711, or about 80 years after Mohammed died (in 632AD), Malik's son, Abd El-Wahd (who ruled from 705-715), reconstructed the Christian-Byzantine Church of St. Mary and converted it into a mosque. He left the structure as it was, a typical Byzantine "basilica" structure with a row of pillars on either side of the rectangular "ship" in the center. All he added was an onion-like dome on top of the building to make it look like a mosque. He then named it El-Aksa, so it would sound like the one mentioned in the Quran. Therefore Mohammed could never have had this mosque in mind when he compiled the Quran, since it did not exist for another

71

three generations after his death. Rather, as many scholars long ago established, it is logical that Mohammed intended the mosque in Mecca as the "Sacred Mosque," and the mosque in Medina as the "Furthest Mosque. Jerusalem never held any sanctity for Muslims, but only for the Jews, (Reference: Dr. Manfred R. Lehmann, a writer for the Algemeiner Journal). The Dome on the Rock is a political ploy against Judaism and not as a religious act. There is no valid Islamic claim to Jerusalem in the religious sense.

Change of qibla from Jerusalem to Mecca. Muhammed was driven out of Mecca by the Arab community and fled to Medina which had three Jewish tribes. Muhammed presented himself to the Jews as God`s final prophet. But the Jews would not leave the Torah for his teachings. When Muhammed finally accepted that the Jews will not leave Judaism to follow him, he changed the qibla (direction of worship) from Jerusalem (the qibla of the Jews), which he had done for the initial years of his mission, to the Kabah (originally the pagan house containing idols) in Mecca, thus renouncing Jerusalem as a religious site in preference of Mecca. He gathered the pagan desert tribes, made a temporary truce (the Hudaibiya Treaty) with the Jewish Quraysh, (also spelled Koraish), tribe but then killed them at the Khaidar Oasis when he had grown military strength.

Al Tabari reported that it was not until Muhammed heard the Jews say "Muhammed and his companions do not know where their qibla was until we directed them" that he decided to change his prayer direction to Mecca (The History of Al Tabari: The Foundation of Community translated by M.V. Mc Donald, annotated by W. Montgomery, 1987 Vol V11 p 24-25). The change of qibla from Jerusalem to the Kabah in Mecca occurred 16 months after the start of the Hijrah (flight to Medina) era.

Temple Mount is the site of the Jewish Temples which were successively built on the Mount. The first Temple was built 2956 years ago by King Solomon, son of David and is described in minute detail in the Torah. This Temple was destroyed by the Babylonian conquerer, Nebuchadnezzar (2370 years ago). The second Temple was built by Cyrus, the King of Persia (today called Iran) who paid for its reconstruction and ordered the return of the Jews exiled to Babylon. King Herod added to the Second Temple for 46 years. After the Jews revolted against Roman Rule, Titus burnt the second Temple 1930 years ago. Carvings on the Arch of Titus in Rome depict Titus's triumphal march through Rome parading the Temple vessels including the great Menorah (Candelabra). The Romans carved a record of the Jewish temple in stone! The Romans sent the Jews in exile for 1878 years, yet a Jewish presence remained.

Ploys to obliterate the historic connection of Jews and Christians to the land of their religion. Judea and Samaria were renamed Province Syria Palestina by the Romans to hide the fact that these lands belonged to the Jews. Judea, Samaria, Cesarea, Galilee are places where Jesus preached, and Nazareth, his home town and Bethlehem where he was born and Jerusalem where he was condemned by Pontius Pilot (the fifth prefect of the Roman province of Judea (praefectus Iudaeae, from AD26 -36) and died. The historic connection to these Jewish lands is also the heritage of all Christians worldwide.

Ploys to obliterate Judaism. The Jews had lived in Israel for at least 2000 years before Muhammed was born. Jesus was born in Bethleham 500 years before Muhammed. Temple Mount is the site of two temples, one of which is Solomon's Temple and is considered the holiest site in Judaism. Dome on the Rock and Al-Aqsa mosque were built over the ruins of the magnificent Roman period Temple and stand there to-day denying access to the temple ruins. There is substantial archeological and historical evidence of the Temples also in Islamic literature. Identified as Solomon's Temple, the underground area of the Temple Mount is known as Solomon's stables in Jewish and Islamic literature.

Further destruction has been undertaken by the Islamic land trust to destroy Judeo-Christian ruins beneath Temple Mount by excavations, so as to deny any connection between Judaism and Christianity and Jerusalem (Daniel Levin, Denial on Temple Mount, The Forward, Oct 23, 2009). In the El-Marwani project without coordinating with Israel, tons of material from Temple Mount were excavated and transported away in hundreds of trucks to dumps.

In the 1967 two unexploded bombs were found inside the Armenian (Christian) monastery. Further destruction within modern times include tomb headstones carried away from the Jewish cemetery to obliterate the Jewish presence. The Christian quarter contains the church of the Holy Sepulchre, viewed by many as Christianity's holiest place.

The Agreements. The agreements and concessions made to the Caliph of the Ottoman Empire in 1922, who lost the war thus ending their raids on the Mediterranean countries, the Devshirme system (introduced in the 14th Century in which Christians and Jews has to surrender 20% of their male children to the state who converted them to Islam and used them as soldiers), and the sergoli (which recruited young boys as servants in the women's quarters of the sultan), are more generous than the Mohammedan Rules of War: kill all the males of fighting age, enslave the women and children, seize all the land and wealth and keep it.

The current legal scenario. In the fog of war that engulfs the conflict, there is a need to maintain clarity by keeping to the terms of agreements. Israel's legal title and rights to all its present territory are recognised by an act of international law made in the post- World War 1 San Remo Agreement, which was then further recognised and incorporated in subsequent binding acts, from the Covenant of the League of Nations to Article 80 of the United Nations' Charter. None of the national and political rights have been revoked, nullified or superseded by any subsequent act of international law. The Oslo Accords prohibit the establishment of any activity of the Palestinian Authority in Jerusalem.

The Political Scenarios. The Hamas Charter states their aim is to "wipe Israel off the map" and their actions speak louder than their written words. The Hamas-Muslim Brotherhood aim to make a Caliphate out of Egypt, Gaza and Israel. This is the reality on the ground. It is greed for religious power and the revenue that comes from such power (Zaki Ameen). The Muslim Brotherhood is a political force in Egypt. Egypt's former president Morsi was the president of the Muslim Brotherhood. His removal from power started with people's protests. Morsi tried to quickly build a dictatorship. Morsi awarded himself total executive control, allowing himself to bypass judicial procedures. However there were street protests. His superiors in the Muslim Brotherhood told him to 'Shut up. You make this decree.' The Brotherhood saw the decision to ram through the constitution as their only option. A significant proportion of the population had started to realise that Morsi didn't have any power. Absolutely nothing. It was the Maktab Irshad (the Brotherhood's management board) who had full power. President Mahmud Abbas has been unable to control terrorism. The gun is louder than dialogue. International actors foment war. Iran aids Hamas in various ways. Iran sent Hamas in Gaza a ship laden with ammunition. Hezbollha, a state within a state in Lebanon, supported by Iran aims to annihilate Israel.

A two-state solution. That East Jerusalem as defined by the pre-1967 municipal boundaries would be the capital of Palastine and West Jerusalem, the capital of Israel is untenable, impractical, ignores Muslim attempts to destroy Jewish and Christian holy sites and the rights of Jews and Christians to their religious heritage. Muslims have continually demonstrated their intention to destroy all evidence of a Jewish and Christian connection to Jerusalem.

East Jerusalem contains The Temple Mount and The Western Wall (Jewish); The Dome on the Rock monument and Al Aqsa Mosque (Muslim); the Church of the Holy Sepulchre (Christian).

The Term "West Bank" refers to a geographical location not to a nation of people. This term refers to land west of the river Jordan from the perspective of Jordan because this land belonged to Jordan until Jordan provoked a war against Israel and lost it to Israel. In terms of Islamic war rules, the West Bank is spoils of war belonging to Israel. The proper name of the West Bank is Judea and Samaria. Judea is historically Jewish land. Hence the West Bank belongs to Israel by war and by historical association.

The six-day war was provoked by Syria, Egypt and Jordan. In the 1967 war against Israel, Israel conquered the Sinai, the West bank, the Golan Heights, East Jerusalem and Gaza. The West Bank and East Jerusalem had previously belonged to Jordan since the 1948-49 Arab-Israeli war not to Palestinians. The Gaza strip was seized by Israel from

Egypt, but Israel withdrew from this territory in 2005. Israel seized land in the Sinai Peninsula from Egypt but gave this back as part of a peace agreement with Cairo. The Golan Heights were captured from Syria in the 1967 war. The Fourth Geneva Convention does not apply to the West bank because this was a defensive war. It is a matter of principle that if a country attacks another, defence is not negotiable. It is a Right. If the attacker is given back the land, then this sets a president for further attacks. Moreover "land for peace" is coercion.

The two-state solution has never been an option, not even a talking point because Hamas and the Muslim Brotherhood clearly call for Israel to be wiped off the map. Moreover there are at least two Islamic practices that give Muslims a major advantage: (i) The principle that criminal guilt does not exist in Sharia. There is no concept of penal law in Islamic Law (Schacht 1982, p187). Murder is not a crime but falls under "blood money" ie the murderer pays money to the family's victim. (ii) Such payment is thwarted by the many verses of the Quran calling for the killing of Jews and Christians and the suppression of all religions.

The Oslo Accords and the two-state solution have constantly been derailed by Hamas, Fatah and splinter groups of terrorists demonstrating a rejection of peace. Since the proposal for a two-state nation solution which was accepted by Arafat, Hamas has responded with intifidas and a high density campaign of guerrilla warfare using tactics such as ambushes, sniper attacks and suicide bombings targeting civilian places, suicide bombs carried by children, car bombs, bus attacks, a practice of militant leaders hiding among civilians in densely populated areas, thus turning them into human shields, hitting kindergartens with anti-tank missiles, snipers killing Israeli babies, kidnapping and killing Israeli teenagers including those tricked by a pretence of friendship, kidnapping of both soldiers and civilians including children, shootings, assassinations, stabbings, stoning, lynching, rockets and mortars launched into Israel from Gaza on a daily basis, including shelling with Qassam rockets, bombardments of cities, use of smuggling tunnels between Gaza and Egypt to obtain ammunition, tunnels into Israel to facilitate ambush, concrete given by Israel to Gaza to build homes used for guerrilla tunnels; using Gaza hospitals and UN schools to hide weapons and launch missiles turning them into war zones; Palestinian militants attacked and shot a pregnant woman and her four young daughters. Amnesty international classified it as a crime against humanity and stated that it "reiterates its call on all Palestinian armed groups to put an immediate end to the deliberate targeting of Israeli civilians."

Israel at peace with its neighbours. Islamic Principles derived from the Quran have from its inception sought and achieved the destruction of Jews, Christians, pagans, and all other beliefs in the Arabian Peninsula. Moreover Islam does not, like democracy, evolve because the Quran is regarded as the unchanging will of Allah. Bedouin (preIslamic) cultural practices are fundamental to Islam. The security of an individual of a tribe rested with the tribe. The tribe protected the interests of the individual. Honour is central to tribal culture. A loss of honour must be addressed by killing the offending person in order to regain honour. Hence, the neighbouring countries, all of which have tried to overrun Israel but have failed, now suffer from a loss of honour. Further, in Islam oaths (agreements) are temporary, "until something better comes along" when a Muslim regards the oath to be at an end. In Western society oaths are binding, ie Oaths are indicative of truth and hence cannot be altered after being taken without adequate negotiation.

Western practices are not appropriate to bring peace to the Middle East due to their directly opposing philosophies as demonstrated several times: Where Israel withdraws, terrorists enter. Israel withdrew from Gaza after winning it in the 6-day war. Hamas and the Muslim Brotherhood entered and took the land. Israel withdrew from S. Lebanon after winning it in the 6-day war. Hezbollha (an allay of Iran) entered giving rise to a state within a state in Lebanon. Saad Rafik Al-Hariri born in Saudi, (son of Lebanese Prime Minister Hariri assassinated in 2005) has been Prime Minister of Lebanon from 2009 to 2011 and from 2016. He is now part of a coalition composed of *Hezbollah* (a terrorist organisation), the Amal Movement, the Free Patriotic Movement, and the Progressive party that was expected to run as a unified block in the elections of 2018.

Some major terrorist attacks. An Islamic Jihad suicide bomber detonated himself in the Tel Aviv coastline Dolphinarium dancing club on June 1,2001, killing several civilians. The attack hampered American attempts to negotiate cease-fire; The stand-off at the Church of the Nativity with Palestinian militants in Bethlehem while Palestinian civilians and priests were inside; Abduction of Gilad Shalit while on duty, exchanged for over 1000 Palestinian terrorists after five years of being kept in a dark underground cell. In addition there are threats to peace from Fatah-Hamas splinter groups and conflict within Fatah itself which further terrorism. A major stumbling block to peace arises from the support for terrorism by Iran with the supply of weaponry and support for suicide bombing. The 4 October suicide bombing at Maxim restaurant, Haifa, claimed the lives of 21 Israelis, sponsored by Syria and Iran Islamic Jihad, and Hezbollah carried out the terrorist attack.

Lack of good will. Mahmud Abbas, the president of the Palestinian Authority has made no real efforts to stop the terrorism. S.47:35 Hilali-Khan "So be not weak and ask not for peace (from the enemies of Islam) while you are having the upper hand. God is with you and will never decrease the reward of your good deeds." Arafat while speaking to the UN Council in English, spoke of peace, but once in Palastine, speaking in Arabic, he worked the Palestinians in a frenzy against Israel. Taqiyya is not a sin when used in the interests of Islam. In 1993, Arafat broke the Oslo accords with Israel. Financing a military and training his police, Arafat declared war on Israel in 2000.

"War is deceit" said Muhammed, narrated Jabir bin Abdullah. "Deceit is war" Bukhari vol4 book52, Hadith number 269. Lack of goodwill for peace results from several Quran verses, including the Mohammedan concept: "No two religions can exist in the Peninsula of the Arabs." This is now echoed in Israel and Muslim majority countries.

Refugee scenarios. The UN Security Council (2334). There are two, not one type of refugee populations created by the Arab-Israeli conflict: Israeli refugees who were driven away by the violence and not only Gazans. Following the 1948 Arab-Israeli war, instigated by Arabs, the Old City was captured by Jordan, the Jewish Quarter was completely sacked by Arab forces. The quarter was besieged and all its

Jewish residents were forced to leave en mass. Fifty-eight synagoges were destroyed. The ancient Jewish cemetery on Mount Olives was desecrated and the tombstones were carted away and used for construction and paving roads to destroy evidence of Jewish presence. Jordan destroyed the Jewish villages of Atarot and Neve Yaakov just north of Jerusalem. Thousands of Arab refugees from West Jerusalem were settled in the previous Jewish areas of East Jerusalem. Jordan went so far as to declare Jerusalem its second capital. Just because one type of refugee has been kept alive by UNRWA, while the other has been dealt with by people who refused to be instrumentalized and chose to move on with their lives, the tragedy and claims on *both* populations require attention.

Israel, the only Democracy in the Middle East. Israel is a democracy with a Jewish majority. Christians living in Jerusalem have an innate religious sense for peace. Christians worldwide have a right to visit Jerusalem in peace. It is their heritage. To-day, Egypt has struggled towards democracy but has failed due to the Muslim Brotherhood and Hamas terrorism because they want to turn Egypt, Gaza and Israel into a Caliphate which would provide them with power, stolen wealth and taxes. Even under President El- Sisi, with whom Netanyahu has been developing mutually beneficial security relations, prominent figures in state run press disseminate anti-Israeli conspiracy theories. Turkey has struggled towards secularism but the recent coup has caused a turning towards Islamization. Lebanon had achieved a high level of secularism until Hezbollha appeared. The Iranian revolution put an end to the rule of the Shah, who had a programme of modernization and Westernization. Persia as Iran was known before 1935, was one of the greatest empires of the ancient world and had Zoroastrian religion. Iran became an Islamic republic in 1979 when the monarch was overthrown and clerics assumed political control under supreme leader Ayatollah Kkomeini. Pro reform outlets were closed and their writers and editors imprisoned. Iran has been described by media freedom advocates as "among the five biggest prisons in the world" for journalists.

Recent history. When the Ottoman Sultan, Suleiman lost the war, Ottoman land including former Ottoman territories came under the 1922/23 British Mandate. The British lopped off 85% of the

Ottoman province "Palestine" (name given by the Romans) and created Transjordan. The land west of the river Jordan (West Palestine) was left for a Jewish homeland promised to the Jews with a Balfour Declaration. Yet once the British started to be dependent on Arab oil, they started limiting Jewish migration to Palestine. A large influx of Arabs (mainly Muslim), from Egypt, Syria and elsewhere migrated to Palestine looking for a better life, looting rather than working. Therefore, all current Muslim inhabitants of Samara, Judea and Gaza have their roots in Egypt and could potentially move back to Egypt just as more than half the Jewish population of Israel (which also has 23% Muslim) are descendents of Jews who had to flee or were ethnically cleaned by Muslims who are now doing the same to Christians as there are no more Jews left among them.

Jerusalem cannot be dissected. The Old city of Jerusalem, the heart of Judaism for more than 3,000 years and the seat of Christianity for 2,000 years, is the heritage of Jews and Christians. It should in no way be given up to be an Islamic country, and a terrorist one. The UN Security Council has completely ignored the heritage of Christianity in Jerusalem to the advantage of Islamic interests.

Yasser Arafat in 1967 made a political claim that Temple Mount is the third holiest site for Islam, including all Jerusalem. His uncle, the grand Mufti of Jerusalem, Haj Amin Al-Husseini used to initiate riots in Hebron and Jerusalem in 1929 by claiming that the Jews were attacking the Al-Aksa mosque and killing Muslims in his war against Jews. Husseini later became a confidant of Hitler begging him to come to Jerusalem in WW11. Israeli Prime Minister Benjamin Netanyahu (2017), lamented: "The greatest obstacle to the expansion of peace today is not found in the leaders of the countries around us. The obstacle is public opinion on the Arab street, public opinion that has been brainwashed for years by a distorted and misleading presentation of the State of Israel."

Indeed, it is 40 years since Egyptian President Anwar Sadat's historic visit to the Knesset, where Sadat announced: "I have come to you so that together we might build a durable peace based on justice to avoid the shedding of one single drop of blood from an Arab or an Israeli." Anwar

Sadat, whose peace pact with Israel earned him the Nobel Peace Prize was gunned down on October 6, 1981, by four of his military officers during an annual parade.

What has been achieved so far? In 2018, The UN Resolution was approved: "Status of Jerusalem. The capital of the State of Israel. For 128, against 9, abstentions 35.

The Muslim subjugation and slaughter continued throughout the Middle East, Persia (to-day Iran), Asia and North Africa, with three unsuccessful waves into Europe. This is documented history. The classical Christian populations in the Middle East consisted of Copts, Greeks, Armenians and Arameans, the latter being the indigenous people of Southeast Turkey, Iraq, Syria and Lebanon. The Arameans include the traditionally Aramanic-speaking churches of the Syria Orthodox, Syriac Catholics, Chaldeans, Nestorians (also known as Assyrians), Maronites, Melkite Orthodox and Melkite Catholics. It is reported that Christianity in the biblically historic lands such as Iraq, Syria and Turkey will be at an end by 2030.

3

Law and Order

Whereas Democracy seeks to make the punishment fit the crime, Islam maintains Law and Order through punishments specified in the Quran and Hadiths. The vast majority of Muslims and most Islamic scholars consider both the Quran and Sahih hadiths to be the valid source of Sharia, with Quranic verse 33.21 (SAHIH INTERNATIONAL "There has certainly been for you in the Messenger of Allah an excellent pattern for anyone whose hope is in Allah and the Last Day and (who) remembers Allah often," which states that Muhammed is the example. Traditional Sharia courts, unlike modern Western courts, do not use jury or prosecutors on the behalf of society.

Fatwas are a formal ruling or interpretation on a point of Islamic law given by a qualified legal scholar (known as a mufti). In 1989 the Ayatollah Khomeini of Iran issued a fatwa ordering Muslims to kill Salmon Rushdie because of his book, "The Satanic Verses" which was considered blasphemous.

Hadd and Hakk crimes. There are two broad categories of crimes: Hadd and Hakk crimes. Hadd crimes are crimes against God (Hakk/Haq Allah meaning the "right of God" and also "the truth of God"). Under Islamic Law, they are mandated and fixed by God as revealed through Muhammad, and as such immutable, unable to be altered or abolished by people, jurists or parliament. Hadd crimes cannot be pardoned by the victim or by the state, and the punishments must be carried out in public. All other criminal matters are regarded as against Humans (Hakk/Haq Adami), including murder and bodily injury and are treated as disputes between individuals with an Islamic judge deciding the outcome based on Sharia Fiqh such as Hanafi, Maliki, Shafi'i, Hanbali and Jafari followed in the Islamic jurisdiction. For crimes against humans (Hakk Adami), Islamic law prescribes a retaliatory punishment analogous to the crime (qisas) or monetary compensation (diya), and for other crimes the form of punishment is left to the judge's discretion (tazir). Hadd punishments range from public lashing to publicly stoning to death, amputation of hands and feet and crucifixion. Different punishments are prescribed for different scenarios and there are differences of opinion regarding specifics within and between legal schools. Examples of offenses incurring Hadd punishments include zina (unlawful sexual intercourse), unfounded accusations of zina, homosexuality, impurity, drinking alcohol and highway robbery, and others.

Zina, the Sin of unlawful sexual intercourse. Zina includes pre-marital sex and extra-marital sex. Although stoning for zina is not mentioned in the Quran, all schools of traditional jurisprudence agreed on the basis of hadith that it is to be punished by stoning if the offender is muhsan (adult, free, Muslim, and married). Unfounded accusation of zina is punished by 80 lashes. The Quran is clear about punishments for sex outside marriage. Fornicators are to be publically flogged with one-hundred lashes and let a party of believers witness the punishment (Q 24:2), "The woman and the man guilty of adultery or fornication - flog each of them with a hundred stripes. Let not compassion move you in their case, in a matter prescribed by Allah, if ye believe in Allah and the Last Day, and let a party of the Believers witness their punishment." The crime of "accusation of illicit sex or rape against chaste women without four witnesses" is a Hadd punishment based on Quranic verses 24:4, 24:6, 9:66 and 16:106, among others. "And those who accuse chaste women and do not bring four witnesses, flog them with eighty stripes and do not accept their witness thereafter. Indeed they themselves are impure."

There are certain standards for proof that must be met in Islamic law for zina punishment to apply. In the Shafii, Hanbali, and Hanafi law schools Rajm (public stoning) or lashing is imposed for religiously prohibited sex only if the crime is proven, either by four male adults witnessing at first hand the actual sexual intercourse at the same time or by self-confession. For the establishment of adultery, four male Muslim witnesses must have seen the act in its most intimate details. Shia Islam allows substitution of one male Muslim with two female Muslims, but requires that at least one of the witnesses be a male. The Sunni Maliki school of law consider pregnancy in an unmarried woman as sufficient evidence of zina, unless there is evidence of rape or compulsion. If a person alleges zina and fails to provide four consistent Muslim witnesses, or if witnesses provide inconsistent testimonies, they can be sentenced to eighty lashes for unfounded accusation of fornication itself a hadd crime. The Hudood (Hudud) Ordinance in Pakistan led to the jailing of thousands of women on zina-related charges, were used to file "nuisance or harassment suits against disobedient daughters or estranged wives." The sentencing to death of women in Pakistan, Nigeria, Sudan for zina caused international uproar, being perceived as not only too harsh, but an "odious" punishment of victims not wrongdoers.

According to a well-known, though by no means universally accepted hadith, those who engage in homosexual acts are to be put to death. Classification of homosexual intercourse as zina differs according to a legal school. Supporting Hadd punishments are Islamic revivalists such as Abul A'la Maududi who writes that in a number of places the Quran "declares that sodomy is such a heinous sin" that it is the duty of the Islamic State to eradicate this crime and punish those who are guilty of it.

Public executions are a requirement for crimes of impurity. Oriana Fallici (international journalist) IN: The Rage and the Pride (2002), relates an example of law enforcement against impurity, the torture and death of twelve young men regarded as impure, executed in Dacca stadium with bayonet blows to the torso and abdomen in the presence of twenty thousand faithful who applauded in the name of God "Allah akbar, Allah akbar." A little boy who tried to save his brother, was crushed by combat boots. Moreover the audience organised itself into a line and crushed the bodies into a bleeding carpet, thundering: "Allah akbar."

Floggings for moral crimes have been carried out since the codification of Islamic law in Sudan in 1991 and continue. In 2012 a Sudanese court sentenced Intisar Sharif Abdallah, a teenager, to death by stoning in the city of Omdurman under article 146 of Sudan's Criminal Act after charging her with "adultery with a married person." She was held in Omdurman prison with her legs shackled, with her 5-month-old baby. She was released on July 3, 2012 after an international outcry.

Islamic Republic of Iran stoned to death four offenders in Kerman. By the late 1980s, Mauritania, Sudan, and the United Arab Emirates had "enacted laws to grant courts the power to hand down Hadd penalties." During the 1990s Somalia, Yemen, Afghanistan, and northern Nigeria followed suit. In 1994 the Iraqi president Saddam Hussein, issued a decree "ordering that robbers and car thieves should lose their hands." Brunei adopted Hadd laws in 2014. Enforcement of Hadd punishments has varied from country to country. In Nigeria local courts have passed several stoning sentences for zina, all of which were overturned on appeal or left unenforced. During the first two years when Shari`a was made state law in Sudan (1983 and 1985), a Hadd (hudud) punishment for theft was inflicted on several hundred criminals, and then discontinued though not repealed.

The requirement of four male witnesses before a rape victim can seek justice has been criticized as leading to "hundreds of incidents where a woman subjected to rape, or gang rape, was eventually accused of zina" and incarcerated, in Pakistan. Hundreds of women in Afghanistan jails are victims of rape or domestic violence, accused of zina, when the victim failed to present witnesses. In Pakistan, over 200,000 zina cases against women under the Hudood laws were under way at various levels in Pakistan's legal system in 2005. In addition to thousands of women in prison awaiting trial for zina-related charges, rape victims in Pakistan have been reluctant to report rape because they feared being charged with zina. The resulting controversy prompted the law to be amended in 2006, though the amended version has been criticized for continuing to blur the legal distinction between rape and consensual sex.

The Hadd crime of theft is referred to in Quranic verse 5:38 "And (as for) the male thief and the female thief, cut off (from the wrist joint) their (right) hand as a recompense for that which they committed, a punishment by way of example from Allah. And Allah is All Powerful, All Wise." A person's right hand is amputated, whether he is a Muslim or a non-Muslim subject of the Islamic state. It can also be amputation of the right hand and left foot or vice versa based on the expression of Min khilaf in Q5:33 and Q7:124. Notwithstanding these Quran verses against theft, the killing of infidels allows the seizing their land, wealth, women and children. It sets up a dualistic situation. The crime of "robbery and civil disturbance against Islam" inside a Muslim state, according to some Muslim scholars, is referred to in Quranic verse 5:33.

The crime of intoxication is referred to in Quran verse 5:90, and its Hadd punishment is described in hadiths. "O ye who believe! Intoxicants and gambling, (dedication of) stones, and (divination by) arrows, are an abomination, of Satan's handwork. eschew such (abomination), that ye may prosper." Sunan Abu Dawud, Book 38, Number 4467,Narrated Mu'awiyah ibn AbuSufyan "The Prophet said: If they (the people) drink wine, flog them, again if they drink it, flog them. Again if they drink it, kill them." The Hanafis forbid drinking alcoholic beverages other than wine only if it leads to drunkenness, while other schools forbid all alcoholic beverages. It is punished by 40 to 80 lashes, depending on the legal school.

Rebellion is considered a Hadd crime. Quran 5:33 is clear "The punishment of those who wage war against Allah and His Messenger, and strive with might and main for mischief through the land is: execution, or crucifixion, or the cutting off of hands and feet from opposite sides, or exile from the land: that is their disgrace in this world, and a heavy punishment is theirs in the Hereafter." Sahih International 8:39 "And fight them until there is no fitnah and (until) the religion, all of it, is for Allah. And if they cease, then indeed, Allah is Seeing of what they do." Fitnah is translated to mean various acts such as resistance to

Islam, defined in the prior verse as an unwillingness to believe (8:38). Quran 33:57–61, "Those who annoy Allah and His Messenger, Allah has cursed them in this World and in the Hereafter, and has prepared for them a humiliating Punishment. Truly, if the Hypocrites, and those in whose hearts is a disease, and those who stir up sedition in the City, desist not, We shall certainly stir thee up against them: Then will they not be able to stay in it as thy neighbours for any length of time: They shall have a curse on them: whenever they are found, they shall be seized and slain (without mercy)."

The criteria for which Muhammed would kill a person. Sahih Bukhari (83:37), emphasises the criteria for which Muhammed would kill a person: "Allah's Apostle never killed anyone except in one of the following three situations: (1) A person who killed somebody unjustly, was killed (in Qisas,) (2) a married person who committed illegal sexual intercourse and (3) a man who fought against Allah and His Apostle and deserted Islam and became an apostate." al-Muwatta of Imam Malik (36.18.15) realized: "The Messenger of Allah said, "If someone changes his religion, then strike off his head."" Reliance of the Traveller (Islamic Law) 08.1, "When a person who has reached puberty and is sane voluntarily apostatizes from Islam, he deserves to be killed." 08.4 affirms that there is no penalty for killing an apostate. Tabari 17:187 relates the words of a group of Christians who had converted to Islam, but realized their error after being shocked by the violence and looting committed in the name of Allah. "By God, our religion (din) from which we have departed is better and more correct than that which these people follow. Their religion does not stop them from shedding blood, terrifying the roads, and seizing properties." "And they returned to their former religion." The price of their decision to return to a religion of peace was that the men were beheaded and the woman and children enslaved by caliph Ali.

The crime of Apostacy, the Sin of Treason. Leaving Islam (apostacy) for another religion or for atheism, is regarded as one of the Hadd crimes liable to capital punishment in traditional jurisprudence. Many Hadith establish the death sentence for apostates The most reliable Hadith collection contains numerous accounts of Muhammad and his companions putting people to death for leaving Islam. Sahih Bukhari (52:260), The Prophet said, "If somebody (a Muslim) discards his religion, kill him." Muhammad clearly and unambiguously lays out that the penalty for leaving the religion of Islam is execution. The idea that apostates should be executed is not a fringe view. Rather, it is the view of the five greatest schools of Islamic law: the Sunni Hanbali, Hanafi, Maliki, and Shafi'i schools, and the Shi'i Ja'fari school. Rejection of Islam or conversion to another religion is punished by death. There is also a consensus by all four schools of Sunni Islamic jurisprudence (i.e., Maliki, Hanbali, Hanafi, and Shafii), as well as classical Shiite jurists, that apostates from Islam must be put to death. The process of declaring a person to be an apostate is known as Takfir and the disbeliever is called a Murtad. Al-Muwatta of Imam Malik (36.18.15) "The messenger of Allah said "Whoever changed his religion, then kill him." Reliance of the Traveller (Islamic Law) 08.1: "When a person who has reached puberty and is sane voluntarily apostasizes from Islam, he deserves to be killed." Averroes (d. 1198), the renowned philosopher and scholar of the natural sciences, who was also an important Maliki jurist, provided this typical Muslim legal opinion on the punishment for apostasy: "An apostate is to be executed by agreement in the case of a man, because of the words of the Prophet, "Slay those who change their din (religion)." Asking the apostate to repent was stipulated as a condition prior to his execution. The contemporary (i.e.,1991) Al-Azhar (Cairo) Islamic Research Academy endorsed manual of Islamic Law, Umdat al-Salik (pp. 595-96) endorses: "Leaving Islam is the ugliest form of unbelief (kufr) and the worst. When a person who has reached puberty and is sane voluntarily apostasises from Islam, he deserves to be killed. In such a case, it is obligatory to ask him to repent and return to Islam. If he does it is accepted from him, but if he refuses, he is immediately killed."

Apostasy is taken so seriously by Muslims such that it spawned the first of many serious internal wars. Immediately after Muhammad's death, several Bedouin tribes wanted to leave Islam and return to their preferred religion. In a conflict known as the Riddah (apostasy) Wars they were slaughtered in such places recalled as `Garden of Death` and `Gulley of Blood`during the first caliph Abu Bakr's aggressive and violent campaign to force submission (and keep the tribute payments flowing back to Mecca). Within months, a great many people were dead, including Muslims who had memorized the Quran by heart. As Abu Bakr, Muhammad`s closest companion, explained in a letter at the time, his prophet "struck whoever turned his back to Him until he came to Islam, willingly or grudgingly." Thus, did Abu Bakr promised to "burn them with fire, slaughter them by any means, and take women and children captive" from any who left Islam, (al-Tabari v10 p.55-57). Ali, the fourth (Rightly guided Caliph) and Muhammed`s son-in-law burned people alive who wanted to follow their conscience. An old man (Rumahis Mansur regretted leaving Christianity and vowed not to remain Muslim, was quickly beheaded by Ali (Al-Tabari v17 p191). In 1400 years, there has never been a system of Islamic law that did not prescribe the death penalty for Muslims choosing to leave Islam. Even in modern, ostensibly secular Islamic countries with constitutions "guaranteeing" freedom of religion, there is de facto enforcement of this law with intimidation and the vigilante murder of apostates. A modern day (2018) example is the ISIS terrorists accusing Abu Zmat of being an "apostate" for smuggling weapons to Hamas`s armed wing, Al-Qassam in Gaza, and smuggling dozens of people from Al-Arish in the Sinai into Gaza strip. He was beheaded.

The crime of Blasphemy. The Quran admonishes against blasphemy. The verses 5:33-34 and 33: 57-61 most commonly justified punishment for blasphemy. Various fiqhs (schools of jurisprudence) of Islam have different punishments for blasphemy, depending on whether the blasphemer is Muslim or non-Muslim, man or woman. The punishment can be fines, imprisonment, flogging, amputation, hanging, or beheading. Support in the Quran and Sunnah for the death penalty for blasphemy is also found in this verse: "Indeed, the penalty for those who wage war against Allah and His Messenger and strive upon earth (to cause) corruption is none but that they be killed or crucified or that their hands and feet be cut off from opposite sides or that they be exiled from the land. That is for them a disgrace in this world, and for them in the Hereafter is a great punishment," (Q.

5:33). In the case of an insult to Muhammad, the Muslim community is considered to be under an obligation to avenge the insult because the possibility of forgiveness expired upon the death of Muhammad. A wide range of acts are considered blasphemy but the punishment is the same: death. Touching something that has touched a Quran but the individuals were not Muslim is considered blasphemy. A well known case is that of Aishia Bibi (real name Asyan Noreen but called "Bibi" in Pakistan. Al-Shabaab whipped women who were wearing a bra, and whipped men for being beardless; Islamic scholars issued a fatwa declaring yoga as blasphemous, because yoga is a form of spiritual practice in Hinduism.

The crime of hypocrisy. Hypocrisy is defined as "Double-facedness" the person is a believer but the inner self of the person is in disbelief. Hypocrisy is categorized as Hypocrisy against Allah regarding actual faith and Hypocrisy with Allah regarding the necessities of faith. The term "hypocrite" in the Quran refers both to all those who renegade from Islam and also to those who deliberately fail to conform to Islamic rulings and regulations while claiming to be Muslims. In the minds of the victim's family, the daughter or son is regarded as an apostate when she or he refuses to follow the dictates of Islam such as opting for Westernization or running away from an abusive home to gain freedom. Such disobedience is addressed with murder. Disobedience is not allowed to stand in the way of Allah. Surah 58:22 "You shall not find a people who believe in Allah and the latter day befriending those who act in opposition to Allah and His Messenger, even though they were their own fathers, or their sons, or their brothers, or their kinsfolk," Shakir.

The Sin of Non-submission. Law and Order is maintained through family executions in cases of disobedience and "bringing shame" upon their family. Reasons for such honour killing focus on disobedience at adhering to society's social norms. The killers mainly defend their act of murder by referring to the Quran and Islam. The family guardian says that they are merely following the directives set down in their Islamic ethical beliefs. The following are not subject to retaliation: a father or mother (or their fathers or mothers) for killing their offspring or offspring's offspring. A Muslim parent faces no legal penalty under Islamic law for killing his child or grandchild: "not subject to retaliation" is a father or mother (or their fathers or mothers) for killing their offspring," Umdat al-Salik, Relience of the Traveller, Sunni Orthodoxy, 01.1-2. Thus, parents who murder their son/daughter for the sake of "honour," whether owing to issues of chastity, apostasy and the like, incurs no penalty under Sharia. Regarding slaying a boy who refused to go to prayers, "And as for the boy, his parents were believers and feared lest he should make disobedience and ingratitude to come upon them. So they desired that their Lord might give them in his place one better than him in purity and nearer to having compassion" Pickthall. Honour killing incurs no penalty under Sharia. If a parent murders their child for the sake of honour, this is not penalized under Islamic law. Honour killing is committed by the family members, father, mother, brothers, brother-in-laws, even in some cases own sisters. Family honour is one of the core values of Arab society However, honour killing is also extensively practiced by Muslims not only Arabs. The practice of committing homicides in the name of honour has been legitimized by its enshrinement in Sharia Law as an excuse for murder. Honor Killing is widespread in Islamic countries. The Human Rights Directorate in Turkey reported that in Istabbul alone there was one honour killing every week and there were 1,000 during the previous five years. Kurdish immigration from the East contributed to this. According to UNICEF, in 2000 two thirds of all killings in Palestinian territories were honor killings. The Palestinian Authority using a clause in the Jordanian penal code still in effect in the West bank exempts men from punishment for killing a female relative is she brought dishonour to the family. The Article 340 of the Jordanian Penal Code states: "He who catches his wife, or one of his females un-lawfully committing adultery with another, and he kills, wounds, or injures both of them, is excused and benefits from an exemption from penalty." Provisions as Article 340 exist in many Arab countries. Honour killing is practised extensively by Muslims. Kafaya Husayn, a 16-year old Jordanian girl was lashed to a chair by her 32-year-old brother. He gave her a drink of water and told her to receit an Islamic prayer. Then he slashed her throat. Hafaya's crime? She was raped by another brother. 23-year-old Rania Arafat in Jordan was promised to a cousin as a young child. She wanted to marry another man with whom she was in love. She ran away before her forced marriage. She wrote to her parents pleading to let her return home. Her parents promised that she would not be harmed. On her return her brother shot her 5 times in the chest and neck killing her. Amal was strangled by her father as he receited the Quran. Amira was killed by her mother, smothered with a plastic bag because she had been raped by her brothers and got pregnant. Aqsa Pervez was strangled by her father because she did not wear the Hijab. In Pakistan Samia 29, a mother of two boys was shot dead in her lawyer 's office by a man accompanying her mother. In Pakistan Amnesty International documented 10,000 killings per year in 2005. Killings are declared by the police as a domestic case that warrants no involvement. In 2008 a woman was killed in Saudi Arabia for chatting to a man on Facebook. In 2008, in Texas, US, an Egyptian father killed his two girls. It is reported that the girls were very smart, active in soccer and tennis causing conflict with their father.

Punishments for unbelievers. The sword is the standard instrument to impose law and order. The sword is a major symbol in Islam. Saudi Arabia celebrates the sword with a sword festival. There is a sword on the flag. (Q 5:33) states that the punishment for those who sow corruption on the Earth, which can include large swathes of people, is to be executed, crucified, or mutilated. Bukhari (52:73) "Allah's Apostle said, "Know that Paradise is under the shades of swords." The words of Muhammad, prophet of Islam are focused on the use of the sword. Quran 9:5, known as ayat as-sayf or the sword verse, maintains law and order by subduing non Muslims and imposing the practices of prayer and alms giving, "Then, when the sacred months are drawn away, slay the idolaters wherever you find them, and take them, and confine them, and lie in wait for them at every place of ambush. But if they repent, and perform the prayer, and pay the alms, then let them go their way." Quran (9:29) requires Muslims to "Fight those who believe not in Allah nor the Last Day, nor hold that forbidden which hath been forbidden by Allah and His Messenger, nor acknowledge the religion of Truth, (even if they are) of the People of the Book, until they pay the Jizya with willing submission, and feel themselves subdued." "People of the Book" refers to Christians and Jews. According to this verse, they are to be violently subjugated to ensure they pay the Jizya (tax), with the sole justification being their religious status. Surah al-Maìdah (5:33) says: "The punishment of those who wage war against Allah and His apostle is that they should be murdered or crucified." "Killing Unbelievers is a small matter to us" Tabari 9:69. Quran (8:39)"And fight with them until there is no more fitna (disorder, unbelief) and religion should be only for Allah." Sahih International 2:193 "Fight them until there is no (more) fitnah and (until) worship is (acknowledged to be) for Allah. But if they cease, then there is to be no aggression except against the oppressors." The Quran demands that polytheists are to be fought and punished for being non-Muslim (Q 9:5). It demands that Christians and Jews be fought and brought under submission for their beliefs (Q 9:29). The Quran commands that Muslims be harsh against unbelievers, and merciful amongst themselves (Q 48:29). So brutal is sharia that the great Muslim philosopher, Ibn Rushd (Averroes, 1126 – 1198 A.D.), states that although there is disagreement among Islamists as to whether it is allowed in time of war to "slay hermits who have retired from the world, the blind, the chronically ill and the insane, those who are old and unable to fight any longer, peasants, and serfs", he cites as-Shafi'i (c. 767 – 820 A.D.), the founder of one of the four main schools of Islamic jurisprudence, as being in favor of slaying all such people. The intention of wiping out the Jewish tribes is made clear in the Quran verse: "Allah's Apostle said, "The Hour will not be established until you fight with the Jews, and the stone behind which a Jew will be hiding will say. "O Muslim! There is a Jew hiding behind me, so kill him" Bukhari (52:177), meaning that even the stones will betray the Jews.

The obligation to convert unbelievers to Islam impinges heavily on Law and Order. Quran 9:111 endorses this obligation. "Allah has purchased from the believers, their lives and their wealth because the garden is theirs. They fight in the way of Allah and shall slay and be slain." In these modern times the Rakkine Buddhist village (Arakan, Burma, 2012) was attacked by Rohynga Muslims (Youtube through

Google). A youth explained: "Muslims came to our Buddhist village, started to burn our houses. More came with clubs and knives, shouting in our faces: Go away. The whole village ran away. Some came to our house, grabbed me by the neck and poured gasoline over me, telling me: Say Bismilla. If you don`t become Muslim we will kill you. Your Buddha doesn`t help you. They beat me and my mother but we escaped up the mountain. We are lucky to be alive. Why are they killing us?"

Punishment of the Qurayza tribe because they did not want to convert to Islam. The involvement and assistance of Allah in fighting the tribes in Arabia is borne out in the battle against the Qurayza, the first tribe to be attacked which was also wiped out: 600 men slaughtered, women and children enslaved. According to the Hadith, Gabriel is the reason why Muhammad attacked the Banu Qurayza. Narrated Aisha "When Allah's Apostle returned on the day (of the battle) of Al-Khandaq (i.e. Trench), he put down his arms and took a bath. Then Gabriel whose head was covered with dust, came to him saying, "You have put down your arms! By Allah, I have not put down my arms yet." Allah's Apostle said, "Where (to go now)?" "Gabriel said, "This way," pointing towards the tribe of Bani Quraiza. "So Allah's Apostle went out towards them" Sahih Bukhari 4:52:68.

Prior to a military raid on a community, Muhammed`s instructions were: "Fight everyone in the way of Allah and kill those who disbelieve in Allah" (Ibn Ishaq/Hisham 992). This provided the Muslims with an opportunity to enrich themselves. Cutting off someone`s head while shouting "Allahu Akbar" is a tradition of Islam that began with Muhammed. A Companion recounts an episode in which he staged a surprise ambush on a settlement: "I leapt upon him and cut off his head and ran in the direction of the camp shouting "Allah akbar" and my two companions did likewise" (Ibn Ishaq/Hisham 990).

Law and Order at the international level. Soon after the death of Muhammed (634), the jihad fighters burst out of Arabia and a targeted Persian commander who asked the invading Muslims what they wanted. They replied "God has sent us and brought us here so that we may free those who desire from servitude to earthly rulers and make them servants of God, that we may change their poverty into wealth and free them from tyranny and chaos of false religions and bring them to the justice of Islam. Whoever accepts it from us will be safe and we shall leave him alone; but whoever refuses, we shall fight until we fulfil the promise of God." Fourteen hundred years later, in March 2009, Saudi legal expert Basem Alem publically echoed this view: "As a member of the true religion, I have a greater right to invade others in order to impose a certain way of life (according to Sharia), which history has proven to be the best and most just of all civilizations. This is the true meaning of offensive jihad. When we wage jihad, it is not in order to convert people to Islam, but in order to liberate them from the dark slavery in which they live, "until all chaos ceases and all religion belongs to Allah" (Q 8.39). According to the four recognised schools of Sunni jurisprudence, war against infidels will go on perpetually.

Fire, Burning, Boiling water to maintain Law and Order. Burning people and property is a punishment applied in various situations. Burning was a punishment for those Muslims who did not go to prayers. Bukhari (11:626), "Muhammad said: "I decided to order a man to lead the prayer and then take a flame to burn all those, who had not left their houses for the prayer, burning them alive inside their homes."" "Those who disbelieve Our revelations, We shall expose them to the Fire. As often as their skins are consumed We shall exchange them for fresh skins that they may taste the torment" (Q.4:56). "They will wish to come forth from the Fire, but they will not come forth from it. Theirs will be a lasting doom" (Q.5:37)."Lo! the tree of Zaqqum, The food of the sinner! Like molten brass, it seetheth in their bellies As the seething of boiling water. (And it will be said): Take him and drag him to the midst of hell, then pour upon his head the torment of boiling water" (Q44:43-48). Sahih International 2:257 "Allah is the ally of those who believe. He brings them out from darkness into the light. And those who disbelieve, their allies are Taghut. They take them out of the light into darkness. Those are the companions of the Fire; they will abide eternally therein." In these modern times, burning in a cage is a common punishment. A Jordanian pilot who was shot down by ISIS in Syria was burnt alive in a cage. Gaddafi`s wife poured boiling water on the servant`s head.

Eye for an Eye. Sahih International 5:45 "And We ordained for them therein a life for a life, an eye for an eye, a nose for a nose, an ear for an ear, a tooth for a tooth is legal retribution. But whoever gives (up his right as) charity, it is an expiation for him. And whoever does not judge by what Allah has revealed, then it is those who are the wrongdoers." Murder, injury and property damage are not Hadd crimes in Islamic Penal Law-and are subsumed under other categories of Islamic penal law, which are: Qisas (meaning retaliation, and following the principle of "eye for an eye") and Diya ("blood money)", financial compensation paid to the victim or heirs of a victim in the cases of murder, bodily harm or property damage. Diya is an alternative to Qisas for the same class of crimes. Tazir is punishment administered at the discretion of the judge. There is unequal treatment between Muslims and non-Muslims in murder cases. Islam has the clear rule that a Muslim is not to be killed for murder of a non-Muslim, ie verse 5:45 does not apply. Narrated Abu Juhaifa: I asked Ali "Do you have any Divine literature besides what is in the Quran? Or, as Uyaina once said, "Apart from what the people have?" Ali said, "By Him Who made the grain split (germinate) and created the soul, we have nothing except what is in the Quran and the ability (gift) of understanding Allah's Book which He may endow a man, with and what is written in this sheet of paper." I asked, "What is on this paper?" He replied, "The legal regulations of Diyyah (Blood-money) and the (ransom for) releasing of the captives, and the judgment that no Muslim should be killed in Qisas (equality in punishment) for killing a Kafir," Sahih Al-Bukhari, Volume 9, Book 83, Number 50; cf. Volume 1, Book 3, Number 111; Volume 4, Book 52, Number 283 (Hadith). Narrated Ali ibn AbuTalib: Qays ibn Abbad and Ashtar went to Ali and said to him: "Did the Apostle of Allah give you any instruction about anything for which he did not give any instruction to the people in general?" He said: "No, except what is contained in this document of mine." Musaddad said: "He then took out a document." Ahmad said: "A document from the sheath of his sword. It contained: The lives of all Muslims are equal; they are one hand against others; the lowliest of them can guarantee their protection. Beware, a Muslim must not be killed for an infidel, nor must one who has been given a covenant be killed while his covenant holds. If anyone introduces an innovation, he will be responsible for it. If anyone introduces an innovation or gives shelter to a man who introduces an innovation (in religion), he is cursed by Allah, by His angels, and by all the people" Sunan Abu Dawud, Book 39, Number 4515. Narrated Abdullah ibn Amr ibn: "The Prophet said: "A believer will not be killed for an infidel. If anyone kills a Muslim man deliberately, he is to be handed over to the relatives of the one who has been killed. If they wish, they may kill, but if they wish, they may accept blood-wit," Sunan Abu Dawud, Book 39, Number 4491 (hadith).

Acid attacks. The issue of qisas gained considerable attention in the Western media in 2009 when Ameneh Bahrami, an Iranian woman blinded in an acid attack, demanded that her attacker be blinded as well. The concept of punishment under Qisas is not based on 'society' versus the 'individual' (the wrong doer), but rather that of 'individuals and families' (victim(s)) versus 'individuals and families' (wrong doers). Thus the victim has the ability to pardon the perpetrator and withhold punishment even in the case of murder. Bahrami pardoned her attacker and stopped his punishment (drops of acid in his eyes) just before it was to be administered in 2011. Another example of this was reported by Ralph Ellis, CNN March 7, 2015, in which Iran blinded a man in 'eye for an eye' justice. Quote: On Tuesday, a man convicted of blinding another man in an acid attack was himself forcibly blinded in one eye, according to Amnesty International and Tasnim News, a semi-official news website. Amnesty International denounced the sentence. The Western perception of this verse: "Meeting out cruel and inhuman retribution punishments is not justice. Blinding, like stoning, amputation and flogging, is a form of corporal punishment prohibited by international law." It does not allow a person to be rehabilitated.

Overall, the foundations of Law and Order for the Muslims are maintained by whipping adulterers (24.2), amputation and crucifixion (5:33), beheadings and mass murder (8:12, 47:4, 2:191, 9:5, 8.67, 7.4), genocide (8.17), killing and terrorizing kafirs (47.4, 8.60, 3.151), wife beating 4:34), subjugation of women (2.228, 4.11,4.176), torture

(22.19-22), sex-slavery and rape (4:3, 4:24), child molestation (65:4). Law and Order pertaining to Jews and Christians takes the approach of mass murder of tribes or expulsion, as recorded by Sahih Muslim Book 019 Hadith no. 4366 "It has been narrated by Umar b.al-Khittab that he heard the Messenger say, "I will expel the Jews and Christians from the Arabian Peninsula and will not leave any but Muslim."" Indeed, Allah partakes active participation in maintaining Law and Order. "It is not ye who slew them; it is Allah. When thou throwest a handful of dust, it is not thy act, but Allah (Q.8:17).

4

Speech

Beliefs control speech. Beliefs control what one is allowed to say and what one is allowed to think. The word "Allah" is the Arabic word referring to God. It is distinguished from ilah, the Arabic word meaning deity, which could refer to any of the pagan gods worshipped in pre-Islamic Arabia. "Allahhu Akbar" has the meaning "God is greatest." It arose as an exclamation for thanking Allah after winning a battle. Ibn Ishaq/Hishham990, "I leapt upon him and cut off his head and ran in the direction of the camp shouting "Allah Akbar" and my two companions did likewise.

Bismilla (Q.1.1) also known as Bismala, is a phrase in Arabic. The Islamic phrase bismillahi r-rahmani r-rahim means "In the name of God, the Most Gracious, the Most Merciful." It has a special significance for Muslims, who are to begin each task after reciting the verse. This is the phrase recited before each surah of the Quran, except for the ninth. It is used by Muslims in various contexts (for instance, during daily prayer) and is used in over half of the constitutions of countries where Islam is the official religion or more than half of the population follows Islam, including those of Afghanistan, Algeria, Bahrain, Bangladesh, Brunei, Comoros, Egypt, Iran, Iraq, Jordan, Kuwait, Libya, Malaysia,

Maldives, Mauritania, Morocco, Oman, Pakistan, Qatar, Saudi Arabia, Somalia and the United Arab Emirates. The Basmala is used extensively in everyday Muslim life, said as the opening of each action in order to receive blessing from God. In the Indian subcontinent, a Bismillah ceremony is held for a child's initiation into Islam. Reciting the Basmala is a necessary requirement in the preparation of halal food.

Adhan is the Islamic call to daily prayer (salat) five times a day by a muezzin (caller) from a minaret tower of the mosque. Adhan means "to listen." As he recites the adhan, the muezzin usually faces the Kaba in Mecca, although there are other traditions in which he faces the four compass directions in turn. The words of the Adhan include: Allahu Akbar, Allahu Akbar, meaning Allah is the Greatest, Allah is the Greatest. The adhan is also used to call believers to Friday worship at the mosque.

Sirah are biographies of Muhammed the Prophet.

Taqwa. Taqwa means "fear of Allah." Fear of Allah unites all Muslims as equals and distinguishes them from non-Muslims. The Term Taqwa is explained by SAHIH INTERNATIONAL 9:109, "Then is one who laid the foundation of his building on righteousness (with fear) from Allah and (seeking) His approval better or one who laid the foundation of his building on the edge of a bank about to collapse, so it collapsed with him into the fire of Hell? And Allah does not guide the wrongdoing people." Taqwa distinguishes Muslims from non-Muslims. This division excludes non-Muslims from going to paradise, (9:30), particularly the Jews who are cursed by Allah (5:13) because they did not want to leave their Torah to follow Muhammed, but makes paradise available to peoples of all colours if they have Taqwa. Jabir bin Abdallah narrated that Muhammed said in the last sermon (although there is no Quran verse), "Indeed your Lord is one, an arab has no superiority over a non-Arab nor does a non-Arab have any superiority over an Arab; nor a red-skinned person over a black, nor a black over a red one, except by Taqwa. Verily, the most honourable of you in the sight of Allah is the one with the most Taqwa." In the same sermon Muhammed referred to several rules he had instituted and which they had to observe in order to go to paradise. Allah says in the Quran (9:33), "It is he (Allah) who has sent his Messenger with guidance and the religion of truth, in order for it to be dominant over all other religions, even though the Mushrikeen (disbelievers) hate it." "Verily Allah has shown me the eastern and western part of the earth, and I saw the authority of my Ummah (nation) dominate all that I saw" (Saheeh Muslim, hadith 2889).

Shirk. Speaking of partners with Allah, is the cardinal sin (Tafsir al-jalalayn, 385 <u>IN</u>: Spencer (2009) p.189). Jews and Christians are called al-mushrikeen because they ascribe partners with God, i.e. Jews believe their rabbis are lords besides God, whereas the Christians believe in a trinity and profess that Jesus is the Son of God. Wearing a wedding ring is shirk because of the belief that it may strengthen love, because it is showing off, because it imitates non-Muslims. It is not permissible to wear a wedding ring under any circumstances.

Fitnah is disobedience due to shirk and kufr (non-believing).

Ridda Wars are the apostasy wars. The apostasy wars arose soon after Muhammed died and were against Bedouin tribes that wanted to leave Islam.

Taqiyya, Tawriyya, Kitman

Taqiyya is saying something that isn't true, lying for Islam. Tawriyya is a deception. Kitman is lying by omission ie leaving out a part of a verse. Muslims "need" *tawriyya* because it "saves them from lying," and thus sinning. While the Quran is against believers deceiving other believers, for "surely God guides not him who is prodigal and a liar," deception directed at non-Muslims is the norm.

Lying to a Muslim is forbidden and is a sin. Lying to non-Muslims is not only allowed but is encouraged. Taqiyya provides Muslims with the means to lie to a non-Muslim without committing a sin. Al-Taqiyya is the Islamic word for concealing or disguising one's beliefs, convictions, ideas, feelings, opinions, and strategies. Muslims are permitted to lie: (1) to save their lives, (2) to reconcile a husband and wife, (3) to persuade a woman into a bedroom and (4) to facilitate one on his journey. Muslims are permitted to disavow Islam and Mohammed if it is not a genuine heart-felt rejection. Concealment of a truth is not an abandonment of that truth if it benefits Islam.

Christians have also lied but were never given permission to lie. However, a Muslim has no guilt since the Quran and Hadith permit his deception. Mohammed gave permission for a follower to lie exemplified by the killing of the Jewish poet (Ashraf) who had offended Mohammed with his poetry. One can lie to make Islam more attractive to potential converts as they speak of "no compulsion in religion" yet this verse was abrogated by later verses. Muslims have no hope for eternal salvation without their good works, so they must keep working to advance Islam.

Sahih International 24:7 "the curse of Allah be upon him if he should be among the liars". But only for lying to a Muslim. The statement that "The Prophet Muhammad also emphasized the importance of honesty as a central principle of Islam," followed by the hadith "Honesty leads to righteousness." is only valid in the context of Muslim to Muslim relations. "whoever lives his life in dissimulation dies a martyr." Dissimulation means faking. Examples: a Muslim cleric appeared in video counselling Muslims to tell Christians, "I wish you the best," whereby the latter might "understand it to mean you're wishing them best in terms of their (Christmas) celebration." But here the sheikh giggles as he explains: "by saying *I wish you the best*, I mean in my heart "*I wish you become a Muslim*." Once when Hanbal was conducting class, someone came knocking, asking for one of his students. Hanbal answered, "He's not here, what would he be doing here?" all the time pointing at his hand, as if to say "he's not in my hand." The caller, who could not see Hanbal's hands, assumed the student was simply not there and left. If someone declares "I don't have a penny in my pocket," most listeners will assume the speaker has no money on him, though he might have dollar bills, just literally no pennies. A man who swears to Allah that he can only sleep under a roof, when caught sleeping atop a roof, he exonerates himself by saying "by roof, I meant the open sky." This is legitimate. "After all," Munajid adds, "Quran 21:32 refers to the sky as a roof."

The Muslim claim to Jerusalem is an example of Taqiyya. Sahih International 17:1, "Exalted is He who took His Servant by night from al-Masjid al-Haram to al-Masjid al- Aqsa, whose surroundings We have blessed, to show him of Our signs. Indeed, He is the Hearing, the Seeing." Yet Aishia stated that "the apostle's body remained where it was but God removed his spirit by night" IN: Spencer 2009 (p.131); Ibn Ishaq, The Life of Muhammad, p183. In the dream, he"visited" a place referred to as *masjid el-aksa*, which means "the farthest mosque". Yet in Mohammed's time, Jerusalem was ruled by the Byzantine Christians, and there were no mosques at all in Jerusalem, not on the Temple Mount or anywhere else. When Surah 17:001 was revealed, about 621AD, the Sacred Mosque already existed in Mecca, but where was "the farthest mosque?" Palestine had not yet been conquered by the Muslims, and contained not a single mosque. The Ummayad Caliph, in AD 688-691, built the Dome of the Rock, right on the spot of the Jewish Temple. Then in AD 715, to build up the prestige of their dominions, the Umayyads built a second mosque on the Temple Mount, and called this one the farthest mosque (al-masjid al Aqsa). With this, the Umayyads retroactively gave Jerusalem a role in Muhammad's life, and inserted Jerusalem post hoc into the Quran, thus making it more important to Islam.

Words regarded as blasphemy. Blasphemy in Islam is impious utterance or action concerning God, Muhammad or anything considered sacred in Islam and reciting Muslim prayers in a language other than Arabic although other acts are also included. Blasphemy against beliefs and customs covers a wide range of speech: saying that Islam is an Arab religion; prayers five times a day are unnecessary; and the Quran is full of lies (Indonesia); believing in transmigration of the soul or reincarnation or disbelieving in the afterlife (Indonesia); cursing apostles, prophets, or angels; Expressing an atheist or a secular point of view (Malaysia); praying that Muslims become something else (Indonesia); whistling during prayers (Indonesia); reciting Muslim prayers in a language other than Arabic (Indonesia); expressing amusement in Islamic customs (Bangladesh); publishing an unofficial translation of the Quran (Afghanistan); watching a film or listening to music (Somalia), uttering "words of infidelity" (sayings that are forbidden); participating in non-Islamic religious festivals; talking about or trying to convert others from

Islam to Christianity; speaking ill of Allah; slighting a prophet who is mentioned in the Quran, or slighting a member of Muhammad's family; naming a teddy bear Muhammad (Sudan), the Sudanese teddy bear blasphemy case. Gibbons was arrested after allowing her class of 7-year-olds to name a teddy bear "Mohammed" because it is the most common name in Sudan; invoking God while committing a forbidden act. Quranic verses 5:33-34 and 33:57-61 have been most commonly used in Islamic history to justify and punish blasphemers.

Hypocrites. This is a common word used in the Quran. Sahih Bukhari (84:64-65) "During the last days there will appear some young foolish people who will say the best words but their faith will not go beyond their throats (i.e. they will have no faith) and will go out from (leave) their religion as an arrow goes out of the game. So, wherever you find them, kill them, for whoever kills them shall have reward on the Day of Resurrection." This verse from the Hadith is worse than it appears because it isn't speaking solely of apostates, but those who say they believe but don't put their religion into practice. They are called hypocrites. Sahih Bukhari (11:626), The Prophet said, "No prayer is harder for the hypocrites than the Fajr and the 'Isha' prayers and if they knew the reward for these prayers at their respective times, they would certainly present themselves (in the mosques) even if they had to crawl." The Prophet added, "Certainly I decided to order the Mu'adh-dhin (call-maker) to pronounce Iqama and order a man to lead the prayer and then take a fire flame to burn all those who had not left their houses for the prayer along with their houses."

Hard words against Muhammed's scribe. Abu Dawud (4346), "Was not there a wise man among you who would stand up to him when he saw that I had withheld my hand from accepting his allegiance, and kill him?" Muhammad is chastising his companions for allowing an apostate to 'repent' under duress. This person was Muhammad's former scribe, who left him after doubting the authenticity of divine "revelations" upon finding out that grammatical changes could be made. He was brought back to Muhammad after having been captured in Medina.

"War is deceit" was Muhammed's mantra applicable to several situations, not only war. The Prophet had clear words for war: "War is deceit." Ibn al-Munir (d. 1333) writes, "War is deceit, the most complete and perfect war waged by a holy warrior is a war of deception, not confrontation, due to the latter's inherent danger, and the fact that one can attain victory through treachery without harm (to oneself)." Narrated Abu Huraira and Jabir bin Abdullah "The Prophet said, 'War is Deceit'" Sahih Bukhari 4:52:267,268,269. Deceit was used on the Meccans. Muhammad signed a 10-year treaty with the Meccans that allowed him access to their city while he secretly prepared his own forces for a takeover. The unsuspecting residents were conquered easily after he broke the treaty two years later, because some of the people in the city had trusted him at his word. They were wiped out. Relevant verses:

Sahih Bukhari 4:52:270, 5:59:369; 4:52:271; Sahih Muslim, 19:4436; Sahih Muslim 1801; Book 32, Hadith 146. Deceit was used on Usayr ibn Zarim and his thirty unarmed men. Nuaym told the Prophet "I've become a Muslim but my tribe does not know of my Islam. Muhammed said "Make them abandon each other if you can so that they will leave us; for war is deception" Al-Tabari vol 8, p.23, Bukhari (4:52:269). The context of this verse is thought to be the murder of Usayr ibn Zarim and his thirty unarmed men by Muhammad's men after he "guaranteed" them safe passage. The practice of deceit is central to Muhammed's tactics in individual assassinations.

Words of deceit are directed not only as a war tactic but also as a tactic against individual persons. Lying to Ashraf is a Classical example (Bukhari 4:52:271; Bukhari 5:59:369). It has been narrated on the authority of Jabir bin Abdullah, that the Messenger of Allah said: "Who will kill Ka'b Ashraf? He has maligned Allah, the Exalted, and His Messenger." A young Muslim named Muhammad ibn Maslama volunteered on condition that in order to get close enough to Ka'b to assassinate him, he be allowed to lie to the poet. Muhammad bin Maslama said, "O Allah's Apostle! Do you like me to kill him?" He replied in the affirmative. Maslama said: Messenger of Allah, do you wish that I should kill him? He said: "Yes." He said: "Permit me to talk (to him in the way I deem fit)." Muhammed said: "Talk (as you like)." Ibn Maslama traveled to Kab and began to denigrate Islam and Muhammad, saying "This person (i.e. the Prophet) has put us to task and asked us for charity." Kab replied, "By Allah, you will get tired of him." Muhammad said to him, "We have followed him, so we dislike to leave him till we see the end of his affair." Muhammad said to his companions: "As he comes down, I will extend my hands towards his head and when I hold him fast, you should do your job." So when he came down and he was holding his cloak under his arm, they said to him: "We sense from you a very fine smell." He said: "Yes, I have with me a mistress who is the most scented of the women of Arabia." Muhammad said: "Allow me to smell (the scent on your head)." He said: "Yes, you may smell." So, he caught it and smelt. Then he said: "Allow me to do so (once again)." He then held his head fast and said to his companions: "Do your job." And they killed him.

Sufyan says that Ashraf 's wife said: "I hear a voice which sounds like the voice of murder." Ashraf replied "It is only Muhammad b. Maslama and his foster-brother, Abu Na'ila. When a gentleman is called at night even it to be pierced with a spear, he should respond to the call." Quran Chapter 42: The slaying of Kab Bin Al-Ashraf, fully describes the incident. Is Allah the best of deceivers? Quran 3:54 "and they (the disbelievers schemed) and Allah schemed (against the disbelievers). And Allah is the best of schemers." Transliteration: wamakaroo wamakara Allahu wa Allahu khayru almakireena. Literal translation: And they cheated/deceived and God cheated/deceived, and God (is) the best (of) the cheaters/deceivers. The Quran openly states many times that Allah is the 'best deceiver'. The root word used in these verses is *Makr* which means *deception*. The literal translations presented here, referenced from a Muslim website, make this very clear. The word makir (deceit) is always used disparagingly, and never in a positive context. It is often used to describe someone sly and dishonest. This is because of the way a makir deceives - they set out to cheat you by deception. It is highly inappropriate for Allah to use this word to describe himself, especially when two of his names are the truth and the dependable.

Similarly, the verses: Quran 8:30; 10:21, 7:99, 13:42; Bukhari (49:852; 49:857) "He who makes peace between the people by inventing good information or saying good things, is not a liar." Lying is permitted when the end justifies. In our times leaders of the Arab world routinely say one thing to English-speaking audiences and then something entirely different to their own people in Arabic. Yassir Arafat was famous for telling Western newspapers about his desire for peace with Israel, then turning around and using Arabic whipping Palestinians into a hateful and violent frenzy against Jews.

Oaths. Quran (2:225), "Allah will not call you to account for thoughtlessness in your oaths, but for the intention in your hearts" This refers to thoughtless oaths. However, if a man takes an oath then finds something better, he takes the preferred path and makes compensation. "If I take an oath to do something and later on I find something else better than the first one, then I do what is better and make expiation for my oath," (Bukhari 78:618; Bukhari 9:89:260; Muslim 15:4044). This is a principle of compensation, whereby the violation of an oath may be atoned by some other performance. SAHIH INTERNATIONAL 5:88, "Allah will not impose blame upon you for what is meaningless in your mouths, but He will impose blame upon you for (breaking) what you intended of oaths. So its expiation is the feeding of ten needy people from the average of that which you feed your (own) families for clothing them or the freeing of a slave. But whoever cannot find (or afford it), then a fast of three days is required. That is the expiation for oaths when you have sworn. But guard your oaths. Thus, does Allah make clear to you His verses that you may be grateful. Dissolution of oaths is reinforced by SAHIH INTERNATIONAL 66:2, "Allah has already ordained for you (Muslims) the dissolution of your oaths. And Allah is your protector, and He is the Knowing and the Wise." This new principle is confirmed and applied to a case wherein the Prophet himself is concerned: SAHIH INTERNATIONAL 66:1, "O Prophet, why do you prohibit (yourself) what Allah has made lawful for you, seeking the approval of your wives? And Allah is Forgiving and Merciful. Allah has already ordained for you (Muslims), the dissolution of your oaths. And Allah is your protector and He is the Knowing and wise." To subdue Mohammed`s rebellious wives, Allah sent an warning: SAHIH INTERNATIONAL 66:5, "Perhaps his Lord, if he divorced you (all), would substitute for him wives better than you, submitting (to Allah), believing, devoutly obedient, repentant, worshipping, and traveling, (the ones) previously married and virgins." The prophet changed his rulings day by day. This has had the serious result that there appears to be no mode known to Mohammedan Law whereby an oath can be legally binding. Hence if a man having made an oath discovers some preferable course, he is to take that preferable course and make compensation. Narrated Zahdam: "We stayed for a short while (after we had covered a little distance), and then I said to my companions, "Allah`s Apostle has forgotten his oath. By Allah, if we do not remind Allah`s Apostle of his oath, we will never be successful."" So we returned to the prophet and said, "O Allah`s Apostle we asked you for mounts, but you took an oath that you would not give us any mounts; we think that you have forgotten your oath." He said "By Allah and Allah`s willing, if I take an oath and later find something else better than that, then I do what is better and expiate my oath," Bukhari 7:67:427; Sahih Muslim 15:4044.

Hudaibiya. This is an important word that is frequently used in politics. Violating the treaty of Hudaibiya established that a promise to non-Muslims is not obligatory for the believer. Abu Bakr, a military leader, stated: "If I take an oath to do something and later on I find something else better than the first one, then I do what is better and make expiation for my oath" (Bukhari 78:618). This follows the message: "The Prophet said: `War is deceit` (Bukhari 52:269). On violating the treaty of Hudaibiya, Muhammed established an example for his followers: a promise to non-Muslims is not obligatory for the believer. The terms of the treaty specified that any Muslim who flees Mecca for Medina (where Muhammad resided) he must be returned. But when a group of Muslims did exactly that a few weeks after the treaty was signed, Muhammad did not return all of them according to the terms, but kept the women. A verse from Allah arrived to justify his decision (Q.60:10). Allah gave Muhammad His personal permission to break the treaty. Muslims started murdering the Meccans after the treaty was signed. Bukhari 50:891 refers to a man named Abu Basir who embraced Islam and then killed a Meccan. Muhammad sent the man to live on the coast, where he formed a group of seventy Muslims who supported themselves by attacking Meccan caravans. According to the Hadith, he and the other Muslims "killed them and took their property." Muir words it as follows, "They waylaid every caravan from Mecca (for since the truce, traffic with Syria had again sprung up) and spared the life of no one."

Attacking and killing Meccans was an obvious violation of the treaty of Hudaibiya, but the victims did not want war with Muhammad and thus did not march against him. They had little choice but to surrender to him without a fight.

Words used in insults. Insults are a major part of Islam. Many insults are of a general nature directed to all Jews, Christians and pagans. Jews and Christians came under a barrage of colourful insults. According to a hadith recorded in Sunan Ahmed (Hanbali jurisprudence) and Sunan al-Bayhaqi (Shafii jurisprudence), during the course of a discussion about non-Muslims, Calif Omar al-Khatteb, one of Sunni's Islam's "four righteous caliphs" declared: "They are heathens, and the blood of one of them is (like) the blood of a dog." Verse 7:176 compares unbelievers to "panting dogs" with regard to their idiocy and worthlessness; Verse 7:179 says they are like "cattle" only worse; Verse 9:28 says the unbelievers are unclean; Verse 6:111 says they are ignorant; Verse 23:55 says they are helpers of the devil; This is echoed by verses 7:166 and 2:65. A hadith (Bukhari 54:524) says that Muhammad believed rats to be "mutated Jews" (also confirmed by Sahih Muslim 7135 and 7136).

SAHIH INTERNATIONAL 5:60, "Say, "Shall I inform you of (what is) worse than that as penalty from Allah? (It is that of) those whom Allah has cursed and with whom He became angry and made of them apes and pigs and slaves of Taghut. Those are worse in position and further astray from the sound way." The relationship is clearly enshrined in the Quran verse 60:4, "there has arisen between you (infidels) and us (Muslims), enmity and hatred forever, till ye believe in Allah and Him alone" This gives legitimacy to enmity. The Islamic idea is that

Christianity is a "distorted, deformed religion" is explained by Saudi Sheikh Abd Al-Muhsin Al-Qahi. It fuels a great deal of Muslim hatred for Christianity and Christians to this day (Spencer, 2009 p151-152).

Verses 46:29-35 say that unbelieving men are worse than the demons who believe in Muhammad. Non-Muslims are said to have diseased hearts (2:10), disobedient (2:99), stupid (2:171) and deceitful (3:73). Those who disbelieve from among the People of the Book and among the polytheists, will be in Hell fire, to dwell therein. They are the worst of creatures (98:6). "Surely the worst of creatures in Allah's eyes are those who disbelieve" (8:55).

The first Surah of the Quran, Fatiha, 1:5-7 repeated by Muslims 17 times a ends with these words: "Keep us on the right path. The path of those upon whom Thou hast bestowed favors. Not (the path) of those upon whom Thy wrath is brought down, nor of those who go astray. Muhammad was once asked if this pertained to Jews and Christians. His response was, "Whom else?" (Bukhari 56:662, Sahih Muslim 34:6448). Those who engendered Allah's anger" are the Jews and "those who have gone astray are the Chrisians." 5:60 SAHIH INTERNATIONAL Say, "Shall I inform you of (what is) worse than that as penalty from Allah? (It is that of) those whom Allah has cursed and with whom He became angry and made of them apes and pigs and slaves of Taghut. Those are worse in position and further astray from the sound way. Christians and Jews are also condemned and insulted many times (Q. 2:61, 4:48, 4:50, 4:116, 4:47-52, 4:55-56, 4:160, 5:12-5:13, 5:37, 5:51, 5:53, 5:59-60, 5:72-73, 5:79, 18:52, 33:26, 59:14). Verse 60:4 says Muslims will hate the disbelievers forever until they believe in Allah only. The Quran states explicitly that non-Muslims are "guilty" of disbelief (Q.45:31). The worst possible sin is disbelief in or denial of Allah (Q.10:17, 11:18-19, 18:15, 32:22).

Abrogation of Quran verses. The debate on abrogation refers to several ways by which changes could have been brought about in the Quran. Quran 2:106, interpretations in the Quranic Corpus: Sahih International: We do not abrogate a verse or cause it to be forgotten except that We bring forth [one] better than it or similar to it. Do you not know that Allah is over all things competent? Pickthall: Nothing of our revelation (even a single verse) do we abrogate or cause be forgotten, but we bring (in place) one better or the like thereof. Knowest thou not that Allah is Able to do all things? Yusuf Ali: None of Our revelations do We abrogate or cause to be forgotten, but We substitute something better or similar: Knowest thou not that Allah Hath power over all things? SURAH 16:101, SAHIH INTERNATIONAL: And when We substitute a verse in place of a verse - and Allah is most knowing of what He sends down - they say, "You, [O Muhammad], are but an inventor [of lies]." But most of them do not know.

The common view is that Quran verses are abrogated when Muhammed had a subsequent inspiration that is "better," in accordance with the hadith: "If you ever take an oath to do something and later on you find that something else is better, then you should expiate your oath and do what is better." The Meccan verses (50:45; 109:2;109:3; 109:4; 109:5, 109:6; 2:256 which appeared to be benign were later abrogated by the Sword verse (9:5). Some verses are deemed to have been lost. The Verse of Rajam (stoning) for adulterers is not found in the present day Quran. However, Sahih Hadiths testify that there was a verse in the Quran pertaining to the "Stoning Punishment". Umar, the second Caliph of Islam confirms the loss of this verse from the Quran. Abdullah b. Abbas reported that Umar b. Khattab sat on the pulpit of Allah`s Messenger and said: "Verily Allah sent Muhammed with truth and He sent down the Book upon him, and the verse of stoning was included in what was sent down to him. We recited it, retained it in our memory and understood it. Allah `s messenger awarded the punishment os stoning to death (to the married adulterer and adulteress) and, after him, we also awarded the punishment of stoning. I am afraid that with the lapse of time the people (may forget it) and nay say; We do not find the punishment of stoning in the Book of Allah and thus go astry by abandoning this duty prescribed by Allah. Stoning is a duty laid down in Allah`s book for married men and women who commit adultery when proof is established, or if there pregnancy or a confession (Sahih Muslim 17:4194). It was narrated that Aishia said "The verse of stoning and of breastfeeding an adult ten times was revealed and the paper was with me under my pillow. When the Messenger of Allah died, we were preoccupied with his death and a tame sheep came in and ate it" Sunan Ibn Majah 3:9:1944. "The verses of stoning and breastfeeding were in the possession of Aishia in a Quranic copy. When Muhammed died and people became busy in the burial preparations, a domesticated animal entered and ate it" Ibn Hazam Vol 8, Part 11, pages 235 and 236. Ibn Kathir "Uthman burned the rest of the copies which were in the hands of the people because they disagreed on the (correct) reading and they fought among themselves. When they came to take ibn Masud's copy to burn it, he told them, "I know more than Zayd ibn Thabit (whom Uthman ordered to collect the copies of the Quran)." Uthman wrote to ibn Masud asking him to submit his copy for burning, The Beginning of the End Part 7, page 218. Seven readings of the Quran are permitted. Narrated Abdullah bin Abbas "Allah's Apostle said, "Gabriel recited the Quran to me in one way. Then I requested him (to read it in another way), and continued asking hm to receipt it in other ways and then he recited it in several ways till he ultimately recited it in seven different ways" Sahih Bukhari 6:61:513; Sahih Bukhari 4:54:442; Sahih Muslim 4:1785; Sahih Muslim 4:1786; Sahih Muslim 4:1787; Sahih Muslim 4:1788.

Ubayy b. Kab reported that the Apostle of Allah was near the tank of Banu Ghifar that Gabriel came to him and said: "Allah has commanded you to recite to your people the Quran in one dialect. Upon this he said: I ask Allah pardon and forgiveness. My people are not capable of doing it. Then her came a second time and said: "Allah has commanded you that you should recite the Quran to your people in two dialects. Upon this the Apostle said: I seek pardon and forgiveness, my people would not be able to do it...... Allah has commanded that you recite in three dialects.......Then he then came a fourth time and said: .....: Allah has commanded that you recite the Quran to your people in seven dialects and in whichever dialect they would recite, they would be right, Sahih Muslim 4:1789.

Muhammad had scribes write his revelations down for him. One scribe was 'Abdullah Ibn Sa'd Ibn Abi Sarh. As Sarh wrote these revelations down, he frequently made suggestions on improving their wording. Muhammad often agreed and allowed the changes to be made. Eventually, Sarh left Islam thinking that it could not be from God if a mere scribe were allowed to change God's word and went to live in Mecca. After the conquest of Mecca, Muhammad ordered Sarh's death. His foster brother Uthman b. Affan interceded but Muhammed kept silent. When they left Muhammed told his companions "I kept silent so that one of you may strike off his head."

Treaties can also be abrogated. Islamic schools of law, such as the Hanafi, assert that Muslim leaders may abrogate treaties merely if it seems advantageous for Islam. Yasser Arafat, soon after negotiating a peace treaty criticized as conceding too much to Israel, addressed an assembly of Muslims in a mosque in Johannesburg where he justified his actions: "I see this agreement as being no more than the agreement signed between our Prophet Muhammad and the Quraysh in Mecca." In other words, like Muhammad, Arafat gave his word only to annul it once "something better" came along, that is, once the Palestinians became strong enough to renew the offensive. This supports: "The Prophet said: "War is deceit" Bukhari 52:269, which is supported by "Taqiyya."

5

Slavery and Subjugation

Slavery is allowed by Sharia. Quran 24:32, "those whom your right hand possess" refers to slaves. Bernard Lewis translates *ma malakat aymanukum* as "those whom you own." Abdullah Yusuf Ali translates it as "those whom your right hands possess," as does M. H. Shakir. N. J. Dawood translates the phrase more idiomatically as "those whom you own as slaves." The Islamic scholar Muhammed Aashiq LLahi Bulandshaahri (Illuminating Discourses on the Quran vol.1.p.502), explains that during Jihad many men and women become war captives and enslaved as a punishment for disbelief and maintains that slavery has not been abolished in Islam because none of the verses relating to slavery have been abrogated. He blames the disbelievers (kuffar) for shackling Muslims with treatises that prevent enslavement, which he sees as a great boon if every house had a slave. The Quran allows a man to force sexual relations on his slave girls as well as his wives (Q. 4:24, 23:1-6, 33:50, 70:22:30), a situation regarded as sexual abuse and a crime in the West. Saudi national Homaidan Al-Turki in the US was imprisoned for holding a woman as a slave in Colorado. He complained that attacking traditional Muslim behaviours was persecution. Slavery is ordained by the Quran (Surah 33:50) and Sharia Law. A large section of the Sharia is devoted to codifying the practice of slavery (k32.0). The Reliance of the Traveller provides information on the capture of slaves and the sanctioning of forced conversion under duress (k32.0).

Rules for enslavement: (o9.13). When a child or a woman is taken captive, they become slaves by the fact of capture, and the woman's previous marriage is immediately annulled; (o9.14) When an adult male is taken captive, the caliph considers the interests of Islam and the Muslims and decides between the prisoner's death, slavery, release without paying anything, or ransoming himself in exchange for money or for a Muslim captive held by the enemy. If the prisoner becomes a Muslim (before the caliph chooses) then he may not be killed, and one of the other three alternatives is chosen; (o9.12) Whoever enters Islam before being captured may not be killed or his property confiscated, or his young children taken captive; (o4.9) is one of several rules that establish slaves as property, to be traded as a form of restitution; (o20.2) makes it clear that a slave freed as a method of expiation must be a "sound Muslim."

Supremacist ideology. Muhammad's words are the basis for offensive Jihad - spreading Islam by force. Muhammed exhorted his followers to make Islam "Superior over all religions (9:33; 48:28; 61:9). "He who fights for Islam is Superior, Sahih Bukhari (52:65, 3:125), "The Prophet said, "He who fights that Allah's Word (Islam) should be superior, fights in Allah's Cause." Muhammad's words are the basis for offensive Jihad, spreading Islam by force. The supremacist ideology is put forward in the Quran in the Sword verse, 9.5, "And when the sacred months have passed, then kill the polytheists wherever you find them and capture them and besiege them and sit in wait for them at every place of ambush. But if they should repent, establish prayer, and give zakat, let them [go] on their way. Indeed, Allah is Forgiving and Merciful."

Islam is a supremacist ideology in which the social position and worth depends on religion. The social position of non-believers is subordinate to the position of Muslims. Muslims are the best people (Q.3:110). "But not equal are those followers who do not fight" (Q.4:95). Those who resist Islamic rule are to be fought until they are either killed or fully humiliated and forced to acknowledge their inferior status by converting to Islam or by paying a poll-tax and accepting the subjugation of their own religion to Islam. In the Medina phase, Muhammad directed military campaigns to subjugate other tribes and religions, "inviting" them to Islam at the point of a sword and forcing them to pay tribute. He set in motion the aggressive military campaigns that made war against all five major world religions in just the first few decades following his death. In less than 10 years Muhammed and the believers put an end to two formidable kingdoms, the kingdom of the old Achemenides represented by the classical Sassanides and that of the Roman Caesars of Eastern countries thus fulfilling the given mandate, "leaving Arabia only for Muslims." After Muhammed died, they invaded and conquered Palastine, Lebanon, Syria, Iraq, Iran, Anatolia (Turkey), Egypt, Libya, Algeria, Tunisia, Morocco, Afganistan, Pakistan and other "stan" countries, Indonesia, Bangladesh, Chechenya, North and South Africa, etc, giving rise to the largest empire the world has seen and it is still expanding. There are at present, 50 Islam majority counties in the world and several others with minority populations.

Subjugating unbelievers. Interfaith marriage is forbidden. According to all four schools of Sunni law and Shia law, interfaith marriages are condoned only between a Muslim male marries a non-Muslim female from the People of the Book and not vice versa. "Let not the believers take unbelievers for their friends in preference to believers" Q.3:28. Don't believe or trust anyone who is not a Muslim, Q.3:73. Have no unbelieving friends, Kill the unbelievers wherever you find them, Q.4:89. Do not choose disbelievers as friends, Q.4:144. Don't take Jews or Christians for friends. If you do, then Allah will consider you to be one of them, Q.5:51. Don't pray for dead disbelievers or attend their funerals, Q.9:84. Stay away from non-Muslims. They are all liars, Q.9:107. Never help disbelievers, Q.28:86. Don't obey disbelievers and hyporites, Q.33:1. Don't be friends with disbelievers. They are your (and Allah's) enemy, Q.60:1. "O Prophet! Strive against the disbelievers and the hypocrites, and be stern with them. Hell will be their home, a hapless journey's end. Be stern with disbelievers. They are going to Hell," Q.66:9.

Allah is an enemy of unbelievers because they do not believe in Gabriel (Q.2:97-98), "And if this is the cause of their hostility to Gabriel, let them know whoever is an enemy to Allah, His Angels and His Messengers and to Gabriel and Michael will surely find Allah an enemy to such unbelievers." Allah will destroy non-Muslim cultures (Q.7:138-9). Allah will not forgive disbelievers (Q. 9:80), "Do not ask forgiveness for them. If you should ask forgiveness for them seventy times, never will Allah forgive them. That is because they disbelieved in Allah and His Messenger, and Allah does not guide the defiantly disobedient people." Allah punishes disbelievers (Sahih International 35:26) "Then I seized the ones who disbelieved, and how (terrible) was My reproach." Those who disbelieve will never be pardoned by Allah. "Indeed, those who disbelieved and averted (people) from the path of Allah and then died while they were disbelievers, never will Allah forgive them," SAHIH INTERNATIONAL 47:34-35.

Ibn Ishaq/Hisham 992, "Fight everyone in the way of Allah and kill those who disbelieve in Allah until religion is for Allah." (Q.2:193). War is ordained by Allah, and all Muslims must be willing to fight, whether they like it or not. "Fighting has been enjoined upon you while it is hateful to you. But perhaps you hate a thing and it is good for you; and perhaps you love a thing and it is bad for you. And Allah Knows, while you know not" (Q.2:216). SAHIH INTERNATIONAL "Those are the ones of whom Allah knows what is in their hearts, so turn away from them but admonish them and speak to them a far-reaching word." Oppose and admonish those who refuse to follow Muhammad. (Q.4:63) advises: Have no unbelieving friends. SAHIH INTERNATIONAL 4:89 "So do not take from among them allies until they emigrate for the cause of Allah. But if they turn away, then seize them and kill them wherever you find them and take not from among them any ally or helper." Treat converts to Islam well. Kill those who refuse to convert, (Q.9:5; 9:11). SAHIH INTERNATIONAL (9:5) "And when the sacred months have passed, then kill the polytheists wherever you find them and capture them and besiege them and sit in wait for them at every place of ambush. But if they should repent, establish prayer, and give zakat, let them (go) on their way. Indeed, Allah is Forgiving and Merciful." But this promise has not yet materialized: Q 9:11, "For it is written that a son of Arabia would awaken a fearsome Eagle. The wrath of the Eagle would be felt throughout the lands of Allah and lo, while some of the people trembled in despair still more rejoiced; for the wrath of the Eagle cleansed the lands of Allah; and there was peace."

Allah subjugates unbelievers. He will give you victory (Q.9:12-14). Fight disbelievers who are near you, and let them see the harshness in you, (Q.9:123). Tabari 9:69, "Killing Unbelievers is a small matter to us," The words of Muhammad, prophet of Islam."

Ibn Ishaq/Hisham 992, "Fight everyone in the way of Allah and kill those who disbelieve in Allah." Quran (8:59-60), "And let not those who disbelieve suppose that they can outstrip (Allah's Purpose). Lo! they cannot escape. Make ready for them all thou canst of (armed) force and of horses tethered, that thereby ye may dismay the enemy of Allah and your enemy

Ibn Ishaq/Hisham 990, "I leapt upon him and cut off his head and ran in the direction of the camp shouting 'Allah Akbar' and my two companions did likewise." This tradition continue till to-day.

Quran 8.17 "And you did not kill them, but it was Allah who killed them. And you were not, (O Muhammed), when you threw, but it was Allah who threw that he might test the believers with a good test. Indeed, Allah is Hearing and Knowing." This is how it was understood by his companions, and by the terrorists of today." Sahih Bukhari (52:220), Allah's Apostle said "I have been made victorious with terror" (cast in the hearts of the enemy). Sahih International 9:29, "Fight those who do not believe in Allah or in the Last Day and who do not consider unlawful what Allah and His Messenger have made unlawful and who do not adopt the religion of truth from those who were given the Scripture, (fight) until they give the jizyah willingly while they are humbled." Sahih International 47:4, "So, when you meet those who disbelieve (in battle), strike (their) necks until, when you have inflicted slaughter upon them, then secure their bonds, and either (confer) favor afterwards or ransom (them) until the war lays down its burdens. That (is the command). And if Allah had willed, He could have taken vengeance upon them (Himself), but (He ordered armed struggle) to test some of you by means of others. And those who are killed in the cause of Allah, never will He waste their deeds." Allah kills through the hands of Muslims. Quran 8:12, "I will cast terror into the hearts of those who disbelieve. Therefore, strike off their heads and strike off every fingertip of them," Sahih Bukhari (52:256), The Prophet was asked whether it was permissible to attack the pagan warriors at night with the probability of exposing their women and children to danger. The Prophet replied, "They (i.e. women and children) are from them (i.e. pagans)."

Fighting for Allah gets booty for believers. God tells the prophet to wage war against unbelievers and to seize booty (their land, wealth, women and children). Quran (8:67), "It is not for a Prophet that he should have prisoners of war until he had made a great slaughter in the land." Sahih International 8:41"And know that anything you obtain of war booty, then indeed, for Allah is one fifth of it and for the Messenger, and for (his) near relatives and the orphans, the needy, and the (stranded) traveller, if you have believed in Allah and in that which We sent down to Our Servant on the day of criterion, the day when the two armies met. And Allah, over all things, is competent." Sahih International 8:69 "So consume what you have taken of war booty (as being) lawful and good, and fear Allah. Indeed, Allah is Forgiving and Merciful." Ibn Ishaq/Hisham 484, "Allah said, "A prophet must slaughter before collecting captives. A slaughtered enemy is driven from the land."

Allah made believers heirs to the lands of unbelievers. "And he made you heirs to their land and their dwellings and their property and to a land which you have not yet trodden, and Allah has power over all things (Q.33:27). Allah will grant Muslims authority and power over all people: "Allah has promised, to those among you who believe and work righteous deeds, that he will, of a surety, grant them in the land, inheritance (of power), as He granted it to those before him; that He will establish in authority their religion" (Q.24:55). "Seize their land, encroach on them, pressure and punish them." "See that we gradually reduce the land (in their control) from its outlying borders?" (Q.13:41; 21:44). "We shall punish them gradually from directions they perceive not" (Q.68:44). "As for those who disbelieve, garments of fire will be cut out for them; boiling fluid will be poured down on their heads, whereby that which is in their bellies, and their skins too, will be melted; And for them are maces of iron. Whenever, in their anguish, they would go forth from thence they are driven back therein and (it is said unto them): Taste the doom of burning fire" (Q.22:19-22). http://www.tafsirq.com/en/2-al-baqara/verse-98.

Expulsion of Jews, pagans, Christians. The command is to seize their land and property, pressure them to pay tax. Muslim (1:33) "the Messenger of Allah said: I have been commanded to fight against people till they testify that there is no god but Allah, that Muhammad is the messenger of Allah." The strategy of subjugation of Jews is a divine command revealed to Muhammed. Sahih Bukhari (53:392), "While we were in the Mosque, the Prophet came out and said, "Let us go to the Jews." We went out till we reached Bait-ul-Midras. He said to them, "If you embrace Islam, you will be safe. You should know that the earth belongs to Allah and His Apostle, and I want to expel you from this land. So, if anyone amongst you owns some property, he is permitted to sell it, otherwise you should know that the Earth belongs to Allah and His Apostle."

Pay tax or die. Sahih Muslim (19:4294), "When you meet your enemies who are polytheists invite them to three courses of action. If they respond to any one of these, you also accept it and withhold yourself from doing them any harm. Invite them to (accept) Islam; if they respond to you, accept it from them and desist from fighting against them. If they refuse to accept Islam, demand from them the Jizya. If they agree to pay, accept it from them and hold off your hands. If they refuse to pay the tax, seek Allah's help and fight them." The only acceptable position of non-Muslims to Muslims is subjugation under Islamic rule as stated in 9:29. (Q.9:29), "Fight against those who believe not in Allah, nor in the Last Day, nor forbid that which has been forbidden by Allah and His Messenger and those who acknowledge not the religion of truth (Islam) among the people of the Scripture (Jews and Christians), until they pay the Jizyah with willing submission, and feel themselves subdued." Jizya is the money that non-Muslims must pay to their Muslim overlords. Muslims are ordered to fight unbelievers (including Christians, Jews, pagans and all others) until they either convert to Islam or accept living *in a state of humiliation and subjugation* under Islamic law paying the Jizya tax (which is often too high and oppressive such that some Jews were constrained to offer their children), and paid once a month kneeling infront of the Mullah who pulls the man's beard and hits him on the chin, and wearing identification symbols (necklaces by Jews, belts by Christians, an obvious illustration of compulsion).

Muhammad clearly established that people of other religions have to pay a poll tax to Muslims called the *jizya,* as a reminder of their inferior status. This abrogates an earlier verse stating that there is *"no compulsion in religion"* and it destroys any pretense that Islam is merely a religion and not a political system. Ishaq 956 & 962, *"He who withholds the Jizya is an enemy of Allah and His apostle"* The words of Muhammad. Muslim scholars say that non-Muslims are fought "only if they refuse to pay the jizya, *Willingly.*" This is irrational. Who would pay a poll tax and one that was so high that that it was oppressive, driving the Jews to offer their children, "*Willingly*"? Ibn Warraq, 1995 p231, explains "Those families who could not pay the crushing Jizya /poll tax were obliged to hand over their children and to deduct this from the Jizya." For at least 300 years, Christians suffered the humiliation of **Devshirme**. Introduced by the Ottoman, Sultan Orkhan (1326-1359) it consisted of the annual taking of a fifth of all the Christian children in the conquered territories (12,000 to 8,000). Converted to Islam, these children aged fourteen and twenty, were trained to be janissaries or infantry men. These Christian children came from Serbs, Bulgarians, Armenians, Albanians and the Greek aristocracy. On a fixed date all the fathers had to appear with their children in the public square. Recruiting agents chose the most sturdy and handsome in the presence of a Muslim judge. Any father who shirked was severely punished. The recruiting agents took more than they should and sold the surplus back to their parents. This went on till 1656. However a parallel system in which children between six and ten were taken to be trained in the seraglio (women's apartments in an Ottoman palace) of the sultan continued until the 18 century. The

Devshirme was an infringement of the rights of the dhimmis indicating that their rights were not secure. The kharaj was a kind of land tax. The peasant no longer owned his land but worked on it as a tenant. This was a right conferred by Allah over conquered land. Higher commercial and travel taxes than those of Muslims had to be paid by the dhimmis. Church leaders were imprisoned and tortured until ransoms were paid for them, causing many villagers to flee. In lower Egypt the Copts were utterly ruined by taxes and revolted in 832. The Arab governor burnt their villages, vineyards, gardens and churches. Those not massacred were deported.

The Quran specifically addresses Christians, Jews, Polytheists, Hindus and atheists

Christians are unbelievers (Q.98:5-6) and blasphemers (Q.5:17, 5:73) who have invented a lie about Allah (Q.10:68-69) by ascribing partners to Allah (reject the Trinity). Inventing a lie about Allah is the worst of sins (Q.7:37, 29:68) and for this reason Christians are condemned to Hell (Q.10:70). Although one (early Medinan) verse seems to say that righteous Christians will go to heaven, this is abrogated by later verses that make it very clear that Christians must cease being Christian (ie reject the Trinity) or suffer eternal torment for their beliefs (Q. 5:72-73). Jews are also cursed by Allah (Q.5:13). The Quran assures Muslims that Jews are wicked (Q.4:160-161), because they have distorted the word of Allah (Q.2:75; Q.18:27). The Quran assures believers that Jews and Christians have *"diseased hearts"* (Surah al Maidah QS 5:52). Allah has raised enmity between them until the day of resurrection (Q.5:14). Only Jews and Christians who submit to Islamic subjugation and pay the Jizya are protected (Q.9:29 & Ibn Ishaq 956 and 962).

Sahih Bukhari (52:177), Allah's Apostle said, "The Hour will not be established until you fight with the Jews, and the stone behind which a Jew will be hiding will say. "O Muslim! There is a Jew hiding behind me, so kill him." meaning that even the stones obey Allah. Tabari 7:99, The morning after the murder of Ashraf, the Prophet declared, "Kill any Jew who falls under your power."

Quran (9:5) "So when the sacred months have passed away, then slay the idolaters wherever you find them, and take them captive and besiege them and lie in wait for them in every ambush, then if they repent and keep up prayer and pay the poor-tax, leave their way free to them." According to this verse, the best way of staying safe from Muslim violence is to convert to Islam do prayer (salat) and pay the poor tax (zakat). The popular claim that the Quran only inspires violence within the context of self-defense is seriously challenged by this passage.

Preferential treatment for Muslim murderers: a Muslim is not to be killed for the murder of a non-Muslim. Qisas is not available to non-Muslims. Islam has the clear rule that a Muslim is not to be killed for the murder of a non-Muslim: Narrated Abu Juhaifa: I asked 'Ali "Do you have anything Divine literature besides what is in the Qur'an?" Or, as Uyaina once said, "Apart from what the people have?" 'Ali said, "By Him Who made the grain split (germinate) and created the soul, we have nothing except what is in the Quran and the ability (gift) of understanding Allah's Book which He may endow a man with and what is written in this sheet of paper." I asked, "What is on this paper?" He replied, "The legal regulations of Diya (Blood-money) and the (ransom for) releasing of the captives, and the judgment that no Muslim should be killed in Qisas (equality in punishment) for killing a Kafir (disbeliever)." Of relevance: Sahih Bukhari 9:83:50, Sahih al-Bukhari 1:3:111, 4:52:283, Sunan Abu Dawood, 39:4515. The vast majority of Muslim scholars hold this view. Narrated Ali ibn AbuTalib: "Qays ibn Abbad and Ashtar went to Ali and said to him: "Did the Apostle of Allah give you any instruction about anything for which he did not give any instruction to the people in general?"" He said: "No, except what is contained in this document of mine." Musaddad said: "He then took out a document. Ahmad said: "A document from the sheath of his sword. It contained: The lives of all Muslims are equal; they are one hand against others; the lowliest of them can guarantee their protection. Beware, a Muslim must not be killed for an infidel, nor must one who has been given a covenant be killed while his covenant holds. If anyone introduces an innovation, he will be responsible for it. If anyone introduces an innovation or gives shelter to a man who introduces an innovation (in religion), he is cursed by Allah, by His angels, and by all the people" (Sunan Abu Dawud, Book 39, Number 4515). Narrated Abdullah ibn Amr ibn al-As: "The Prophet said: "A believer will not be killed for an infidel. If anyone kills a man deliberately, he is to be handed over to the relatives of the one who has been killed. If they wish, they may kill, but if they wish, they may accept blood-wit""(Sunan Abu Dawud, Book 39, Number 4491). Muhammad gave the verdict (fatwa) that a Muslim cannot be killed for killing a non-Muslim. "Killing believers is the most heinous crime in the world," Q.4: 93. Quran 4:92 "No believer shall kill another believer, unless it is an accident" If this occurred then there must be expiation: "It is not for a believer to slay another believer unless by mistake. And he who has slain a believer by mistake, his atonement is to set free from bondage a believing person and to pay blood-money to his heirs, unless they forgo it by way of charity. And if the slain belonged to a hostile people, but was a believer, then the atonement is to set free from bondage a believing person."

Islam has the clear rule that a Muslim is not to be killed for the murder of a non-Muslim. Islam incorporates the ultimate devaluation of non-Muslims in the most obvious way by teaching that a Muslim may be punished with death for murdering a fellow Muslim, but this does not apply to a non-Muslim. Bukhari 83:17, Narrated "Abdullah: Allah's Apostle said, Sunan Ibn Majah 21:2660, "It was narrated from Ibn Abbas that the Prophet said "A believer should not be killed in retaliation for the murder of a disbeliever and a person who has a treaty should not be killed during the time of the treaty."" The Quran's "Law of Equality," which assigns human value and rights based on gender, religion and status, is the polar opposite of equality in the sense intended by Western liberal tradition, which ideally respects no such distinction because human life is equal. Sahih International 4:93, "But whoever kills a believer intentionally, his recompense is Hell, wherein he will abide eternally, and Allah has become angry with him and has cursed him and has prepared for him a great punishment." The destruction of the world is lighter on Allah than the killing of one Muslim man (Tirmidhi). The wiping away of the World means less to Allah than a believer to be killed unjustly (Ibn Maja). This contrasts with the value put on the lives of women and children exposed in wars. Sahih Bukhari (52:256), "The Prophet was asked whether it was permissible to attack the pagan warriors at night with the probability of exposing their women and children to danger. The Prophet replied, "They (i.e. women and children) are from them (i.e. pagans)." In this command, Muhammad establishes that it is permissible to kill non-combatants in the process of killing a perceived enemy. This provides justification for the many Islamic terror bombings. Muslim (19:4321-4323) are three separate hadith in which Muhammad shrugs over the news that innocent children were killed in a raid by his men against unbelievers.

What is the worth of lives? Christian and Jewish life is worth one third of a Muslim life. Christians and Jews are not considered fully human in that the penalty for killing one of them is limited to one-third of the compensation due for unintentionally killing a Muslim. Muhammad was once asked if this pertained to Jews and Christians. His response was, *"Whom else?"* (Bukhari 56:662). Since Allah makes such a strong distinction between Muslims and those outside the faith, it is only natural that Muslims should incorporate disparate standards of treatment into their daily lives. The Quran tells Muslims to be compassionate with one another but ruthless against the infidel: "Muhammad is the messenger of Allah. And those with him are severe against the disbelievers and merciful among themselves" *(Q.48:29,Bukhari 52:256).*

According to a Sahih hadith, Muhammad said the life of a non-Muslim is not sacred. Narrated Anas bin Malik: Allah's Apostle said, "I have been ordered to fight the people till they say: `None has the right to be worshipped but Allah.` And if they say so, pray like our prayers, face our Qibla and slaughter as we slaughter, then their blood and property will be sacred to us and we will not interfere with them except legally and their reckoning will be with Allah." Narrated Maimun ibn Siyah that he asked Anas bin Malik, "What makes the life and property of a person sacred?" He replied, "Whoever says, `None has the right to be worshipped but Allah, faces our Qibla during prayers, prays like us and eats our slaughtered animal, then he is a Muslim, and has got the same rights and obligations as other Muslims have." Sahih Bukhari 1:8:387.

The sanctity of Muslim blood. "The blood, wealth and honour of the Muslim are sacred to all Muslims" (Muslim). "Allah has made sacred upon you the blood, wealth and honour of each other, just as the sacredness of this day of yours in this land of yours in this month of yours." (Bukhari). "The blood of a Muslim who confesses that none has the right to be worshipped but Allah and that I am His Apostle, cannot be shed except in three cases: In Qisas for murder, a married person who commits illegal sexual intercourse and the one who reverts from Islam (apostate) and leaves the Muslims." (Bukhari 83:50). Abdullah ibn Umar narrated that he saw the Messenger of Allah making tawaf at the Kabah and saying "How delightful you are, and how great is your scent. How magnificent you are and how great is your sanctity. But by the one in whose hand is the soul of Muhammed, the sanctity of a believer, his wealth and his blood is greater in the sight of Allah than your sanctity, and we do not think of him except good" (Ibn Majah). "One drop of Muslim blood is worth more than the Kaba and its surroundings" (Bukhari). According to the highly respected Quranic exegesis of Ibn Kathir an early Quranic commentator and Tabiun, Sayid ibn Jubayr (who lived at the time of Prophet Muhammad) had said, "He who allows himself to shed the blood of a Muslim is like he who allows shedding the blood of all people. He who forbids shedding the blood of one Muslim is like he who forbids shedding the blood of all people" In addition, Al-A`raj said that Mujahadit reported on a commentator of the Quran, Mujahid ibn Jabr (a student of Ibn Abbas; a paternal cousin of Muhammad) while commenting on verse 5:32, "He who kills a believing soul intentionally, Allah makes the Fire of Hell his abode. He will become angry with him and curse him and has prepared a tremendous punishment for him, equal to if he had killed all people, his punishment will still be the same."

Quran 5:32 "Whoever kills an innocent human being, it is as if he killed all mankind and whoever saves one human being it is as if he saved all mankind." Yet Quran verses command the murder of those who leave Islam (apostates) (Bukhari Vol9, no17; Relience of the Traveller chapter 08.0-08.4), and those who are against Islam.

Quran 32-33: "On that account, We, ordained for the Children of Israel that if any slew a (Muslim), unless it be for murder or for spreading mischief in the land – it would be as if he slew the whole people... The punishment of those who wage war against Allah and his apostle, and strive with might and main for mischief through the land is execution or crucifixion or the cutting off of hands and feet from opposite sides, or exile from the land."

The highest grade in Paradise is reached by Jihadists. Muslim (20:4645), "It has been narrated on the authority of Abu Sa'id Khudri that the Messenger of Allah said (to him): "Abu Sa'id, whoever cheerfully accepts Allah as his Lord, Islam as his religion and Muhammad as his Apostle is entitled to enter Paradise." He (Abu Sa'id) wondered at it and said: "Messenger of Allah, repeat it for me." He (the Messenger of Allah) did that and said: "There is another act which elevates the position of a man in Paradise to a grade one hundred (higher), and the elevation between one grade and the other is equal to the height of the heaven from the earth." He (Abu Sa'id) said: "What is that act?" He replied: "Jihad in the way of Allah! Jihad in the way of Allah!" Quran (9:111), "Allah hath purchased of the believers their persons and their goods, for theirs (in return) is the garden (of Paradise): they fight in His cause, and slay and are slain, a promise binding on Him in truth, through the Law, the Gospel, and the Quran, and who is more faithful to his covenant than Allah? Then rejoice in the bargain which ye have concluded: that is the achievement supreme." How does the Quran define a true believer? Quran (48:29), "Muhammad is the messenger of Allah. And those with him are hard (ruthless) against the disbelievers and merciful among themselves"

The Pact of Umar for non-Muslims: treatment of non-Muslims. The pact of Umar for Christians and Jews, is explained in detail IN: Spencer, (2009) p192. The Pact of Umar, (Al-Turtushi, Siraj al-Muluk, pp.229-230), describes the Status of Non-Muslims under Muslim Rule. The Pact of Umar is the political agreement forced by the Caliph Umar on the Christians of Syria.

- We heard from 'Abd al-Rahman ibn Ghanam [d. 697] as follows: When Umar ibn al-Khattab accorded peace to the Christians of Syria, we wrote to him as follows: In the name of God, the Merciful and Compassionate. This is a letter to the servant of God Umar [ibn al-Khattab], Commander of the Faithful, from the Christians of such-and-such a city. When you came against us, we asked you for safe-conduct (aman) for ourselves, our descendants, our property, and the people of our community, and we undertook the following obligations towards you:
- We shall not build, in our cities or in their neighbourhood, new monasteries, Churches, convents, or monks' cells, nor shall we repair, by day or by night, such of them as fall in ruins or are situated in the quarters of the Muslims.
- We shall keep our gates wide open for passers by and travellers. We shall give board and lodging to all Muslims who pass our way for three days.
- We shall not give shelter in our churches or in our dwellings to any spy, nor bide him from the Muslims.
- We shall not teach the Quran to our children.
- We shall not manifest our religion publicly nor convert anyone to it. We shall not prevent any of our kin from entering Islam if they wish it.
- We shall show respect toward the Muslims, and we shall rise from our seats when they wish to sit.
- We shall not seek to resemble the Muslims by imitating any of their garments, the qalansuwa, the turban, footwear, or the parting of the hair. We shall not speak as they do, nor shall we adopt their kunyas.
- We shall not mount on saddles, nor shall we gird swords nor bear any kind of arms nor carry them on our- persons.
- We shall not engrave Arabic inscriptions on our seals.
- We shall not sell fermented drinks.
- We shall clip the fronts of our heads.
- We shall always dress in the same way wherever we may be, and we shall bind the zunar round our waists

- We shall not display our crosses or our books in the roads or markets of the Muslims. We shall use only clappers in our churches very softly. We shall not raise our voices when following our dead. We shall not show lights on any of the roads of the Muslims or in their markets. We shall not bury our dead near the Muslims.
- We shall not take slaves who have been allotted to Muslims.
- We shall not build houses overtopping the houses of the Muslims.
- We accept these conditions for ourselves and for the people of our community, and in return we receive safe-conduct.
- If we in any way violate these undertakings for which we ourselves stand surety, we forfeit our covenant (dhimmi), and we become liable to the penalties for contumacy and sedition.
- Umar ibn al-Khittab replied: Sign what they ask, but add two clauses and impose them in addition to those which they have undertaken. They are: "They shall not buy anyone made prisoner by the Muslims," and "Whoever strikes a Muslim with deliberate intent shall forfeit the protection of this pact."

When I brought the letter to Umar, may God be pleased with him, he added, "We shall not strike a Muslim."

6

Women in Islam

Women in pre-Islamic Arabia. Before Islam, bedouin women worked alongside their husbands and enjoyed a considerable amount of personal freedom and independence. Leading a non-sedentary life the Arab woman was not cloistered nor veiled, was very active and held in good esteem. Women were not restricted to the home. Muhammed`s wife Khadijja was a business woman. She married Muhammed, gave him a job in her business such that he went on trading journeys with the caravans he was later to attack and plunder in order to support his followers. The Hadith reveals that "Ansari women had the upper hand over their men." Women in Medina had more rights and authority than their Quraish counterparts. Mecca, the home of the Quraish tribe, where Muhammad came from was a religious hub. Women in Mecca were more subdued than those living anywhere else in Arabia particularly Medina that was a more cosmopolitan city having Jews and Christians as its inhabitants. Muhammad's wives enjoyed the emancipating atmosphere of Medina and were starting to exercise their relative freedom. This attitude angered Muhammed. Muhammad was angry with his wives` newfound liberties and rebelliousness, such that he threatened to divorce them all. The fact that there is so much emphasis in the Quran and in hadith about the importance of women being obedient to their husbands is indeed an indication of Muhammad's own desire to control his young and rebellious wives, (Quran 4:34).

The Prophet's view of women. The strength of women in pre-Islamic Arabian society caused Muhammad to say: "most of the dammed in hell are women." The Prophet said: "I looked into Paradise and I saw that the majority of its people were the poor. And I looked into Hell and I saw that the majority of its people are women" (Sahih Bukhari 1:6:31; al-Bukhari, 3241; Muslim, 2737). The theologian al-Ghazali, produces a view of women as deceitful, evil, immoral, mean and noxious. Ali (600-661), Muhammed's cousin and son-in-law and fourth caliph (the "rightly guided" Rashidun caliph), regarded "The entire woman is evil and what is worse is that is a necessary evil." Quran verses are clearly explicit regarding how Allah and Muhammed view the deficiencies due to being a woman. Narrated Abu Said Al-Khudri: The Prophet said, "Isn't the witness of a woman equal to half of that of a man?" The women said, "Yes". He said, "This is because of the deficiency of a woman's mind" Sahih Bukhari 3:48:826. Narrated Abu Sa'id al-Khudri: "Once Allah's Messenger (i.e. Muhammad) went out to the Musalla (place of prayer) (to offer the prayer) of 'Id-al-Adha or Al-Fitr prayer. Then he passed by the women and said, "O women! Give alms, as I have seen that the majority of the dwellers of Hell-fire were you (women)." They asked, "Why is it so, O Allah's Messenger?" He replied, "You curse frequently and are ungrateful to your husbands. I have not seen anyone more deficient in intelligence and religion than you. A cautious sensible man could be led astray by some of you." The women asked, "O Allah's Messenger! What is deficient in our intelligence and religion?" (Bukhari 7:62:125). He said, "Is not the evidence of two women equal to the witness of one man?" They replied in the affirmative. He said, "This is the deficiency in her intelligence (Bukhari 6:301). Isn't it true that a woman can neither pray nor fast during her menses?" The women replied in the affirmative. He said, "This is the deficiency in her religion." (Sahih Bukhari 1:6:301). *This is a circular argument*. Narrated 'Abdullah bin Abbas: The Messenger then said, "I saw Paradise (or Paradise was shown to me), and I stretched my hand to pluck a bunch (of grapes), and had I plucked it, you would have eaten of it for as long as this world exists. Then I saw the (Hell) Fire, and I have never before, seen such a horrible sight as that, and I saw that the majority of its dwellers were women." The people asked, "O Allah's Apostle! What is the reason for that?" He replied, "Because of their ungratefulness." Do they disbelieve in Allah (are they ungrateful to Allah)?" He replied "They are not thankful to their husbands and are ungrateful for the favours done to them. Even if you do good to one of them all your life, when she sees some hardness from you, she will say, "I have never seen any good come from you." Sahih Bukhari 7:62:125 "Women are looked down upon because they curse." Narrated Aisha who said: "O Messenger of Allah, do women have to engage in jihad? He said: "Jihad in which there is no fighting: Hajj and Umrah. And because women are not able to fight because they are (physically) weak." "Women are and always were, weak. They stay behind (from Jihad) like women who are weak." "God favoured them with the strongest children, the sons." Women's faults as seen by Muslim men include: deceit, ingratitude, insatable lust. Ali (600-661), the prophet's cousin said: "The entire woman is evil and what is worse is that it is a necessity. It is easy to get pleasure from them but they give you big headaches too." "All the misfortunes and woes that befall men come from women" says Ghazali. "If anything presages a bad omen it is: a house, a woman, a horse. Never will a people know success if they confide their affairs to a woman." Al-Ghazali in his Book of Council for Kings, lists some of God's 18 punishments for women. These include mensuration, childbirth, pregnancy, not having control over her person, marriage to a stranger and separation from mother and father, liability for divorce but inability to divorce, having only one husband, disqualification for rulership and judgeship.

Fatima, Muhammed's daughter enjoyed double standards. The husband of Fatima, Muhammed's daughter was not allowed to have more than one wife. "I heard Allah's Apostle who was on the pulpit, saying, "Banu Hisham bin Al-Mughira have requested me to allow them to marry their daughter to Ali bin Abu Talib, but I don't give permission, and will not give permission unless 'Ali bin Abi Talib divorces my daughter in order to marry their daughter, because Fatima is a part of my body, and I hate what she hates to see, and what hurts her, hurts me" (Bukhari 7:62:157). Allah gave Muhammed a privilege "O Prophet, We have made lawful to you those of your wives, whose dowers you have paid, and those women who come into your possession out of the slave-girls granted by Allah, and the daughters of your paternal uncles and aunts, and of your maternal uncles and aunts, who have migrated with you, and the believing woman who gives herself to the Prophet, if the Prophet may desire her. This privilege is for you only, not for the other believers" (Maududi vol. 4, p. 111).

Subjugation women. Men are in charge of women. Surah International 4:34, "Men are in charge of women by (right of) what Allah has given one over the other and what they spend (for maintenance) from their wealth. So righteous women are devoutly obedient, guarding in (the husband's) absence what Allah would have them guard. But those (wives) from whom you fear arrogance, (first) advise them; (then if they persist), forsake them in bed; and (finally), strike them. But if they obey you (once more), seek no means against them. Indeed, Allah is ever Exalted and Grand." Husbands are a degree above their wives: "Of course, men are a degree above them in status" (Sayyid Abul A'La Maududi, The Meaning of the Qur'an, vol. 1, p. 165).

Muhammed gave male believers a major advantage that was to drastically transform their lives. He made them "in charge of women" Sahih Muslim 9:3511. He gave men power over women. He turned women into possessions belonging to men. Islam places men in charge of women because this is Allah 's commandment. "Men are in charge of women", because Allah hath made the one of them to excel the other, and because they spend for their maintenance of their wealth (Sur 4:34). Yet, Muhammed 's first wife Khadijja was a business woman in the caravan trade and provided Muhammed with sustenance. After her death he became poor and had to resort to organising raids on the same caravans to support himself and his followers. Men 's authority over women and the obedience of women owed to men are divinely inspired by the Quran (Sura 4:34). Muslim jurists are unanimous in their understanding that men are superior to women by virtue of their reasoning abilities, their knowledge and supervisory powers. (Q2.228; Bukhari 6:301) "and the men are a degree above them (women)." Since a man has financial responsibility for the family, they argue that he should have total power over the woman.

Islamic criteria for good women: Good women are obedient. "Good women are the ones who are obedient to God and to their husbands" (Q4:34). "So righteous women are devoutly obedient, guarding in (the husband`s) absence what Allah would have them guard. But those (wives) from whom you fear arrogance, (first) advise them; (then if they persist), forsake them in bed; and (finally), strike them. But if they obey you (once more), seek no means against them. Indeed, Allah is ever Exalted and Grand." Women are constrained to the house. For a woman to leave the house is against the will of God and against the principles of Islam. Ghawji gives a list of conditions that a woman must observe when she leaves the house, "you women do not have the right to walk among men. Stick to the sidewalks." She must no go beyond a 30- kilometre limit without her husband. When in a friend`s house she must remain covered as there may be a man hiding, Ibn Warraq (2003). Ghazali (the greatest Muslim after Muhammed) said, among other things: "She should stay at home and get on with spinning, She should not go out often, must not be well-informed, not communicate with neighbours, seek to satisfy her husband in everything, not leave the house without his permission. If given permission to leave the house she must put on old clothes, take deserted streets, avoid markets, make sure no stranger hears her voice. If a friend of her husband calls, she must not open the door."

Women`s choice of work is strictly restricted. Women are not free to choose their work, certain jobs are forbidden to them, even in so-called liberal Muslim countries. Orthodox Islam forbids women from working outside the home. Women are not allowed an education. Omar, the second Caliph (581-644) said "Prevent women from learning to write. Say no to their capricious ways." He also said: "Adopt positions opposite those of women." "Impose nudity on women because clothes are one reason for leaving the house." Islamic law forbade women to assume any posts of public responsibility, in particular the post of member of parliament. Islam specifically forbids certain professions such as head of state, judge, imam, head of armed forces. The duty of a wife is to attend to the husband's needs. The hadiths on which Islamic Laws are based, describe a woman's role: to stay at home, to be immediately ready for all he needs, to obey him (a religious duty). "Her duty is to stay at home to satisfy the sexual appetite of her husband," said Ghazali who was called "Proof of Islam." The husband can beat his wife, if she does not make herself beautiful for him, refuses his sexual demands, leaves the house without permission, neglects her religious duties. AYAT al-Baqarah 2:223 "Your wives are a place of sowing of seed for you, so come to your place of cultivation however you wish and put forth (righteousness) for yourselves. And fear Allah and know that you will meet Him. And give good tidings to the believers." This means that a husband uses his wife as he pleases, including anal intercourse. This verse corroborates these traditions: Narrated Sahihul Jami 5259, the Prophet said: "It is not right that a human should prostrate to another human, but if it were right for a human to prostrate to another human being I would have ordered a woman to prostrate to her husband, due to the greatness of his rights over her."

"By him in whose hand is my soul, if from his foot to the crown of his head there was a wound pouring forth with pus and she (his wife) came and licked that then she would still not fulfilled his right" reported by Imaam Ahmad, 12153; Saheeh al-Jaami 7725, and in: http://www.quran.mu/the-righteous-wife.html. This website provides detailed information on the duties of a Muslim wife: Serving her husband, carrying out what is needed in his house, such as bringing up and educating the children, preparing meals and housework. It is obligatory to serve her husband unrestrictedly, including serving him, traveling with him, making her available to him, and so on just as it is obligatory for her to obey the parents since obedience due from her transfers to the husband. She serves her husband, looks after his children and his wealth. The rights of women are food, shelter and clothing. "And they (women) have rights (over their husbands as regards living expenses, etc.) similar (to those of their husbands) over them (as regards obedience and respect, etc.) to what is reasonable" (al-Baqarah 2:228).

135

Sexual inequality. Sex is seen from the point of view of the male Muslim. A woman's duties towards her husband are derived from Allah. "A woman cannot fulfil her duties towards God without first having accomplished those that she owes her husband. A woman who dies and with whom the husband is satisfied will go to paradise." A wife should never refuse herself to her husband even if it is on the saddle of a camel. Yet a man can marry up to four women though Muhammed had several more. Q4:3 "Marry women of your choice, two or three or four, or whatever number of amah (sex slaves) you can own." Islam is clearly and openly favourable to sex, including fantasies of the "infinite orgasm" and "the perpetual erection" which are rewards for men in Paradise. Sex is seen only from a male view. A woman's sexuality is regarded as unholy. However, some *Fiqh* scholars "have concluded that women have the right to orgasm during sex and to fight in combat." Yet a woman without a clitoris because it has been cut off through genital mutilation is denied an orgasm.

The husband has control on divorce. A husband can divorce his wife by saying "I divorce you" three times. Divorced women are obliged to "keep themselves in waiting for three menstrual courses and it is unlawful for them, if they believe in Allah and the Last Day, to hide whatever Allah might have created in their wombs. Should their husbands desire reconciliation during this time they are entitled to take them back into wedlock" Surah al-Baqarah 2:228. However, outside this situation, a wife may remarry her ex-husband if and only if she marries another man, they have sex, and then this second man divorces her. The Quran in Sura 2:230 says: "And if the husband divorces his wife (for the third time), she shall not remain his lawful wife after this (absolute) divorce, unless she marries another husband and the second husband divorces her. (In that case) there is no harm if they (the first couple) remarry" (Maududi, vol. 1, p. 165).

Slave-girls are the sexual property of their male owners. The Quran in Sura 4:24 says: "And forbidden to you are wedded wives of other people except those who have fallen in your hands (as prisoners of war)" Maududi, vol. 1, p. 319. Suras 4:3; 23:5-6; 33:50; 70:22-30, permit male slave-owners to have sex with their slave-girls. Suras 23:5-6 and 70:22-230 allowed men to have sex with them in the Meccan period, during times of peace before Muhammad initiated his skirmishes and wars while being based in Medina. Asking about using coitus interruptus, Muslims were advised: "It is better for you not to do so (practice coitus interruptus). There is no person that is destined to exist, but will come to existence, till the Day of Resurrection" Bukhari. That means that these enquiring Muslims should stop doing coitus interruptus, but instead go all the way with the enslaved sex slaves. Fate controls who should be born. While many armies have criminal soldiers who commit this wrong act, the Quran codifys rape in a sacred text.

Womens'worth at Law. Women are considered inferior to men, and they have less rights and duties from the religious point of view. Women 's testimony in a court of law is worth half that of a man. The evidence of Muslim women is admitted only very exceptionally and then only from twice the number required of men. A woman before a judge is worth half of that of a man, (2:282). A woman's life is worth half that of a man. As regards blood-money, evidence, and inheritance, a woman is counted as half a man. The consequences of a law pronouncing on women, only within their role in the family fails to protect those women who need protection from their families. By failing to protect women from violence such as domestic abuse, rape, marital rape and honour killing, the state fails to provide the rights available to a full citizen. By ignoring issues of gender- based violence and granting lenient punishments to the perpetrators of violence against women, the state actually reinforces women's exclusion from the rights of citizens. Family laws require women to obtain a male relative 's permission to undertake activities that should be theirs by right. This increases the dependency women have on their male family members in economic, social and legal matters. Where adult women must obtain the permission of their fathers, brothers or husbands in order to attain a passport, travel outside their country, start a business, receive a bank loan, open a bank account and get married, Human Rights are excluded.

In Turkey, in November 2014, the Turkish PM, Erdogan made headlines by announcing at a summit on "Women and Justice" in

Istanbul that women are not equal to men "because it goes against the laws of nature." Women are seen as wives and mothers not as individuals. Emma Sinclair-Webb, an Istanbul-based senior researcher for Human Rights Watch told IBTimes UK, "From the very top of the government comes a discourse denying the equality of men and women and calling on women to have at least three children." Iranian universities ban women from 80 fields of study.

Choosing a husband. A girl is not allowed to choose her husband. This is done by her guardian or father. Refusing to marry the man chosen by her guardian, trying to elope, marrying above one's caste, issues of chastity and apostasy are reasons for honor killing. Speaking with an unrelated man, rumoured pre-marital loss of virginity, an extra-marital affair, refusing forced marriages; marrying according to their will; or even women and girls who have been raped, can stain or destroy the family honour. Therefore, family members (parents, brothers, or sisters) kill the victim in order to remove the stain, and protect the honour of the family. Provisions such as Article 340 exist in many Arab countries' Penal Codes. Therefore, the practice of murder in the name of honour constitutes a grave barrier to a woman's access to justice since honour is articulated as a valid defense for murder in many Arab Penal Codes. This in itself is a complete disregard for Article 2 (c) of the United Nations Declaration on the Elimination of Violence against Women. It is in response to Surah 4:15 "If any of your women are guilty of lewdness, take the evidence of four (reliable) witness from amongst you against them; if they testify, confine them to houses until death do claim them. Or God ordain for them some (other) way." In this verse, Allah gives Muslim men the right to imprison for life their women (female family members) whom they believe to be "guilty of lewdness." It is left to them to decide what constitutes lewdness.

Azam Kamguian (2005), p. 99, describes in more detail, cases of murdering women because they refused to marry the man chosen by her parents, http://www.islam-watch.org/.

The Hijab, Veil, Burqa are imposed by Imams not the Quran. The word 'hijab' in the Quran has nothing to do with the Muslim women's dress code. It is a FATWA by Imams. The word 'hijab' means `barrier`and is used in several contexts: Quran 7:46, 33:53, 38:32, 41:5, 42:51, 17:45. Antonie Wessels, 1972 IN: A Modern Arabic Biography of Muhammed, p.141, quotes Haykal who relates that the use of a barrier was not required for the wives of Muhammed until after the battle for Al-Khandaq, when Muhammed went to Zaynab's house to talk to her husband but he was not there. The wind blew Zaynab's skirt and he saw Zaynab's legs and fell in love with her. From this arose the custom that Muhammed's wives had to talk to visitors from behind a barrier. The situation was originally only for Muhammed's wives. This avoided that the visitors fell in love with any of his wives. Moreover, a Quran verse was revealed which prohibited anyone to marry his wives, even after he dies. The context of this verse is the wedding of Muhammed and Zaynab and the behaviour of the wedding guests. Quran 33:53 "O believers do not enter the prophet's houses until leave is given to you." The following verse described how visitors are to conduct themselves: Quran 33: 53-54. "When you ask his wives for something do so from behind a partition (hijab). That is purer for your hearts and theirs. It is not right for you to offend Allah's Messenger, just as you should never marry his wives: that would be grievous sin in Allah's eyes. Allah has full knowledge of all things, whether you reveal them or not." In this verse, nowhere is a face veil mentioned. Furthermore, it is actually addressing the believing men, not the wives of the Prophet, asking the men to speak to the prophet's wives from behind a partition. It says: "When you (ie the believing men) ask his wives for something, do so from behind a barrier." Although verse 33:53-54 is addressing the believing men, and not the prophet's wives, yet women got lumbered with a veil. Marriage to the Prophet's wives after his death is forbidden unlike ordinary widowed women. The wives of the Prophet were required to speak to anyone from behind a barrier/curtain because they were not like other women: Q.33:32-33, "O ye wives of the prophet. Ye are not like other women. If ye keep your duty (to Allah), then be not soft of speech lest he in whose heart is a disease aspire to you, but speak with appropriate speech."

Women are instructed to use the shawl to cover their cleavage, not their head. In verse 24:31, the Quran says: "Tell the believing women to avert their eyes, and safeguard their private parts, and not to expose their attractions except what is visible. And let them wrap their shawls (khimar) around their breast lines, and reveal their attractions only before their husbands" Sahih Buhkhari 33:59. "O Prophet. Tell thy wives and thy daughters and the women of the believers to draw their cloaks close around them when they go abroad. That will be better, that so they may be recognised and not annoyed" Sahih Bukhari 33:53. The Quran, does not command the prophet's wives to wear niqab, nor the ordinary believing women. Face veil does not feature in verse 33:53 at all, but says: "And if you were to ask the wives of the Prophet for something, ask from behind a curtain."

There is no teaching in the Quran for any women of the world to cover their faces when outside. The Quran does not require that women use head scarfs, only that they dress decently: cover their breasts and private parts, Quran 24:31. God tells women to use their cover (Khimar being a dress, shawl, coat) to cover their bosoms not their head. Quran 24:31 "And tell the believing woman to lower their gaze and be modest and to display of their adornment only that which is apparent and to draw their veils over their bosoms and not to reveal their adornment save to their husbands or fathers or husbands' fathers, or their sons or their husbands' sons, or their brothers or their brothers' sons or sisters' sons, or their women, or their slaves, or male attendants who lack vigour, or children who know naught of women's nakedness. And let them not stamp their feet so as to reveal what they hide in their adornment. And turn unto Allah together, O believers, in order that ye may succeed."

The word 'hijab' appears seven times in the Quran. Five of them as 'hijab' and two times as 'hijaban', these are the verses: 7:46 (barrier), 33:53 (partition), 38:32 (curtain), 41:5 (partition), 42:51 (partition/Allah speaks from behind a partition), 17:45 (a concealed partition) and 19:17 (screen). 17:45, "and when you receit the Quran, we put between you and those who do not believe in the Hereafter, a concealed partition". None of these 'hijab' words are used in the Quran in reference to what the traditional Muslims call today 'hijab', that being the head cover for Muslim women.

http://www.quranicpath.com/finerpoints/3353niqab.html, explains the word for "barrier" in its various contexts. In the Quran, this word is never used in the context of women's dress but used only in its meaning as a 'barrier'. For example: Quran 17:45 "When you recite the Quran, we place an invisible barrier ("hijab") between you and those who do not believe in the Hereafter." Qur'an 17:46 "We have put covers on their hearts that prevents them from understanding it, and heaviness in their ears." "It is not fitting for a man that Allah should speak to him except by inspiration, or from behind a barrier ("hijab"), or by sending a messenger to reveal with His permission, whatever He wills: for He is Most High, Most Wise" (Qur'an 42:51).

And he said, "Truly do I love the love of good, with a view to the glory of my Lord," until (the sun) was hidden in the barrier ("hijab") (of night). (Quran 38:32). The term "barrier" is also used in the context of a barrier between those in paradise and those waiting to enter. Quran 7: 46 "Between them is a veil. And on the Heights are men who know them all by their marks. And they call unto the dwellers of the Garden: Peace be unto you! They enter it not, although they hope (to enter)." All these verses indicate an invisible barrier. And the following verse is an example of the word being explicitly used by ordinary people of Arabia to mean a psychological barrier at the time of the Prophet: "And they say: Our hearts are protected from what you call us to, and in our ears there is a deafness, and between us and you there is a barrier ("hijab")" (Quran 41:5). Therefore, it is possible that Allah is calling believing men to put up a psychological barrier between themselves and the Prophet's wives, and view them as they would their own mothers, rather than as ordinary believing women with whom marriage is eligible (i.e. to not develop a liking with the intention of marriage).

The tradition of covering the head was practiced thousands of years before Muslim scholars claimed the hijab as a Muslim dress code. Religious Jewish women cover their heads in the synagogues, at weddings and religious festivities. This Jewish tradition is a cultural not a religious one. In Saudi Arabia the men wear a head cover but this has not yet become a required Islamic dress code. In North Africa there is a tribe that requires men to wear a hijab rather than women.

Sharia Law requires coverage because when a man meets a woman he must lower his eyes. Therefore by wrapping women, men do not have to lower their eyes. The imposition that a woman covers her head and face is an invention of men. Imposing that a woman covers her head and face is subjugation, denying freedom and equality of dignity (Article 1, Charter of Human Rights). It is against Article 3 which confers "liberty" on women and against Article 5 which protects women from degrading treatment. It is an affront to ALL women.

Zahra Eshraghi, the grand daughter of the Ayatolla Khomeni declared: "Under Islamic law a woman is there to fill her husband's stomach and raise children. Journalist Moaveni, author of "Lipstick Jihad", noted that by removing the hijab, women are showing they are a force to be reckoned with.

Says Izzettin in: https://answers.yahoo.com : "It is really too regrettable that millions do not or misunderstand the Quran. There is no indication to covering either head or chest or neck or shoulder. I feel deep sadness when I see a Muslim female wrapped in black even if she had never read the Quran." In Nur chap 24, verse 30 is directed to males, verse 31 to the females. In both there is clear order to subdue the vision and protect the perianal (farj: area around anus, between it and the sex organs).

Covering one's head to any extent introduces a risk to safety and national security for obvious reasons such as making identification of persons who did criminal activity is impossible. In Western countries there are cameras in shops, streets, homes, for purposes of safety and security. Covering one's head thwarts this security. Moreover, terrorists are known to wear womens' clothing as a coverup. As a symbol of religion it imposes that religion on everyone else who has to live with women with covered heads. In the West, where people are allowed to wear what they wish, putting a woman behind the veil is not modesty. It is domination, subjugation, control, coercion. "It's like a cage. I wish men could also be trapped like this, so they understand how much we suffer," said a woman in Afganistan. Those who hide girls are robbing them of their childhood

Majid Rafizadeh reports on the protest of women in Iran. January 24, 2018. Women took to the street recently in the front lines of protests in the Islamic Republic of Iran. The demands of the women were clear: Remove Sharia law, eliminate the obligatory hijab, improve the rights of women, and not to treat women as slaves and second-class citizens. "I am sick of Hijab, Sharia law and Sharia police said the women protesters." Women are sick of the Sharia police monitoring them constantly for what they wear, what they say, what they drink, where they go, and what kind of relationships they have" says Leila, a young Iranian woman. What now is the fate of these women? In the Islamist Republic of Iran arrested women are faced with atrocities such as rape, torture or execution. Some die in detention surreptitiously. The Iranian regime brutally cracked down on the protesters. It killed more than 20 people and injured many more. The regime also arrested more than 3,700 people, including young girls and women. In the Sharia court, ambiguous charges are brought against them such as "*Moharebeh*" or "Waging war against God", a capital offense in Iran. Similarly, "insulting Islam," "being corrupt on earth," "endangering the national security," "insulting the Supreme Leader," or "insulting Allah (God)" by defying the rules. With no due or fair process, the detainees are also denied access to lawyers. The Islamist judiciary of Iran has already announced that some of the detainees face the death penalty.

Female Genital Mutilation (FGM). Genital Mutilation is founded on the customs of the Prophet. FGM attempts to control women's sexuality, and uses unrelated ideas about purity and modesty. Genital mutilation takes place from birth to the first young years. Typically carried out by a traditional circumciser with a blade or razor, with or without anaesthesia, FGM is concentrated in 27 countries in Africa, as well as in Yemen and Iraqi Kurdistan, and practised to a lesser extent elsewhere in Asia and among diaspora communities around the world. The age at which it is conducted varies from days after birth to puberty. In half the countries for which national figures are available, most girls are cut before the age of five. The procedures differ according to the ethnic group. They include removal of the clitoral hood and clitoris, and in the most severe form (known as infibulation) removal of the inner and outer labia and closure of the vulva. In this last procedure, a small hole is left for the passage of urine and menstrual blood, and the vagina is opened by intercourse and childbirth. There is profuse bleeding because major blood vessels are close to the genitals and there are problems with passing out urine and menstruation. The girl may struggle ferociously, in which case the incisions may become uncontrolled and haphazard. The girl may be pinned down so firmly that bones may fracture. The removal of the labia exposes delicate tissues to infections and allergies. Without labia the risk and discomfort are extreme. Born a whole woman, removal of the clitoris from her body robs her of her fundamental right to an orgasm. A woman with FGM has lost the use of an essential organ. She is disabled. FGM is a crime against humanity. The result is that the woman cannot have sex until she marries and her husband makes her pregnant by forcing himself when he wants a child. Once she gives birth, she is sown up again, only to be forced open when her husband deems it. Mutilation of the genitals of a woman is an invention of men to ensure that a man is sure that the baby is his. In these modern times there are scientific ways to prove paternity.

Health effects depend on the procedure, but can include recurrent infections, allergies, chronic pain, cysts, an inability to get pregnant, complications during childbirth and fatal bleeding. There are no known health benefits.

WHO has banned the practice. The UN banned FGM in 2012 recognizing FGM as a human-rights violation. In December 2012 the General Assembly passed resolution 67/146, "Intensifying global efforts for the elimination of female genital mutilations," recognizing FGM as an "irreparable, irreversible abuse that impacts negatively on the human rights of women and girls"

Whatever the practice's origins it became linked to female slavery. Slaves were sown up to make them unable for conception. In 1799 the Egyptians practised excision, so that slaves could not get pregnant. Mackie cites the Portuguese missionary Joao dos Santos, who in 1609 wrote of a group inland from Mogadishu who had a "custom to sew up their females, especially their slaves being young to make them unable to conceive, which makes these slaves sell dearer, both for their chastity, and for better confidence which their masters put in them." The English explorer William Browne wrote in 1799 that the Egyptians practised excision, and that slaves in that country were infibulated to prevent pregnancy. Thus, Mackie argues, a "practice associated with shameful female slavery came to stand for honour." The practice is rooted in gender inequality, attempts to control women's sexuality, using ideas as purity, modesty and aesthetics. It is usually initiated and carried out by women, who see it as a source of honour, and who fear that failing to have their daughters and granddaughters cut will expose the girls to social exclusion. Over 125 million women and girls have experienced FGM in the 29 countries in which it is concentrated.

FGM has been outlawed or restricted in most of the countries in which it occurs, but the laws are poorly enforced. Egypt finally outlawed FGM in 2008 after at least two partial bans. Two incidents had attracted international attention. In 1994 CNN broadcast images of a child undergoing FGM in a barber's shop in Cairo, and in 2007 a child died during an FGM procedure. The death prompted the Al-Azhar Supreme Council of Islamic Research, the country's highest religious authority, to rule that FGM had no basis in Islamic law, and the government banned it in July 2007 by ministerial decree. Conducting FGM was added as a criminal offence to the country's penal code in June 2008. The first charges under the new law were laid in 2014 after a girl died; a doctor was charged with manslaughter and the girl's father with complicity. In France FGM is covered by a provision of the country's penal code dealing with violence against children. Doctors are obliged to report FGM. The reaction was that Westerners ought not to intervene, and it took the deaths of two girls in 1982, one of them three months old, for that attitude to change. In 1999 a woman was sentenced to eight years' imprisonment for having performed FGM on 48 girls. Over 100 parents and two practitioners had been prosecuted by 2012. Canada recognized FGM as a form of persecution in July 1994, when it granted refugee status to Khadra Hassan Farah, who had fled Somalia to avoid her daughter being cut. FGM is outlawed by section 268 of the Criminal Code of Canada. It is an offence in the UK under the Prohibition of

BILL KHAN

Female Circumcision Act 1985 to perform FGM on children or adults, and an offence under the Prohibition of FGM Act to arrange for it outside the country for British citizens or permanent residents. Despite having been banned since 1985 FGM in the UK still takes place. Spain made FGM illegal in 2003

There have been international efforts since the 1970s to persuade practitioners to abandon it, and in 2012 the United Nations General Assembly, recognizing FGM as a human-rights violation, voted unanimously to intensify those efforts. The United Nations and WHO have banned FGM.

7

Marriage Rules

Islam imposes clear rules on women through Chastity and subjection to Guardianship.

Chastity. Chastity is imposed on women but not on men. A chaste woman is described as "A chaste woman is one who has been preserved within her house like a jewel, never having been involved in kissing, touching, petting or any form of promiscuous relationships with men other than her husband." Mohammad Qotb, a well-known Muslim writer says: "A girl is simply the guardian of her honour. She does not have the right to make use of it (her sexual organ) nor invite anyone to violate it. It is a case not only of her honour but also of her parent's honour, her family, society and all Humanity."

Guardianship. A woman is under the guardianship of a male Muslim. In traditional Islam, the literal definition of `wali` means `custodian` or `protector`. The guardian (wali) of the bride can only be a free Muslim. The *wali* of the bride is normally a male relative of the bride, preferably her father. The Wali mujbir is a technical term of Islamic law which denotes the guardian of a bride. It is a condition of guardianship in marriage that both the guardian and his ward share the same faith. Therefore, a non-Muslim man cannot have guardianship over a Muslim woman, even if he is her father. This is according to the unanimous agreement (*ijma*) of the Muslims. Likewise, a Muslim man does not have the right of guardianship over a non-Muslim woman, even if she is his daughter, Ibn al-Mundhir, al-Ijma (74). A woman is not free to choose her guardian. It is assigned by family relation. Once she is married, she becomes the charge of her husband's guardianship.

The Prophet said: "Any woman married without the consent of her guardian, then her marriage contract is void, and the ruler is the guardian for a woman who has no guardian" Sunan Abi Dawud (2083), Sunan al-Tirmidhi (1101,2). If a Muslim woman's guardian is a non-Muslim and he marries her to a Muslim man, then the contract will be legally valid. The contract of an Islamic marriage is concluded between the guardian (wali) of the bride and the bridegroom, not between bridegroom and bride. The bride normally is present at the signing of the marriage contract, but this is not mandatory. In this context, it is meant that the silence of the bride is considered consent. The system of guadianship limits the rights of women further. A woman of legal age cannot conclude her own marriage contract. Her legal guardian (her wali) alone has this right. If she is a virgin, her legal guardian can force her to marry someone else of his choice. She cannot choose her husband.

Islam distinguishes between two types of marriages: One is the classical marriage or nikah, an Arabic word for marriage which means coition: a contract that falls under the catergory of Sales/Transactions and has no time limit. The other is the temporary marriage or Mutà: a contract that falls under the category of rents and leases and is temporary. Oriana Fallici (2004), IN: The Force of Reason, p. 103, describes her own experience of a temporary marriage.

Nikah Marriage. Who can a man marry in the classical (nikah) marriage? The Quran verses describe who a man can and cannot marry. Prohibition is based on relationships. There are several rules which prohibit marriage due to certain relationships. In pre-Islamic Arab tradition, the son could inherit his deceased father's other wives as a wife. This changed. 4:23, 24: "Prohibited to you (for marriage) are: Your mothers, sisters, father's sisters, mother's sisters, brothers' daughters, sisters' daughter, foster-mothers (who gave you suck). Foster sisters; your wives' mothers; your step-daughters under your guardianship, born of your wives to whom you have gone in, but no prohibition if ye have not gone in. Those who have been wives of your sons proceeding from your loins; and two sisters in wedlock at one and the same time, except for what is past; for Allah is Oft-forgiving, Most Merciful." Quran 4:24 "And forbidden to you are wedded wives of other people except those who have fallen in your hands (as prisoners of war)." When a married woman becomes spoils of war her marriage is annulled, Maududi vol. 1, p. 319 and she became available for use as a sex slave by her master.

Privileges for Muhammed. However, Allah made special conditions for Muhammed. Quran 4:3. Sura 33:50, "O Prophet! We have made lawful to thee the wives to whom thou hast paid their dowers, and those whom thy right hand possesses out of the prisoners of war whom Allah has assigned to thee; and daughters of thy paternal uncles and aunts, and daughters of thy maternal uncles and aunts, who migrated with you (from Makka) with thee; and any believing woman who dedicates her soul to the Prophet if the Prophet wishes to wed her. This is only for thee and not for the Believers. We know what We have appointed for them as to their wives and the captives whom their right hands possess, in order that there should be no difficulty for thee. And Allah is Oft-Forgiving, Most Merciful." Sura 33: 51 "You, (O Muhammad), may put aside whom you will of them or take to yourself whom you will. And any that you desire of those (wives) from whom you had (temporarily) separated, there is no blame upon you (in returning her). That is more suitable that they should be content and not grieve and that they should be satisfied with what you have given them, all of them. And Allah knows what is in your hearts. And ever is Allah Knowing and Forbearing."

Abu Bakr gave his daughter in marriage to Muhammed even though Abu Bakr protested that this was not correct. Aisha's marriage to Muhammed was contrary to tradition because Aishia was Muhammed's foster niece. Narrated Ursa: The Prophet asked Abu Bakr (her father) for Aishia's hand in marriage. Abu Bakr said: "But I am your brother". The Prophet said "You are my brother in Allah's religion and His book, but she (Aishia) is lawful for me to marry." Muhammed convinced the little girl by telling her a story about seeing her as a baby. Narrated Aisha "Allah's Apostle said to me, "You were shown to me twice (in my dream) before I married you. I saw an angel carrying you in a silken piece of cloth, and I said to him, "Uncover (her)," and behold, it was you. I said (to myself), "If this is from Allah, then it must happen" Sahih Al-Bukhari, Volume 9, Book 87, Number 140; Number 139). Bukhari vol.7, 65. Aishia sums up the whole scenario. Narrated Aishia, "I used to look down upon those ladies who had given themselves to Allah's Apostle and I used to say, "Can a lady give herself to a man? But when Allah revealed: "You (O Muhammed) can postpone (the turnoff) whom you will of them (your wives), and you may receive any of them whom you will; and there is no blame on you if you invite one whose turn you have set aside (temporarily) (33:51), I said to the Prophet, "I feel that your Lord hastens in fulfilling your wishes and desires," Sahih Bukhari 6:60:311.

Double Standards for Fatima. Inspite of the allowance of four wives, Muhammad would not allow polygamy for his son-in-law Ali, because an extra wife would hurt Muhammad's first daughter Fatima, by his first wife Khadijah. Fatima was married to Ali. However, Ali managed to take a slave girl as concubine. Narrated Al-Miswar bin Makhrama: "I heard Allah's apostle who was on the pulpit, saying, "Banu Hisham bin Al-Mughira have requested me to allow them to marry their daughter to Ali Bin Abu Talib, but I don't give permission, and will not give permission unless Àli bin Abu Talib divorces my daughter in order to marry their daughter, because Fatima is part of my body, and I hate what she hates, and what hurts her hurts me," Sahih Bukhari 7:62:157.

Who can a woman marry? A Muslim woman may not marry a non-Muslim man (Quran 2:221-230). A woman has no right to the custody of her children from a previous marriage when she remarries. A woman is in a less advantageous position in divorce and child custody. Women who marry foreigners are denied the right to extend citizenship to their husbands, yet men can extend their nationality to their wives and children. Only fathers, not mothers can independently pass citizenship to their children. Where a woman is widowed, divorced or abandoned or if her husband is not a national in the country where the couple reside, her children have no access to citizenship and to its rights (access to education, health care, land ownership and inheritance). This inequality not only denies women their rights as citizens. It also denies children their basic rights as human beings.

The marriage contract. One Muslim jurist explained: "marriage for a Muslim male is "the contract by which he acquires the reproductive organ of a woman with the express purpose of enjoying it" (Bousquet p.118). A woman does not own her vagina ("al bud"). She has no right over her sexual organ. She has no right to make use of it nor the right to invite anyone to use it. When she marries, it is a contract to allow him to use her vagina. The converse is not the case. A woman does not have the exclusive right to her husband's reproductive organ. The reproductive organ of the husband is not exclusively reserved for one woman, remains the possession of the husband who can use it with an unlimited number of women (wives and concubines), Sura 4:3. She can only demand to be fed, clothed and housed because she is totally dependent on him. The marriage contract includes the age of the bride and the dowry.

The age of marriage. Muhammed set the fate of women by setting the example by his marriage to Aishia when she was six years old and consummated the marriage when she was nine years old (Muslim 8:3309; Bukhari 58:234; Bukhari 6:298). Narrated Aishia "Allah's Apostle married me when I was six years old and I was admitted to his house when I was nine years old" Sahih Muslim 8:3310. She was 18 years old when he died aged 62. Muhammed's wives were not allowed to marry even after his death, by a revelation which Muhammed had received from God, IN: Spencer (2009).

The dowry. There are set conditions. The future husband pays a dowry to his wife and with this payment she becomes his lawfully wedded wife. If no dowry is paid, the marriage contract is invalid (Maliki opinion). The dowry is agreed upon at the time of marriage. If the dowry is not specified, then she is entitled to the dowry that "is given to a woman similar to her." Mahr Mu'ajjal (promptly given dower) is given at the time of the marriage when the groom hands over to the bride a sum of money called Mahr (dower) which is a token of his willing acceptance of the responsibility of bearing all necessary expenses of his wife. This is the original meaning of Mahr. There are two ways of presenting the Mahr to the bride. One is to hand it over at the time of the marriage, in which case it is known as Mahr Mu'ajjal, or promptly given dower, or to give the stated amount after the contract.

During the time of the Prophet Mahr Mu'ajjal was the accepted practice and the amount fixed was generally quite minimal. Muhammed married Aisha in Mecca when she was a child of six years and lived with her in Medina when she was nine. She was the only virgin that he married. Her father, Abu Bakr, married her to him and the apostle gave her four hundred dirhams, IN: Ibn Ishaq, Sirat Rasulullah (The Life of Muhammad), translated by Alfred Guillaume (Oxford University Press, Karachi, tenth impression 1995), p. 792). The giving of Mahr by 'Ali to Fatimah (Muhammed's daughter), illustrates how this custom occurred. After the marriage had been arranged, the Prophet asked Ali if he had anything he could give as dower in order to make Fatima his lawfully wedded wife. Ali replied: "I swear by Allah that I have nothing, O Messenger of Allah." The Prophet then asked: "Where is the coat of armour I once gave you?" Ali replied that it was still in his possession. The Prophet then instructed him to send the coat of armour to Fatima, thereby making his union lawful. This then was the sum total of Fatima's dower, explained in: http://www.islamweb.net/en/article/97117/islam-on-dowry. Al-Tabari said: "Give women their mahr as something that is required and obligatory." He also said: It was narrated from Qatadah: "And give to the women (whom you marry) their Mahr (obligatory bridal-money given by the husband to his wife at the time of marriage) with a good heart." He said it is obligatory. And it was narrated from Ibn Jurayj: "And give to the women (whom you marry) their Mahr (obligatory bridal-money given by the husband to his wife at the time of marriage) with a good heart." he said: "it is obligatory and the amount is to be named." It was narrated from Ibn Zayd concerning the verse "And give to the women (whom you marry) their Mahr (obligatory bridal-money given by the husband to his wife at the time of marriage) with a good heart" The Arabic word nihlah (translated here as "with a good heart") means: obligatory. "And give to the women (whom you marry) their Mahr (obligatory bridal-money given by the husband to his wife at the time of marriage) with a good heart; but if they, of their own good pleasure, remit any part of it to you, take it, and enjoy it without fear of any harm as Allah has made it lawful" al-Nisa' 4:4, Ibn Kathir, Tafsir Ibn Kathir, vol 2 pp 376-77.

In contrast, in Indian states such as Kerala, Tamil and others, the groom receives substantial amounts of gold which, it is claimed to be the reason why Arabians frequently marry in India.

Tafseer al-Tabari,4/241. Allah has made the Mahr obligatory for the man, who must give it to the woman, and not vice versa. This is what is indicated by the texts of the Quran and also in the texts of the Sunnah. For example, al-Bukhari narrated from Sahl ibn Sa'd that a woman came to the Messenger of Allah and said: O Messenger of Allah, I offer myself to you (in marriage). She stood there for a long time, then a man said: O Messenger of Allah, marry her to me if you have no need of her. He said: "Do you have anything that you could give to her as a dowry?" He said: "I have nothing but this izaar of mine." He said: "Look for something, even if it is a ring of iron." So, he looked but he could not find anything. The Messenger of Allah said: "Do you know anything of the Quran?" He said: "Yes, Soorah such and such, and Soorah such and such." He said: "I give her to you in marriage in return for what you know of the Quran." Narrated by Bukhari, 4741; Muslim, 1325.

Conditions in marriage. 4:34 "SAHIH INTERNATIONAL, "Men are in charge of women by (right of) what Allah has given one over the other and what they spend (for maintenance) from their wealth. "Men are managers of the affairs of women because Allah has made the one superior to the other" (Maududi, vol. 1, p. 329). Maududi informs us that men are not superior to women in a moral way, that is, in honour and excellence, but men "have been endowed with certain natural qualities and powers that have not been given to women or have been given in a less degree." The website (http://www.islamweb.net/en/article/97117/islam-on-dowry) explains: "For largely biological reasons, women are well adapted to domestic pursuits while men, for similar reasons, are better suited to work outside the home. These physical and mental differences between men and women are, in practice, what underlay Islam's division of familial responsibilities into internal and external spheres, with the woman dealing exclusively with the home and family and the man providing the funds." A Muslim man must have final control in the relationship. In a tradition Muhammed details the qualities of a wife, including that "she obeys when instructed" and the husband "is pleased to look at her". The clause "men have been endowed with certain natural abilities" degrades womankind's abilities. Maududi in stating the meaning in Sahih International 4:34: "Men are in charge of women by (right of) what Allah has given one over the other and what they spend (for maintenance) from their wealth, explains that a can only expect that she be fed, clothed and housed. The Muslim marriage means that a woman puts herself sexually at the disposition of her husband next to three other wives and an unlimited number of concubines. Muslim jurists insist that in return for using them, wives receive gifts, so the marriage is not about love. She is turned out and replaced as soon as she ceases to please. It is obligatory for a woman to let her husband have sex with her immediately when he asks her. "A wife should never refuse herself to her husband even if it is on the saddle of a camel." It is not lawful for a wife to leave the house except by the permission of her husband. A wife may not leave the house if her husband does not permit it. She may not be visited by friends and relatives if he does not wish it. A woman must be obedient and this obedience is grounded in her obedience to God. To go to paradise a woman must accomplish: prayers, fasts, guards her chastity and obey her husband. Traditions support this: The woman who dies and with whom the husband is satisfied, will go to paradise. Righteous women are devoutly obedient, guarding in (the husband's) absence what Allah would have them guard.This was a new situation for women who in pre-Islamic times were socially strong, organised and commanded the sex market (Women of flags), setting the operational rules, charging payment in the form of silver rings and bracelets and selecting who the father was of a born child such that he was made responsible to pay maintenance.

The wife has no sexual rights. A husband could enjoy his wife in any way he pleases. Some men enjoyed their women from the front and from the back. When asked about this, Muhammed produced Sura 2.223 "Your women are as your field. Go unto them as you will." That includes anal sex. There is no consultation with women. "Your women are a tilth for you (to cultivate) so go to your tilth as ye will" Quran (2:223). This verse likens a woman to a field (tilth), to be used by a man as he wills. In this verse, Allah also gives divine sanction for anal sex.

Wives and concubines. The Quran allows men to have four wives (Surah: 4:3). "If you fear that you cannot act justly towards the orphans, then marry such women as seem good for you; two three, four of them. But if you fear that you cannot do justice, then one only, or those you possess. It is likelier then that you will not be partial." As well as marrying four wives, Muslim men can also force sex on slave girls, "those whom your right hand possess" (33:50; 23:5-6;4:24). Islam allows marriage to pre-pubescent girls, stipulating that Islamic divorce procedures "shall apply to those who have not yet mensurated" (65:4). According to Q 65:4, sexual relations with females who have not yet had their menstrual cycle (i.e prepubescent girls) is permissible. Mohammed married 15 women and consummated his marriages with 13 (al-Tabari vol.9 p.126-127). Bukhari vol.1 Book 5 ch.25 no.282 p.172-173). As well as wives Muhammed possessed several concubines. He relegated his wives to either consecutive days or according to some accounts all in one night, Bukhari (62:6).

"The Prophet used to go round (have sexual relations with) all his wives in one night, and he had nine wives." Bukhari (5:268), narrated Anas, "The Prophet used to visit all his wives in a round, during the day and night and they were eleven in number." I asked Anas, "Had the Prophet the strength for it?" Anas replied, "We used to say that the Prophet was given the strength of thirty men." Volume 1, Book 5, Number 268: Narrated Qatada: Anas bin Malik said, "The Prophet used to visit all his wives in a round, during the day and night and they were eleven in number." I asked Anas, "Had the Prophet the strength for it?" Anas replied, "We used to say that the Prophet was given the strength of thirty (men)." And Said said on the authority of Qatada that Anas had told him about nine wives only (not eleven).

Volume 1, Book 5, Number 270: Narrated Muhammad bin Al-Muntathir:on the authority of his father that he had asked Aisha about the saying of Ibn Umar (i.e. he did not like to be a Muhrim while the smell of scent was still coming from his body). Aisha said, "I scented Allah's Apostle and he went round (had sexual intercourse with) all his wives, and in the morning he was Muhrim (after taking a bath)." Volume 1, Book 5, Number 282, Narrated Anas bin Malik. "The Prophet used to visit all his wives in one night and he had nine wives at that time." *Yet* Muhammad also said that it was impossible to treat all wives *equally*.

Non-believers who are "spoils of war", and "that which your right hand possesses" do not have any rights, are concubines, sex slaves and the Muslim owner can do whatever he wants to them including rape.

Domestic violence. Q 4:34 provides for husbands to beat their wives if they "fear disobedience." In the Quran this belief is driven home by giving the husbands the right to beat their wives "into submission" Domestic violence is embedded in the Quran. The "Wife beating Handbook written by Imam Mohammed Kamal Mustafa of the Spanish Islamic Councillors, provides instructions of how to beat the wife. The blows must inflict psychological suffering, not only physical, to lead to her subjugation. Sura 4:34 "But those (wives) from whom you fear arrogance, first advise them; (then if they persist), forsake them in bed; and (finally), strike them. But if they obey you (once more), seek no means against them. Indeed, Allah is ever Exalted and Grand." The Rules for female disobedience are: warn, forsake in bed, beat. Beating aims to achieve subjugation of the woman. In his commentary, Ruhul Maani, Sheik Sayed Mahmud Allusi gives four reasons to beat a wife: if she refuses to beatify herself for him, if she refuses sex when he asks for it, if she refuses to pray or do ablutions, if she goes out of the house without a valid excuse.

Narrated Abdallah b. Zama: "None of you must flog his wife as he flogs a slave, and then have sexual intercourse with her in the last part of the day." Another version is, "One of you has recourse to whipping his wife as a slave and perhaps he lies with her at the end of the day." Rifa'a divorced his wife whereupon Abdur Rahman bin Az-Zubair Al-Qurazi married her. Aisha said that the lady (came), wearing a green cover (and complained to her (Aisha)) of her husband and showed her a green spot on her skin caused by beating). When Allah's Apostle came, Aisha said, "I have not seen any woman suffering as much as the believing women. Look! Her skin is greener than her clothes!" Reported in Muslim Book 009, Number 3506 by Jabir b. Abdullah reported, "Abu Bakr came and sought permission to see Allah's Messenger. He found people sitting at his door and none amongst them had been granted permission, but it was granted to Abu Bakr and he went in. Then came Umar and he sought permission and it was granted to him, and he found Allah's Apostle sitting sad and silent with his wives around him. He (Umar) said: I would say something which would make the Holy Prophet laugh, so he said: Messenger of Allah, I wish you had seen (the treatment meted out to) the daughter of Khadija when she asked me some money, and I got up and slapped her on her neck. Allah's Messenger laughed and said: They are around me as you see, asking for extra money. Abu Bakr then got up went to Aisha and slapped her on the neck, and Umar stood up before Hafsa and slapped her saying: You ask Allah's Messenger (for that) which he does not possess. They said: "By Allah, we do not ask Allah's Messenger for anything he does not possess." Then he withdrew from them for a month or for twenty-nine days."

The following report is narrated by Aisha, Muhammad's favorite young wife. The context is about Muhammad leaving the house, to visit a graveyard and pray over the dead. Aisha followed him. She returned just before he did, but he noticed she was out of breath and he asked her why. She told him, and apparently fearing for his life as he saw her in the shadows, he punished her. Says Aisha: "He struck me on the chest which caused me pain" (Muslim, vol. 2, no. 2127). So Muhammad committed domestic violence on his young wife.

Umar b. al-Kattab reported the Prophet as saying: "A man will not be asked as to why he beat his wife" (vol. 2, no. 2142). Muslims believe that this policy expresses the divine will of Allah for all times and places.

Surah 2:222 says, "They will question thee concerning the monthly course, and do not approach them till they are clean. When they have cleansed themselves, then come unto them as God commanded you.

Truly, God loves those who repent and he loves those who cleanse themselves." Yet Muhammad's wives had to be available for the prophet's fondling even when they were having their menstrual period. (Sahih al-Bukhari Volume 1 Book 6 Hadith 300). Sahih al-Bukhari Volume 1 Book 6 Hadith 298 and 300, Narrated 'Aisha: "The Prophet and I used to take a bath from a single pot while we were Junub (being impure due to sexual intercourse). During the menses, he used to order me to put on an Izar (dress worn below the waist) and used to fondle me. While in Itikaf, he used to bring his head near me and I would wash it while I used to be in my periods (menses)." Itikaf is a period devoted to prayer in the mosque, during which time no earthly activities are allowed. Itikaf is an Islamic practice consisting of a period of staying in a mosque for a certain number of days, devoting oneself to prayer during these days and staying away from worldly affairs, yet Muhammed still went to Aisha.

Sahih Bukhari, Volume 1, Book 6, Number 299 and 300, Narrated Abdur-Rahman bin Al-Aswad, (on the authority of his father), Aisha said: "Whenever Allah's Apostle wanted to fondle anyone of us during her periods (menses), he used to order her to put on an Izar and start fondling her." However, verse 2:222 states otherwise: "They ask you about menstruation. Say: "It is a state of impurity; So, keep away from women in the state of menstruation, and *do not approach them until they are cleansed*. And when they are cleansed, then come to them as Allah has commanded you. Truly, Allah loves those who abstain from evil and keep themselves pure." Volume 1, Book 6, Number 294, Narrated Aisha, "While in menses, I used to comb the hair of Allah's Apostle" Volume 1, Book 6, Number 295, Narrated Urwa, "A person asked me, can a woman in menses serve me? And can a Junub woman come close to me?" I replied, "All this is easy for me. All of them can serve me, and there is no harm for any other person to do the same." Aisha told me that she used to comb the hair of Allah's Apostle while she was in her menses, and he was in Itikaf (in the mosque). He would bring his head near her in her room and she would comb his hair, while she used to be in her menses." Volume 1, Book 6, Number 299, Narrated Aisha, "The Prophet used to lean on my lap and recite the Quran while I was in menses." Volume 1, Book 6, Number 297, Narrated Um Salama

"While I was laying with the Prophet under a single woolen sheet, I got the menses. I slipped away and put on the clothes for menses. He said, "Have you got Nifas (menses)?" I replied, "Yes." He then called me and made me lie with him under the same sheet."

Sahih Bukhari, Volume 1, Book 6, Number 311, Narrated Aisha, "A woman asked the Prophet about the bath which is taken after finishing from the menses. The Prophet told her what to do and said, "Purify yourself with a piece of cloth scented with musk." The woman asked, "How shall I purify myself with it" He said, "Subhan Allah! Purify yourself (with it)." I pulled her to myself and said, "Rub the place soiled with blood with it." Sahih Bukhari Volume 1, Book 6, Number 319; Volume 1, Book 6, Number 320, Narrated Zainab bint Abi Salama, Um-Salama said, "I got my menses while I was lying with the Prophet under a woolen sheet. So, I slipped away, took the clothes for menses and put them on. Allah's Apostle said, 'Have you got your menses? 'I replied, 'Yes. Then he called me and took me with him under the woolen sheet." Um Salama further said, "The Prophet used to kiss me while he was fasting."

Divorce: Rules for the waiting period. There are rules regarding when sex can take place when marrying young girls, divorced women and captured women. It is a precaution to ensure that the women are not already pregnant. Allah clarifies the waiting period of the woman in menopause and the one whose menstruation has stopped due to her older age. Her 'Iddah' is three months instead of the three monthly cycles for those who menstruate, which is based upon the Ayah in Surat Al-Baqarah.2:228. "The same for the young, who have not reached the years of menstruation. Their 'Iddah' is three months like those in menopause," Ibn Kathir Quran interpreter, on Quran 65:4. Ibn Kathir clearly mentions women in menopause as well as young girls, who have not reached the years of menstruation. Tafsir Jalalain of Imam Jalaluddin Mahalli and Jalaluddin Suyuti also interpret the verse in the same way, "And (as for) those of your women who no longer expect to menstruate, if you have any doubts, about their waiting period, their prescribed (waiting) period shall be three months, and (also for) those who have not yet menstruated, because of their young age, their period shall (also) be three months" Tafsir Jalalain on Quran 65:4. These two famous Mufassirs interpret "Those who haven't not menstruated yet" in verse 65:4 to be prepubescent girls. Quran 65:4, (Tifsir Al-Razi) "a man stood up and asked, O Messenger of Allah, "What is the iddah of those girls that have not yet reached the age of mensuration?" It is then revealed "Those who haven't mensurated yet, their iddah is also three months." Tafsir Abu-Hayyan, on Quran 65:4 "Those who have not menstruated yet" denotes those who have not menstruated because of being young. In all these greatest of Tafsirs, what is common is that all of them interpret the phrase "Those who have not menstruated" in Quran 65:4 as "Those girls who have not reached the age of menstruation due to their young age." Sura (65:4) lays down rules for divorce and sets the prescribed period for divorce.

Divorce process. Divorce depends on the husband. Muhammed made it easy to get rid of any wife. A Muslim man divorces his wife by saying "Talaq" ie "I divorce you" three times. The word "Talaq" actually means "leave." Another way for the husband to get rid of the wife is to desert her. A man who wanted to get rid of his wife deserted her and she then lost her marriage rights. So, this Ayah was revealed: The Ruling concerning Desertion on the Part of the Husband, Tafsir Ibn Kathir: "Allah states, and thus legislates accordingly, that sometimes, the man inclines away from his wife, sometimes towards her and sometimes he parts with her. In the first case, when the wife fears that her husband is steering away from her or deserting her, she is allowed to forfeit all or part of her rights, such as provisions, clothing, dwelling, and so forth, and the husband is allowed to accept such concessions from her. Hence, there is no harm if she offers such concessions, and if her husband accepts them. This is why Allah said, "there is no sin on them both if they make terms of peace between themselves." He then said, "and making peace is better than divorce." Allah's statement means, coming to peaceful terms, even when it involves forfeiting some rights, is better than parting. Abu Dawud At-Tayalisi recorded that Ibn "Abbas said, "Sawdah feared that the Messenger of Allah might divorce her and she said, "O Messenger of Allah! Do not divorce me; give my day to Aisha. And he did, and later on Allah sent down, "And if a woman fears cruelty or desertion on her husband's part, there is no sin on them both" Ibn Abbas said, "Whatever (legal agreement) the spouses mutually agree to is allowed." At-Tirmidhi recorded it. In two Sahihs, it is recorded that "Aisha said that when Sawdah bint Zam`ah became old, she forfeited her day to Aisha, and the Prophet used to spend Sawdah's night with Aisha. There is a similar narration also collected by Al-Bukhari. Al-Bukhari also recorded that Aisha commented "And if a woman fears cruelty or desertion on her husband's part, that it refers to, "A man who is married to an old woman, and he does not desire her and wants to divorce her. So, he says, "I forfeit my right on you." So, this Ayah was revealed."

It is legally essential that the wife be a virgin when she asks for a divorce. Once marriage has been consummated the woman's sexual rights vanish. According to the Shiites a woman can only ask for a divorce in case of ablation of her husband's penis. According to the Malekites and Hanefites, once the marriage has been consummated, the woman has no rights at all. He only has to have sex once. On divorcing, his family will raise the children. In some sects she can raise the children, but if she marries, the former husband takes the children. Women are not automatically guardians of their children; in regard to marriage and divorce her position is less advantageous than that of the man; her husband may even beat her, in certain cases (Schacht 1982 p.126, 127). If one suspects his wife of adultery and cannot find four reliable eyewitnesses, he may testify himself four times (Q24: 6).

A wife can ask for a divorce only if she is still a virgin. If a husband has sexual relations once, she loses all her rights in this field. If he divorces her (for the third time), she shall not be lawful to him after that until she has wed another spouse and then if he divorces her it shall be no offence for either of them to return to each other, if they think they can keep within the bounds of Allah. "Those are the Bounds of Allah. He makes them plain to people to know" Quran 2:230. Women may not divorce their husbands in this way. After a Muslim man tells his wife he is divorcing her she must wait for the monthly periods in order to determine if she is pregnant or not. If the divorcing couple have children, they go to the father. He owes his wife no financial or other support. Marriage can give rise to a hostage situation since the Quran directs that if the couple "would be unable to keep the limits ordained by Allah", then "there is no blame on either of them if she gives something for her freedom" or in Pickthall's translation "ransom herself." After 3 talaqs, divorce is irrevocable. After a man divorces his wife three times, he cannot marry her again unless she marries another husband and he divorces her (Q.2:230). This has led to the phenomenon of temporary husbands. She takes her children with her but if she marries again, she loses her children. Her options: To stay unmarried and have her children or to marry and loose her children. The woman has total insecurity. Hence instead of keeping four wives which is expensive, it is cheaper to marry and divorce and hence change the wife several times (al-Ghazali; Ibn Warraq (2003) p.320) and Case histories: Women in Pakistan <u>IN</u>: Ibn Warraq (2003) p. 321.

Adultery: The punishment is stoning to death if married, lashings if not. Stoning is the punishment for married adulterers while lashing is for an unmarried adulterer. "The woman or man found guilty of sexual intercourse, lash each one of them with a hundred lashes, and do not be taken by pity for them in the religion of Allah, if you should believe in Allah and the Last Day. And let a group of the believers witness their punishment" Quran 24:2. If they are married, the Hadd punishment is stoning. It was narrated that Abu Hurayrah and Zayd ibn Khaalid al-Juhani said: The Messenger of Allah said: "Go tomorrow, O Unays, to this woman and if she admits (to adultery) then stone her." He said: "I went to her the next day and she admitted it, so the Messenger of Allah ordered that she be stoned."

Rape. Islamic law does not contain a true equivalent of the modern concept of rape, which is based on notions of individual autonomy and inviolability of the body, particularly the female body. Rape is, at its most basic level a violation of another person's sexual autonomy. Most jurists hold that rape is committing zina (unlawful sex, adultery) by force. This basic definition of rape as "coercive zina" meant that all the normal legal principles that pertained to zina, its definition, punishment and establishment through evidence, were also applicable to rape. The prototypical act of zina was defined as sexual intercourse between a man and a woman over whom the man has neither a conjugal nor an ownership right. What distinguished an act of zina from an act of rape, for the jurists, was that in zina, both parties act out of their own volition, while in an act of rape, only one of the parties does so. Jurists admitted a wide array of situations as being "coercive" in nature, including the application of physical force, the presence of duress, or the threat of future harm either to oneself or those close to oneself; they also included in their definition of "coercion" the inability to give valid consent, as in the case of minors, or mentally ill or unconscious persons. Muslim jurists from the earliest period of Islamic law agreed that perpetrators of coercive zina should receive the ḥadd punishment, but that the ḥadd punishment should not be applied to victims of coercive or non-consensual zina.

Certain classical jurists (Al-Tabari and Maliki Ibn al-'Arabi) and others (The Religious Council of Egypt among others) have classified the crime of rape not as a subcategory of zina, but rather a separate crime of violence under hirabah (forced and violent taking), i.e. a violent crime causing disorder in the land in the manner described in the Quran (5:33) as fasad (destructive mischief). According to the Mālikī, Ḥanbali, and Shafi schools of law, the rape of a free woman consisted of two violations: a violation against a "right of God" (Haqq Allah), provoking the Hadd punishment; and a violation against a "human" (interpersonal) right (Haqq Adami), requiring a monetary compensation. The amount of this compensation, they reasoned, should be the amount that any man would normally pay for sexual access to the woman in question, that is, the amount of her dower (ṣadaq or mahr).

Rape in marriage. The question arises whether sex with little girls in marriage can be considered as rape (violation of her sexual autonomy), since a child is not in a position to give consent based on a good understanding of sex with an adult man. Rape in marriage arises from the dictates of the Quran. Wives and concubines are expected to endure the husband's/master's advances at any time. When Muhammed and his followers destroyed a tribe, all males are killed and women enslaved as concubines by "same day marriage" which is a cover for rape. Muhammed married Safiya after beheading her father, torturing her husband and massacaring her entire tribe. He took Rayhana, a

15-year-old girl of a Jewish Rabbi (Bani Quraiza) after massacring all the men and boys. He married Juwariyah after massacaring all the men, robbing all the wealth and taking women and children as slaves.

However reporting a rape is also regarded to mean a confession of adultery under Sharia Law if four male witnesses cannot be found to confirm the victim's claim *in great detail*. Raped women are punished, the rapist goes free. The media regularly report atrocities against raped women. Thousands of female protesters took to the streets of Istanbul, Ankara and Mersin to protest at the brutal murder of Ozgecan Aslan, a tragic death which is a symbol of the growing trend of violence against women in Turkey. Aslan, a student at Cag University in the southern city of Tarsus, was stabbed to death after resisting a rape attempt by a bus driver while she travelled home. Her burned remains were discovered in a river bed three days after she disappeared. A woman can be executed for killing her rapist in Self Defence. Reyhaneh Jabbari was 19 when she stabbed her attacker in trying to defend herself. He died. In October 2014, 7 years later, the regime executed her.

Cousin marriages. It is proven that cousin marriages result in a high frequency of heart disease and mental illnesses which is compounded by daily indoctrination of males. Cousin marriages have been the norm for at least 1400 years in the Middle East. Consider that since 600 AD, generations following generations have been inbred. This is known to result in an accumulation of genetic defects, lung and heart problems, and schizophrenia. This is coupled with indoctrination and rote learning since young, which destroys the ability for cognative development (critical thinking). On the contrary, critical thinking and rational arguments are fundamental to Western Democracy.

Temporary marriages, temporary husbands, temporary wives. It is the custom in many Islamic countries to use temporary marriage. These are used to circumvent the marriage laws. Such marriages can last only a few hours. Example: a man goes to a house, asks to marry a girl, usually 16 years old, pays the parents the sum of money, goes to a hotel and has sex for two weeks, then disappears and divorces her. The girl cannot find her husband so she goes back to her parents. A divorced woman is regarded as shamed. Her only option is to go into prostitution. But girls do not want this. They want marriage and a family. Temporary marriages are legal under Sharia. The media regularly produce comments on this. A photo shows a beautiful girl of about 17 years being married to a gnarled old man with whom one would not want to rub shoulders let alone have sex. The "marriage," which has a local Islamic cleric's blessing, can be as short as 15 minutes and the woman is paid a "fee" for her "services." The marriage and divorce contracts are set up by a cleric before the parents release the girl to the man. The girl gets pregnant and faces the dangers of childbirth. Many young girls die in childbirth. These "marriages" are most common between older men and teenage girls. Secular individuals see this as "Islamicized" prostitution.

There are also cases of a man tricking the girl into thinking that he is marrying her only to be taken to a hotel for two weeks, then he disappears and she has no choice but to go back home. She is then dishonoured and cannot face society. Case details IN Spencer (2009) p.160 and IN: Zaki Ameen (2009). Hillman further explains that Zawaj al Mutah (contract marriage), is similar to Zawaj al Misyar (travellers' marriage, meaning the marriage is over after travelling is done), Zawaj al Urufi (marriage of convenience or marriage just for sex only), and Zawaj al Siry (secret marriage so that the old wives do not need to know). Niqa Mut'ah is practised by Muslim Shia. Muslim Sunni called it by a different name: Zawaj al Misyar. The name can be different, but the practice is exactly the same. Unfortunately, most of the time, the Indonesian girls and her families do not realize that the marriage will only last as long as the vacation period. Condoning temporary wives, "those of whom ye seek content (by marrying) give them unto them their portion as a duty. There is no sin in what ye do by mutual agreement." According to the verse 4:24 of the Quran temporary marriage is allowed in Islam and the marriage described in this verse cannot be usual marriage. This verse says when you did Mutah you must pay their dowries.

Surat An-Nisa 4:24: "And (also prohibited to you are all) married women except those your right hands possess. This is the decree of Allah upon you. And lawful to you are (all others) beyond these (provided) that you seek them (in marriage) with (gifts from) your property, desiring chastity, not unlawful sexual intercourse. So for whatever you enjoy (of marriage) from them, give them their due compensation as an obligation. And there is no blame upon you for what you mutually agree to beyond the obligation. Indeed, Allah is ever Knowing and Wise." From this Shite Muslims have gleaned permission to enter into marriages that have a time limit. The couple may marry for one night or a month.

Child Brides. Sex with pubescent girls is allowed by the Quran. Sur 65:4 clearly says, Muslim men can marry (and divorce) little girls who have not yet reached menstruation age. This means that Muslim men were allowed to marry little girls. Muhammad established an appalling precedent for abuse of young girls which continues to be nurtured by the Muslim faithful. For example, in Iran a fatwa was given about Quran 65.4, "A man can marry a girl younger than nine years of age, even if the girl is still a baby being breastfed. A man, however is prohibited from having intercourse with a girl younger than nine, but other sexual acts such as foreplay, rubbing, kissing and sodomy is allowed. A man having intercourse with a girl younger than nine years of age has not committed a crime, but only an infraction if the girl is not permanently damaged. If the girl is permanently damaged, the man must provide for her all her life. But this girl will not count as one of the man's four permanent wives"

Sex with children is prohibited in the West. It is called paedophilia. Every Muslim paedophile finds justification and validation for taking children as brides and the ignorant parents, who are often poor, let their little girls to be raped for the greed of money. Sex with children results in torn vagina and anus. Many get to suffer from fistula disease resulting from early intercourse and pregnancy. Videos of cemeteries full of children who died in childbirth have been shown on Google. What age to marry young girls? The Quran equates marriageable age to a mature and sound judgment (as is required to give them their inheritance). Quran, 4:6 "And test the orphans until they reach a marriageable age; then, if you find them to be mature of mind/sound in judgment, hand over to them their possession." Marriageable age is equated to sound judgement, an age in which a person can responsibly handle their possessions. Is a girl sound in judgement at the age of 9 to 12? Does such a child have a mature intellectual level? Those years are meant to be a time of learning, a crucial time in which a child shapes her personality by exploring different paradigms and attaining valuable experiences on life. Such situations are rapes of children, since children have not developed and matured in sexual awareness to comprehend sex. While sexual intercourse may be painful for adult women, the situation of an eight-year-old child's vagina being forced open has consequences of being irreparably torn and the urinary bladder damaged. The psychological impact of such sexual imposition on a child is extreme. A child giving birth to a child severely endangers the life of both. Videos have been shown on Google of cemeteries full of children who have died in childbirth. Child mothers risk that the baby dies in the womb and has to be cut out, incontinence and miscarriages. The vagina is torn and the mother child becomes incontinent, that is, cannot hold urine and faeces because of torn structures, hence urine and faeces continually fall from her body.

Media Reports: London 17 February 2015 - Malawi has passed a law banning child marriage, raising the minimum age to 18 in a country where half of girls end up as child brides.

Case: RABAT, Morocco, 28 March 2012 – The death of 16-year-old Amina Filali, in the town of Larache, Morocco, has prompted outrage around the world. Amina's life was shattered by a double tragedy: She was raped at age 15, and then, after reporting the assault, she was forced to marry her rapist. After five months of marriage, during which she endured repeated beatings, Amina committed suicide by ingesting rat poison.

Case: An eight-year-old child bride has died in Yemen of internal bleeding sustained during her wedding night after being forced to marry a man five times her age, she suffered from bleeding and uterine rupture which caused her death. Medics couldn't save her life.

Case: In 2010, the case of Elham Mahdi Al-Assi, a 12-year-old girl died three days after she was married to a much older man. Her death was the result of severe bleeding caused by tears to her genital and anal area. Her husband tied her up and raped her.

Case: 2014. Iranian child bride faces execution for killing the man she was forced to marry. "I didn't know who I am or what is life all about," she said soon after being arrested.

Case: Farzaneh Moradi, 28, was executed for murdering her husband. She was forced into marriage at 15 and gave birth at 16.

Case: 17 Feb 2015 Rape and murder of 20-year-old Ozgecan Aslan in Turkey. He stabbed her and beat her to death with an iron bar. He then enlisted the help of his father and a friend to dispose of her body in a river in Tarsus.

Case: A mother talks: Rulla, was 13 years old and attractive. She was still a child, playing with kids in the camp. But the war, hunger, humiliation and fear forced her father in the end to accept the offer. Rulla knew nothing about marriage. Her mother tried to prepare the groom for the fact that he was getting married to a child, not a mature woman. The problem was that Rulla could not forget that she was still a child.

Case: Another mother talks: I had to persuade my daughter to drop out of study and prepare for marriage. She was adamant that she wanted to finish her schooling, but I said that our need was greater. She ran to me sobbing. pale and in shock. He complained Dima howled and wailed whenever he wanted to touch her. She is now broken.

Case: Another mother talks: I could not advise Nour (16 years) on her wedding night. She was too confused and apprehensive to listen. Nour did not look happy like a bride after her wedding. She was in shock. He was always grumbling about her childish behaviour and enraged after once catching her playing football with his young nephews, jumping and running like a little child. There was a huge gap in thinking between Adil and Nour. Around the world 10 million children are not at school today as a result of being married off as child brides.

The International Legal Obligations on Child Marriage (2011) protect women and children through terms that recognise: That Child Marriage is Harmful and Discriminatory; The Right to Full and Free Consent into Marriage; The Right to Choose a Spouse; The Right of Children to Express Their Views Freely; The Right to Non-Discrimination; The Right to Health and Access to Health Information; The Right to Education; The Right to be Free from Physical, Mental, and Sexual Violence; The Obligation to Set a Minimum Age for Marriage and Enforce Registration. In 2014 the UN human rights experts set out states' obligations to set 18 as the legal minimum age of marriage, establishing and implementing marriage registration, and establishing national compulsory birth registration. The Commission on the Status of Women equality goal in post-2015 targets violence against women and issues strong language against such violence.

8

Inheritance

In the pre-Islamic period, the Arab family was socially and politically composed of males (*aṣaba*), namely those who were able to fight and defend the common property. At the death of the head of family, the familial estate was transmitted only to males, according to the principle of proximity. Firstly, to those on direct line (descendants and ascendants), then to those on the collateral line (full or consanguine brothers and their sons, paternal uncles and their sons, etc.). This structure reflected the strong unity of the familial group conceived as an association able to defend and offend, thus, implying the social alienation of women, children, and all those persons unable to contribute to the common defence effectively (Santillana,1938, pp. 495-96). There are several schools of thought which differ on several aspects of inheritance. The Quran introduced in the division of the estate the closest women, that is, daughter, wife, sister, and mother, generally giving them a half share of a male. Then verse 4:7 stated that to males as well as to females a fixed share (*farz*) shall be allotted. For this, they are named heirs by quota (*ahl al-farż* or *ahl al-faraeż*). The basic principle governing the inheritance law of Islam is that it is considered as founded on the will of God, who directly imparted such rules in the Quran. From this premise the other principles derive. The system by quota introduced by the Quran constituted a sort of transition from the ancient pre-Islamic to the new order aiming to conciliate the rights of the weakest members of the society.

Titles (*asbab*) giving right to inherit are relationship (*nasab*, *raḥem, qarāba*), marriage (*nekaḥ*), and patronage (*wala*). If a person has more than one title, he is entitled to inherit, based on all of them. Persons entitled to succeed are firstly the heirs by quota, determined by the Quran, the Sunna, and the *ijma* (consensus), namely spouses, parents, grandfathers, grandmothers, daughters, son's daughters, full, consanguine, and uterine brethren. Secondly, there are three categories of agnates: agnates in a proper sense (*aṣaba be-nafsehi*), that is, males related to a deceased person only through males; and patrons are included in this category. Next follow agnates because of another heir (*aṣaba be-gayrehi*), that is, females who are considered agnates because of the presence of a male of their degree (daughters and sons; full or consanguine sisters and full or consanguine brothers). Lastly to be considered are agnates in the presence of another heir (*aṣaba maa gayrehi*), that is, full or consanguine sisters who are considered agnates because of the presence of direct daughters or son's daughters.

Differences of religion, slavery, and homicide are impediments to inheritance. The heir excluded from the inheritance because of such an impediment is considered a dead person. According to a Hadith, a Muslim does not inherit from a non-Muslim, and a non-Muslim does not inherit from a Muslim. A slave does not possess, but he himself is possessed. However, if he is set free before the division of the estate, he is considered a free person. Most jurists (Malikis, Shafi'is, Hanbalis) believe that freedom is required prior to the death of his relative. According to the Quran, the shares are six. The share of two-thirds is attributed to two or more daughters or, in their absence, to two or more son's daughters (4:11); and to two or more full or consanguine sisters (4:176). One half is allotted to one daughter or, in her absence, to a son's daughter (4:11); to the husband when a wife does not leave direct descendants; and to a full or consanguine sister (4:176) "If there are both brothers and sisters, the male will have the share of two females.

One-third is given to a paternal grandfather as his minimum share when he is with the full or consanguine brothers (only for Malikites, Shafiites, and Hanbalites); to the mother when her deceased husband does not leave descendants and when there are two or more brothers and/or sisters (4:12); and to two or more uterine brothers and/or sisters (4:11). One-fourth is allotted to the husband when his deceased wife leaves descendants, and to the wife when her husband does not leave descendants (4:12). The share of one-sixth is attributed to the father when the deceased person leaves descendants or son's descendants; to the mother when the deceased person leaves descendants of son's descendants or two or more brothers and/or sisters; to one uterine brother or sister (4:11); to one or more son's daughters when there is a direct daughter; to one or more consanguine sisters when there is a full sister; to a grandfather in the presence of a son; and to one or more grandmothers. Lastly, one-eighth is attributed to one or more wives when her/their deceased husband leaves descendants (4:12). If the wives are two or more, they shall divide their share on equally (Santillana,1938, pp. 506-11). A son's inheritance is twice the size of that of a daughter (4:11).

Can non-Muslim children inherit from their Muslim father? There is no inheritance for the children born to a Christian man who converted to Islam. They get nothing. It all goes to his Muslim wife. The Muslim may inherit from the non-Muslim but not the opposite, based on the Prophet's hadith *al-islam ya`lu wa la yu`la* "Islam dominates and is not dominated", although there are various opinions: http://www. sunnah.org/msaec/articles/inherit.htm.

Al-Zuhayli said in *al-Fiqh al-islami wa adillatuh*: All four schools agree that difference in religion between legator and inheritor, one being Muslim and the other not, precludes inheritance. The Muslim cannot leave anything to the non-Muslim nor the non-Muslim to the Muslim, whether through parenthood or marriage, due to the Prophet's sayings: "The Muslim does not leave anything to the non-Muslim nor the non-Muslim to the Muslim" (Bukhari and Muslim), and "The people of two different religious communities inherit nothing from each other" (narrated by Tirmidhi, Ahmad, Abu Dawud). Egyptian law and Syrian law stipulate: "There is no mutual inheritance between Muslim and non-Muslim."

Al-Zuhayli continues: "Muadh ibn Jabal, Mu'awiya, Ibn al-Hanafiyya, Muhammad ibn Ali ibn al-Husayn, and Masruq, held the view that the Muslim may inherit from the non-Muslim but not the opposite, based on the Prophet's hadith *al-islam ya'lu wa la yu'la*, "Islam dominates and is not dominated" (a hadith narrated by al-Rawyani, al-Daraqutni, al-Bayhaqi, and al-Diya from Aidh ibn Amr) and Ahmad said: "The Muslim inherits from his non-Muslim manumitted slave" due to the general meaning of the hadith *al-wala' li man a'taq*: "The rights of patronage belong to the manumitter" (narrated by Bukhari and Muslim)." The Mufti of Egypt Muhammad Hasanayn Makhluf was asked a question to which he gave this answer in his *Fatawa shar'iyya*: "A man who was Christian and married with a Christian woman, had five children with her, two males and three females, then he became Muslim, married a Muslim woman, and divorced his Christian wife after he made his Islam public. Then he died on the 20th of July 1954. However, the children all remained Christian, and their age is now (in the year 1956 C.E.) as follows: a 22-year old daughter, an 18-year-old daughter, a 17-year-old son, a 14-year old son, and an 11-year-old daughter. It is needed to know which of his children inherit from him, and we thank your honour." Answer: "The inheritance of this deceased Muslim all goes to his Muslim wife." There is no inheritance for the children he left behind as mentioned above, due to their embrace of the Christian religion at the time of his death and the fact that none of them followed him in accepting Islam. "Difference in religion precludes inheritance, as stipulated by the jurisprudents, and Allah knows best."

9

Usuary

Usuary is taking 100% interest. Taking of interest is explicitly prohibited, yet there was a demand for giving and taking interest in the commercial life. Azam 2001, quoting Schacht 1950, explains that in order to observe the religious prohibition and satisfy the need, devices were used. One such device consisted of giving real property as a security for the debt and allowing the creditor to use it, so that its use represented the interest. Another device consisted of a double sale. The prospective debtor sells to the prospective creditor a slave for cash, and immediately buys the slave back from him for a greater amount payable at a future date. This amounts to a loan with the slave as security and the difference between the two prices represents the interest. The Arabic word "Riba" means interest. There are two types of interest, quantity and quality. If one swaps gold for silver it becomes interest in quality. And if one lends $1000 and charge $1500 in payment it becomes interest in quantity. Interest is a major sin because the curse of Allah is on those who charge interest. When you give charity, Allah will increase your wealth: "Allah will destroy Riba (usury) and will give increase for Sadaqat (deeds of charity, alms, etc). And Allah likes not the disbelievers, sinners" (Al-Baqarah: 274-279).

Allah will declare war on those who dabble in "Riba": "O you who believe! Be afraid of Allah and give up what remains (due to you) from Riba (usury) (from now onward), if you are (really) believers" (Al-Baqarah: 278). "And if you do it, then take a notice of war from Allah and His Messenger but if you repent, you shall have your capital sums. Deal not unjustly (by asking more than your capital sums), and you shall not be dealt with unjustly (by receiving less than your capital sums (Al-Baqarah: 279). He said it is the job of the Caliph to wage jihad on people who do riba. Imam Abu Hanifa said any country that uses riba is dar ul Harb and he uses Ayah Q 2:279. Q.2:275: "As for those who devour interest, they behave as the one whom Satan has confounded with his touch." Seized in this state they say: "Buying and selling is but a kind of interest," even though Allah has made buying and selling lawful, and interest unlawful. Hence, he who receives this admonition from his Lord, and then gives up (dealing in interest), may keep his previous gains, and it will be for Allah to judge him. As for those who revert to it, they are the people of the Fire, and in it shall they abide."

The term "riba" in Arabic means 'to grow, to exceed, to increase'. Technically, it denotes the amount that a lender receives from a borrower at a fixed rate of interest. At the time of the revelation of the Quran there were several forms of interest transactions and were designated as riba by the Arabs. Of these one was that the vendor sold an article and fixed a time limit for the payment of the price, stipulating that if the buyer failed to pay within the specified period of time, he would extend the time limit but increase the price of the article. Another was that a man loaned a sum of money to another person and stipulated that the borrower should return a specified amount in excess of the amount loaned within a given time limit. A third form of interest transaction was that the borrower and vendor agreed that the former would repay the loan within a certain limit at a fixed rate of interest, and that if he failed to do so within the limit, the lender would extend the time limit, but at the same time would increase the rate of interest. It is to transactions such as these that the injunctions mentioned here apply.

The Arabs used the word majnun (possessed by the jinn) to characterize the insane. The Quran uses the same expression about those who take interest. Just as an insane person, unconstrained by ordinary reason, resorts to all kinds of immoderate acts, so does one who takes interest. He pursues his craze for money as if he were insane. He is heedless of the fact that interest cuts the very roots of human love, brotherhood and fellow-feeling, and undermines the welfare and happiness of human society, and that his enrichment is at the expense of the well-being of many other human beings. This is the state of his 'insanity' in this world: since a man will rise in the Hereafter in the same state in which he dies in the present world, he will be resurrected as a lunatic.

Many countries do not send troops to fight Muslims around the world but Imam Abu Hanifa has still categorized them as Dar ul Harb. This is because of their riba system, Islam rationality states. They use the accumulated wealth to cheat the people. This puts them at war with Allah and makes the country dar ul Harb. The following Hadith explains to the Ummah how grave riba is: Abu Huraira reported Allah's Messenger said, "Riba has seventy segments, the least serious being equivalent to a man committing adultery with his own mother" (Sunan Ibn Majah (3/337) No. 2274 and Mustadrak al-Haakim (2/43) No. 2259).

10

Individualism

Zhud. Zuhd includes the Islamic concept of asceticism and more specifically the concept of renunciation. Asceticism involves a life of privation that lacks certain comforts and luxuries and early ascetics were often characterized by their poverty. Renunciation involves detachment and an indifference towards worldly items. Both of these concepts require one to shun a life of luxury in favor of a more pious and simple life. According to Al-Qushayri, it is an obligation to renounce that which is prohibited but to renounce that which is lawful and the renunciation of intentions and desires constitutes a virtue. Zuhd is often attributed to Sufism. Sufyan al-Thawri (d. 161H/778CE) described zuhd as preparation for death and not having long term hopes for this life. Sufi master, Rabi'a was quoted to have said in response to a declaration from God, "When I heard this address, I so detached my heart from the world and cut short my hopes that for thirty years now I have performed each prayer as though it were my last and I were praying the prayer of farewell.

Homosexuality. Being Homosexual is an illegal illness according to the Islamic Legal Code. So, the Regime will give you a free gender-reassignment surgery to "cure" you or you can risk being executed.

Homosexuals are thrown off tall buildings. The Prophet said: "Kill the one who sodomizes and the one who lets it be done to him." And (remember) Lout (Lot), when he said to his people: "Do you commit the worst sin such as none preceding you has committed in the Alamin (mankind and jinns)? Verily, you practise your lusts on men instead of women. Nay, but you are a people transgressing beyond bounds (by committing great sins)" (Al-A'raf 7:80-81). The Quran is negative towards sodomy (4:16; 7.80), (26.165), (27:55), (26:166). Q. 4:16 "If two men among you commit indecency, punish them both." Q.7:80 "and Lot said to his people. Do you commit indecent acts that no nation has ever committed before? You lust after men in preference to women. You are a degenerate people."

Sahih International 7.81 "Indeed, you approach men with desire, instead of women. Rather, you are a transgressing people." Quran 27:55 "Will you indeed approach males in lust in place of women?" Quran 26:165-166 "What. Do you approach the males of the worlds and forsake those whom your Lord has created for you for your mates?" Quran (7:80-84) "For ye practice your lusts on men in preference to women: ye are indeed a people transgressing beyond bounds. And we rained down on them a shower (of brimstone)." This is an account that is borrowed from the Biblical story of Sodom. The destruction of the two cities of Sodom and Gomorrah was God's punishment for the two cities for people's immoral behaviour. Only Lot and his daughters were saved. Lot's wife disobeyed God's instruction not to look back, and was turned into a pillar of salt.

Muslim scholars through the centuries have interpreted the "rain of stones" on the town as meaning that homosexuals should be stoned, since no other reason is given for the people's destruction. The story is also repeated in Suras 15:74, 27:58 and Q29:40 "So each We seized for his sin; and among them were those upon whom We sent a storm of stones, and among them were those who were seized by the blast, and among them were those whom We caused the earth to swallow, and among them were those whom We drowned. And Allah would not have wronged them, but it was they who were wronging themselves."

Quran (7:81) "Will ye commit abomination such as no creature ever did before you?" This verse is part of the previous text and it establishes that homosexuality as different from (and much worse than) adultery or other sexual sin. According to the Arabic grammar, homosexuality is called *the* worst sin, while references elsewhere describe other forms of non-marital sex as being "among great sins." Quran (26:165-166), "Of all the creatures in the world, will ye approach males, and leave those whom Allah has created for you to be your mates? Nay, ye are a people transgressing" Quran (4:16),"If two men among you are guilty of lewdness, punish them both. If they repent and amend, leave them alone" This is the Yusuf Ali translation. The original Arabic does not use the word "men" and simply says "two from among you." Abu Dawud (Book 033 hadith 4448), "If a man who is not married is seized committing sodomy, he will be stoned to death." Sahih Bukhari 7:72:774 and 8:82:820, "The Prophet cursed effeminate men (those men who are in the similitude (assume the manners of women) and those women who assume the manners of men, and he said, "Turn them out of your houses." "The Prophet turned out such-and-such man, and Umar turned out such-and-such woman." Al-Tirmidhi, Sunan 1:152, Sunan Ibn Majah 3:20:2561, Muhammad said "Whoever is found conducting himself in the manner of the people of Lot, kill the doer and the receiver." Reliance of the Traveller, p17.2 "May Allah curse him who does what Lot's people did." This is also repeated in three other places. Al-Muwatta 41:11 "Ibn Shihad said "He is to be stoned, whether or not he is muhsan.""

But the Quran does not prohibit using, as passive sex partners, the ancient category of men who by nature lacked desire for women, since such men were not considered "male" as a result of their lack of arousal for women. This kind of man is regarded as gay in modern times but in the ancient world he was identified as an anatomically whole "natural eunch".

Islam goes beyond merely disapproving of homosexuality. Sharia teaches that homosexuality is a vile form of fornication, punishable by death by the sword though there are differenes of opinion. https://www.thereligionofpeace.com/pages/quran/homosexuality.aspx. Regarding lesbianism, there is no doubt among the fuqahaa that lesbiansm is haram and a mjor sin. There is no Hadd for it but it is subject to tazeer (unspecified punishment determined by the qaad (al-Mawsooah al-Fiqhiyyah part 24 p.253).

There are also several other hadith stating (Sunan Abu Dawud 38:4447, Sunan ibn Majah 3:20:2562, "if a man comes upon a man, then they are both adulterers," "If a woman comes upon a woman, they are both adulteresses," "When a man mounts another man, the throne of God shakes," and "Kill the one that is doing it and also kill the one that it is being done to."

Permitted food. "He has forbidden you dead animals, and blood, and the swine, and that which is slaughtered as a sacrifice for other than God." (Quran 2:173) "for that surely is impure" (Quran 6: 145). Scholars may not know why consuming pig meat is forbidden in the Hebrew Torah, they do not know the reason why it is forbidden in the Quran, perhaps because it is forbidden in the Torah. Pigs were not known to preIslamic Arabs. Pliny in his natural history, noted the absence of pork in Arabia. It is unclear why Muhammed would prohibit an animal that was not likely to be found in Arabia. The Quran describes pig flesh as an abomination and not as unclean. Among the Syrians pig flesh was taboo but it was uncertain whether this was because the animal was holy or because it was unclean. Jews had an ambiguous attitude towards swine. There are suggestions that Jews revered swine as divine and met secretly to eat swine flesh as a religious rite.

All animals are subject to infections not only pigs. Trichinosis is a disease caused by a parasitic nematode which is passed to man in uncooked infected meat. It is rarely a serious disease. The parasite was first seen in 1835 and it was in 1859 that it became known that the parasite can be transmitted to humans. It is a disease of cold and temperate regions in Europe and America rather than the Middle East. Cattle sheep and goats transmit diseases to humans. Undulent fever is transmitted from infected cattle and milk. Malta fever was transmitted to man from goats if milk is not pasteurized. Anthrax, a serious disease, is transmitted from sheep and cattle to man. Dietry Laws in the Old Testament have food taboos and are based on the animal's type of locomotion. Cloven hoofed, cud chewing ungulates are proper food for a pastoralist. Thus, the pig which is cloven hoofed but is not a ruminant is excluded. The definition of "proper" meat was based on sacrificial species and became a measure of fitness for all animals in the Israelite diet. It seems that prejudice against pork developed among pastoral peoples living in arid and semiarid regions because pigs were unsuited to the pastoral way of life but were widely used among agricultural people. The pig was used by one group but not by the other. Many scholars ascribe to the notion of group loyalty and allegiance. Where populations of different religions live side by side food taboos mark the social boundaries. This would prevent competition for the same food source. Such is the case in India where prohibitions occur in casts. Food partitioning is also found in Aboriginal tribes in Australia.

List of Animals permitted and prohibited as food:

1. The animals which are shown as prohibited in the Quran and by tradition, such as swine or pig, pet donkey are undoubtedly prohibited.
2. The animals in which there is no blood at all such as flies, mosquitoes, spiders, cockroach, scorpion, glow warm, white ants, etc are all prohibited (Haram), but locusts are permitted without slaughter (zibha).
3. The animal which contains blood but it does not flow such as snakes, lizard, house lizard, forest lizard etc are prohibited.
4. The animals which live under the earth such as rat, muskrat, bandicoot, mongoose, etc. are all prohibited.
5. The animals which are born in water and live therein such as frog, crab, alligator, tortoise etc. All are prohibited but the fish, even dead is permitted. Prawns are disputed, those who call it fish it is permitted for them and those who do not declare it as fish for them it is disapproved to the point of being forbidden.
6. The animals containing flowing blood which eat grass, leaves etc. But they do not inflict wounds with their teeth and do not prey such as camel, goat, sheep, cow, ox, buffalo etc., (pet or stray) deer, stag etc. All are permitted, but the horse is abhorrent.

7. The birds which peck only (To peck the corn is a sign of lawfulness and to tear the flesh with claws is the sign of prohibition.) but do not cause wound with their claws and do not prey such as sparrow, pigeon, dove, partridge, cock, quail, duck, charkavva, lark, crane, mina, parrot etc. are all permitted.

8. The beasts which inflict wounds with their teeth and prey such as tiger, wolf, jackle, fox, leopard, panther, cat, dog, monkey, langoor, bear, hyena are all prohibited.

9. The birds which use their claws for hunting. and inflict injury such as hawks, falcon, sparrow hawk, female hawk, vulture, shikra, latora etc, are all prohibited.

10. The birds which feed upon dead such as vultures and phoenix (Huma) are all prohibited.

11. The animals, among whose parents, one is permissible and the other is prohibited in such cases the mother will be counted (The mule is prohibited when his mother is a she-ass and if the mother is a cow it is lawful and if the mother is mare it is abhorrent.). If the mother is prohibited the kid is also prohibited.

12. The milk of the permitted animal is permitted and of those prohibited is prohibited. Similarly, the eggs of the permitted birds are permitted and the prohibited are prohibited.

Fish that do not have scales is also not fit for consumption, and only the fish that have scales on its body, such as Salmon, Trout, Grey Mullet, etc. are considered to be fit for consumption. Furthermore, if any 'allowed' food is contaminated by food which is not allowed, then that food also becomes unfit for Muslim consumption.

Hallal. If animals such as sheep, cow, chicken, etc. are not slaughtered according the prescribed Islamic way, i.e. in Halaal way, then the consumption of such meat is also unfit for Muslims. Hallal is a method of preparing meat by cutting a neck vein and allowing the blood of the animal to drain out. The assumption is that the flesh is purified of disease- causing organisms and toxins. However, disease causing organisms infest the whole animal, muscles and organs. Toxins in food and medications given to the animal when it gets sick are selectively deposited in the liver. Hence the liver should not be eaten. Fat is also a site of deposition. All animals are subject to infections and can if their flesh is eaten, transmit diseases to humans. Pig flesh infected with Trichinella can be identified because the infection is visible.

Sheep and goats suffer from a wide range of diseases which are transmitted to humans: protozoa (Trypanosoma spp); Babesia spp., Theileria hirci, Anaplasma ovis, Eimeria spp., Toxoplasma gondii, Giardia intestinalis,Sarcocystis spp., Cryptosporidium parvum, Ehrlichia ovina, E. granulosus, helminths: flatworms: Fasciola hepatica, Fasciola gigantica, Fascioloides magna, Dicrocoelium dendriticum, Schistosoma bovis; tapeworms: Echinococcus granulosus, Taenia ovis, Taenia hydatigena, Moniezia spp.; roundworms: (including Hoose (disease)) Elaeophora schneideri, Haemonchuscontortus, Trichostrongylus spp.,Teladorsagia spp., Cooperia spp., Nematodirus spp., Dictyocaulus filaria, Protostrongylus refescens, Muellerius capillaris,Oesophagostomum spp., Neostrongylus linearis, Chabertia ovina, Trichuris ovis Prions: scrapie. Blue tongue virus; Viruses: foot-and-mouth disease, bluetongue disease, maedi-visna, orf, tick-borne encephalomyelitis, peste-des-petits-ruminants virus, sheep pox and goat pox; Bacteria: blackleg, foot rot, caprine pleuropneumonia, contagious bovine pleuropneumonia, chlamydiosis, Johne's disease,listeriosis, fleece-rot, funguses, facial eczema, parasites.

Brucellosis is also called undulant fever is caused by Brucella spp, is highly contagious, caused by skin contact with infected cattle, goats, pigs and sheep or eating raw meat or unpasteurised cheese or drinking unpasteurized infected milk. It causes abortions in cattle, sheep, mares, a wasting disease in chickens; It causes undulant fever in man, headaches, chills, muscle aches and pain. These symptoms persist for years.

In these modern times slaughterhouses are tightly controlled with slaughter legislation to prevent unnecessary suffering of animals. Stunning avoids unnecessary suffering. Orthodox Jewish and Muslim dietary laws forbid the consumption of meat from an animal that is not "healthy and moving" when killed. This would prevent eating the flesh of an animal that is sick or found dead. Stunning is thought to cause injury prior to cutting the throat and is therefore unacceptable, because the animal is not "healthy and moving" before throat is slit. Killing is supposed to be carried out with a single cut with a sharp knife aimed at the jugular and carotid veins. At the time when this method was laid down in Jewish law it was more human than any other available method. Now it is less human than modern methods.

Alcohol and gambling are not allowed. They ask you (O Muhammad) concerning `alcoholic drink` and `gambling`. First Allah sent this verse (Surat 2:219), "They ask you about wine and gambling. Say, "In them is great sin and (yet, some) benefit for people. But their sin is greater than their benefit." And they ask you what they should spend. Say, "The excess (beyond needs)." Thus, Allah makes clear to you the verses (of revelation) that you might give thought. "In them is a great damage, and (some) benefit for men, but the sin of them is greater than their benefit." So, the first rule regarding alcohol: there is a damage, and a benefit, but the damage is much greater. Then Allah sent another verse, making drinking alcohol more strict "O you who believe! Approach not As-Salat (the prayer) when you are in a drunken state until you know (the meaning) of what you utter" Surah Nisa (4:43). This means: never go to Salat (that is Islamic prayer) while you are drunk, because you have to perfectly understand what you are saying. The ultimate forbidding of drinking alcohol is Surah Maida 5:90-91, "O you who have believed, indeed, intoxicants, gambling, (sacrificing on) stone alters (to other than Allah), and divining arrows are but defilement from the work of Satan, so avoid it that you may be successful."

Hand shaking. The social practice of hand shaking is not allowed because men cannot touch women who are not in their family. This goes against western social norms where hand shaking is not only an accepted social behaviour but is infact regarded as a fundamental social necessity as in Switzerland.

Human forms are forbidden. Saudi Arabia issued fatwa against snowmen.

Pictures. Every maker of pictures will go to the fire, where a being will be set upon him for each picture he made, to torment him in hell; Pictures imitate the creative act of Allah (when they are of animate beings). It is unlawful to decorate walls with pictures (generally interpreted as pictures of animate beings).

Co habiting. Living with your boyfriend/girlfriend before getting married is illegal.

Aversion of the cross http://en.islamtoday.net/node/1663: Staurophobia. Example: A blogger asked: "There is a small cross in the lower left-hand corner of my cell phone display screen. It is very small and is camouflaged by a small crescent that covers it. Are we allowed to carry such a cell phone in our pockets? Can we enter the mosque carrying it?" It is well-known in Islamic Law that it is not permissible for a Muslim to wear a cross or wear clothing that is decorated by a cross. Some Muslims are forced to flee from their country because of war, travel to Europe on a forged passport showing a European nationality and wear a cross so that airport employees do not have any doubts. However, it is prohibited to wear a cross because it is a symbol of Christianity unless the person fears imprisonment. "Whoever imitates a people is one of them" Narrated Abu Dawood 4031.

Colours. Aversion of the colour yellow. Green is the colour for Islam. The colour green is associated with the green colour of Muhammed's turban. The colours that were restricted in Islam are Red, yellow and saffron which were used in pagan times. Sura al-Kahf 18:31, "Theirs will be gardens of Eden, wherein rivers flow beneath them, therein they will be given armlets of gold, and will wear green robes of fine silk and gold embroidery, reclining upon throne therein."

Dogs are not allowed. Narrated Abu Talha: The Prophet said, "Angels do not enter a house that has either a dog or a picture in it." Sahih al-Bukhari, book 59, hadith 128/ no 3322 "The Prophet said. 'Angels do not enter a house which has a dog or a picture of a dog in it." Someone asked Abu Tharr, "What feature is there in a black dog which distinguish it from the red dog and the yellow dog?" He said: "O, son of my brother, I asked the Messenger of Allah as you are asking me, and he said: The black dog is a devil." (Muslim, 4:299). There was a tradition that a black dog is a devil (Schacht 2011 pg146).

Music and dancing are not allowed by Sharia. Musical instruments are condemned: One should know that singing or listening to singing is offensive (with the exception of songs that encourage piety).

Eating lizards is not allowed. The Prophet prohibited eating lizards because they might be a lost tribe changed into animals. Schacht (2011) pg146.

Choice of clothing in Islam. Mukhtar Aziz in "The Social and the religious in contemporary Islamic Life". Some new converts to Islam confuse the requirements regarding clothing and gave an example. A new convert was asked why he is dressed like that. He replied that it is an Islamic attire requirement. Aziz explained that, no, it was traditional Pakistani attire. Similarly the burqa is a Saudi and the niqab is aYemeni social traditional attire in the Gulf and Afgahnistan respectively. Azis explains that most Muslim scholars and theologians reject the Bedouin postulation that wearing the niqab is mandatory. Aziz explains: if this is Islamic attire, how would one define the saris worn by Muslim women in Sri Lanka, Mauritania and Sudan and the wide variations worldwide? Aziz explains that the accepted Islamic scholars (faqihs) and Islamic law (fiqh) academics reject the attire of the burqa as a religious obligation.

Renting property. Renting an apartment to two Christian women and a Christian man who is not related to them is not allowed because this is regarded as illicit sex (al-Maaidah 5:2). The rent contract is invalid. The rent must be given to charity as it is regarded as unlawful rent. Similarly renting a premesis to make or sell wine is not permissible.

Personal Hygiene. Hygiene is a religious obligation in Islam. The laws on hygiene are clear and carry a punishment in hell if not adhered to. Personal hygene is a religious requirement. Personal Hygiene is described in the four volumes of Sahih Bukhari. By making it a religious requirement, Muslims are put under mandatory pressure to clean themselves. Cleanliness in Islam is of Three Kinds: (1) Purification from impurity (i.e. to attain purity or cleanliness, by taking a bath (ghusl) or performing ablution (wudoo) in states in which a bath or ablution is necessary or desirable according to Islamic Law; (2) To cleanse one's body, dress or place from an impurity of filth; (3) To remove the dirt or grime that collects in various parts of the body, such as cleaning the teeth and nostrils, the trimming of nails and the removing of armpit and pubic hair. Cleanliness is referred to as "purification" and is required before prayer. "Aisha described how Muhammad answered the call of nature: "The Prophet used his right hand for getting water for ablution and taking food, and his left hand for his evacuation and for anything repugnant" reported in the Sunan of Abu Dawud. Abu Hurairah reported "The Messenger of Allah said: 'Be on your guard against two things which provoke cursing." They (the Companions present there) said: "Messenger of Allah, what are those things which provoke cursing?" He said: "Easing on the thoroughfares or under the shades (where people take shelter and rest)" Reported by Muslim.

"O you who believe! When you intend to offer prayer, wash your faces and your hands (forearms) up to the elbows, rub (by passing wet hands over) your heads, and (wash) your feet up to ankles. If you are in a state of Janaba (i.e. post sexual relations), purify yourself (bathe your whole body)" (Al-Ma'idah 5:6). "Truly, Allah loves those who turn unto Him in repentance and loves those who purify themselves (by taking a bath and cleaning and washing thoroughly their private parts, bodies, for their prayers etc.)" (Al Baqarah 2:222).

Volume 1, Book 5, Number 292: Narrated Ubai bin Kab, "I asked Allah's Apostle about a man who engages in sexual intercourse with his wife but does not discharge. He replied, "He should wash the parts which comes in contact with the private parts of the woman, perform ablution and then pray." Abu 'Abdullah said, "Taking a bath is safer and is the last order."

Certain aspects of personal hygiene are a pre-requisite to performing such duties as prayers and fasting. For example, one must do ablution (Wudhu) before the daily prayers, which is the formal washing of the face, hands and forearms. One of the criteria for cleanliness is washing after the use of the lavatories.

Ghusl is a formal head-to-toe washing and rinsing, ie when all parts of the body are washed with water, including the mouth and the nose. It is mandatory upon the couple after sexual intercourse, or after ejaculation in the case of men, and after the end of the monthly menstruation period or the postpartum period in the case of women. If one does not perform such mandatory Ghusls no form of any prayers will be valid. A Muslim is even prohibited from reading the Quran, if s/he is required to perform such a Ghusl but has not done so. A Ghusl must also be performed for the body of the deceased before burial. Anyone who comes in contact with a dead body must also perform a Ghusl.

Ghusl is required of every Muslim after sexual intercourse, after wet dreams, after child-birth, and after post-partum bleeding (40-days flow of blood) and each month after menstruation.

If one is required to perform Ghusl but cannot find the water to do so, one is required to perform Tayammum, which is to strike the palms of both hands-on earth, or sand to wipe them over the face and the back of the hands. Tayammum ia a method of purifcation, which does not require water, is used instead of ablution (Wudoo) and Ghusl in certain circumstances (i.e. when no water is available). Allah says in the Quran, "But if you are ill or on a journey or any of you comes from answering the call of nature, or you have been in contact with women (i.e. sexual intercourse) and you find no water, then perform Tayammum with clean earth and rub therewith your faces and hands. Allah does not want to place you in difficulty, but He wants to purify you, and to complete His Favor on you that you may be thankful" (Al-Maidah 5:6). There are other Ghusls which are not mandatory but Muslims are encouraged to do, such as Friday Ghusl, first-day-of-the-month Ghusl, Ghusls for the Eids and various other occasions. The clothing one wears must also be free from any unclean substance, otherwise one's prayer will be invalid if the prayer is performed using those cloths. So, if only one drop of urine is splashed on the cloths, then those clothes may not be worn to perform the prayers unless washed. Examples of unclean substances: Urine, Faeces, Semen, Dead body, Blood, Dog, Pig, Non-believer, Wine, Beer. The cleaning 'agents' or 'process' are such things as: Water, Earth, Exposure to direct Sunlight.

Wudoo is a simple ablution, used to wash parts of the body with water. This simple ablution is necessary before prayer in the following cases: after urinating or defecating; if one breaks wind; if one loses consciousness; if one directly touches the genitals; if one becomes excited, leading to a subsequent discharge. The above cases also nullify one's ablution, requiring a fresh one. Allah says in the Quran: "O you who believe! When you intend to offer prayer, wash your faces and your hands (forearms) up to the elbows, rub (by passing wet hands over) your heads, and (wash) your feet up to ankles. If you are in a state of Janaba, purify yourself (bathe your whole body)," Al-Ma'idah: 6.

Abu Hurairah quoted Allah's Messenger as saying, "The prayer of a person who does hadath (passes, urine, stool or wind) is not accepted until he performs the ablution." A person from Hadaramout asked Abu Hurairah, "What is `hadith`?" Abu Hurairah replied, "Hadath" means the passing of wind from the anus," Sahih Al-Bukhari, Volume 1, Book 4, Number 137.

Part of the merits of ablution is that it earns Muslims a special name by which they will be called on the Day of Judgment; the name is Al-Ghurr-ul-Muhajjalun (People of shinning bodily parts), due to performing ablution in proper way. Nu'aim Al-Mujmir reported: "Once I went up the roof of the mosque along with Abu Hurairah). He performed ablution and said, I heard the Prophet saying: "On the Day of Resurrection, my followers will be called Al-Ghurr-ul-Muhajjalun from the traces of ablution and whoever can increase the area of his radiance should do so (by performing ablution in the most perfect manner," Sahih Al-Bukhari, Vol. 1, Hadith No. 138. Al-Ghurr-ul-Muhajjalun "the parts of the body of the Muslims washed in ablution will shine on the Day of Resurrection and the angels will call them by that name." Narrated Uthman ibn Affan "The Messenger of Allah said: He who performed ablution well, his sins would come out from his body, even coming out from under his nails," Sahih Muslim, Book 2, Number 0476.

Keeping the Fitrah, Prophet said, "From the acts of nature are five: circumcision, removing pubic hairs, trimming the mustache, cutting the nails and plucking the hair from under the armpits," Recorded by al-Bukhari and Muslim. It is not allowed to leave them for more than forty nights. This is based on the Hadith of Anas who said, "The Messenger of Allah set a time limit for us for trimming the mustache, trimming nails, removing armpit hairs and removing pubic hairs. They cannot be left for more than forty nights," Recorded by Muslim. Letting them grow long resembles animals and some of the disbelievers.

Sexual etiquette. There is much sexual etiquette that is observed by Muslims, as taught by Islam, where some of them are obligatory and some are desirable. Sex outside marriage is forbidden, and within marriage man and woman may not engage in sexual intercourse when the woman is going through her monthly menstruation period or during postpartum period, or the first minimum period of ten days after childbirth, preferably this period should be up to 40 days after childbirth, this is to ensure the health recovery of the mother. Sex between spouses is forbidden when one is fasting and for a number of particular days when s/he on the Hajj pilgrimage in Makkah (Mecca).

Sex is regarded as a polluting activity which requires washing to get rid of the impurity and become pure again "If ye are polluted then purify yourselves" (Q 5:9). Major pollution such as sexual contact, emission of sperm (and female discharge thought to happen during sexual intercourse), mensuration, after childbirth, requires washing the whole body. The Prophet said "He who leaves but one hair unwashed on his body will be punished in hell accordingly" Minor pollution means that the person cannot pray or touch the Quran. During mensuration a woman is impure and cannot fast, pray, touch the Quran or enter a mosque because of her impurity. A hadith illuminates: "The prophet said, If anyone of you rouses from sleep and performs the ablution, he should wash his nose by putting water in it and then blowing it out thrice, because Satan has stayed in the upper part of his nose all the night." In Western democracies the need to wash oneself is based on scientific knowledge and hygiene and does not need threats of going to hell. There are prophetic traditions and teachings about days of the month when one is recommended to have sex and those days that one is recommended not. These teachings and traditions go on to explain how the days on which a woman conceives affect the health and psychology of the child. It is suggested that even the position of the couple during intercourse affects the well being of the child to be, if the woman conceives.

Mensuration. "O Muhammed, they ask you concerning menstruation. Say: it is an impurity, so keep away from women in their menstruation and do not approach them till they are purified" (Surah Baqarah). Therefore, in the light of the Quran and Hadith, to have intercourse during menstruation in not only strictly prohibited, but a major sin. It has been mentioned in another Hadith, "That person who has intercourse with his wife whilst she is menstruating should give half a dinar in charity," Tirmizhi. If the husband in an uncontrollable desire forces his wife to have intercourse even though she is menstruating, it is obligatory for her to refuse. If she does not do so, she will also be sinful. If the woman refuses despite the insistence of her husband, she will not be sinful, rather she will be rewarded for abstaining from sin and causing her husband to do so too. From those sins which Islam has classified as 'major', one of them is having sexual relations in the state of menstruation. If the husband due to his overriding passions finds it difficult to control himself then during the days of menstruation, separate sleeping arrangements should be made. Furthermore, both parties should continue to repent for this sin thus far.

Tomb Worship. Narrated Aishia and Abdullah bin Abbas: "When the last moment of the life of Allah's Apostle came he started putting his Khamisa on his face and when he felt hot and short of breath he took it off his face, "May Allah curse the Jews and Christians for they built the places of worship at the graves of their prophet." Yet Muslims built a mosque on his tomb. His grave became a place for Muslim pilgrims to visit annually. The Prophet's tomb at Medina, is after Mecca, the site most venerated by Muslims.

APPENDIX

Reference: The Quran, English translation by M.A.S. Abdel Haleem, with Parallel Arabic Text. First published in 2004 this book has been acclaimed in avoiding archaism and cryptic language to produce a version that is faithful to the original. The traditional calligraphic pages are displayed alongside the English translation. This translation is approved byAl-Azhar in Cairo, the world's leading authority on Quranic, Islamic and Arabic studies.

Reference: The Quranic Arabic Corpus is an annotated linguistic resource for the Quran. Seven parallel translations in English are given for each verse are provided. Hence one can be assured of the accuracy of the translation. Example, put verse 88:55 in Google, you get seven translations for this verse by renowned authorities, in the website: http://corpus.quran.com/translation.jsp?chapter=8&verse=55.

Examples of References

Quran 47:4 is a reference to Chapter 47 of the Quran, verse 4. Also written as: Sura 47:4.

In this book, reference to the Quran is written as: Quran 47:4; Q 47:4 and 47:4.

Bukhari 1,3,4 is a reference to Sahih Bukhari, Volume 1, book 3 number 4. Sahih means authorative and authentic. Muslim 012,1234 is a reference to Sahih Muslim, book 12, number 1234. Ishaq 123 is a reference to Ishaq`s Sira, margin note 123.

An important source of information are the earliest surviving written *sira* (biographies of Muhammad and quotes attributed to him) in Ibn Ishaq's *Life of God's Messenger* written c. 767 CE (150 AH). This sira was used verbatim at great length by Ibn Hisham and Al-Tabari.

Another important source may be found in hadith collections, accounts of the verbal and physical teachings and traditions of Muhammad. Hadiths were compiled several generations after his death by followers including Muhammad al-Bukhari, Abu Dawood.

Some words are interchangeable. Mecca, Macchah; Medina, Madinah; Quran, Koran are used interchangeably; Muhammed, Mohammed, Muhammad.

Examples of references from Sharia Law.

Example: 09.0 Jihad. Jihad means war against Kafirs to establish Islam. 09.0 is the reference in the Reliance of the traveller.

Example: Dealing with a rebellious wife.m10.12. When a husband notices signs of rebelliousness.... Ishaq 969.... "Men were to lay injunctions on women lightly for they were prisoners of men and had no control over their persons." Sharia reference number m10.12 allows one to read the original reference which is in Ishaq, index number 969, a note that allows one to look at the Sira (Mohammed`s biography, The Life of Muhammed, A. Guillaume) and verify the truth of the reference.

BIBLIOGRAPHY

CHAPTER 1

Ahmed ibn Naqib Al- Misri (Shihabuddin Abu al-'Abbas Ahmad ibn an-Naqib al-Misri (AH 702-769 / AD 1302–1367). *Reliance of the Traveller.* The Classic Manual of Islamic (Sharia) Law (Umdat Al-Salik). Translated by N. Keller (2001) Amana Publications.

Huntington Samuel P., (1993) The Clash of Civilizations? Foreign Affairs Landmark Article, Summer 1993, Journal of Foreign Affairs, USA.

Huntington Samuel (1996). The Clash of Civilizations and the Remaking of World Order. New York: Simon & Schuster.

Ibn Warraq (2003), Why I am not a Muslim. Promethus books New York.

Ibn Warraq (2012), Why West is Best. Galloway Gal.

Kissinger Henry (2014), "World Order" Penguin Random House, UK

Kamguian Azam (2001), Unveiling Islam & Multicultralism: In Defence of Secularism & Universal Women's Rights. CDWRME Publications.

Russel Bertrand (1920), The Practice and Theory of Bolshevism. London.

Schacht Joseph (1964, 1982), An Introduction to Islamic Law. Oxford University press.

Schacht Joseph (1950), Origins of Muhammedan Jurisprudence, Clarendon Press.

Spencer (2009), The Complete Infidel's book on the Koran, Regnery Publishing Inc.

Saifur Rahman Mubarakfuri (2006), The Sealed Nectar, The Life of the Prophet Muhammed.

Speer Albert (1969) Inside the third Reich: Memoirs. translated by Richard and Clara Winston, with an introduction by Eugene Davidson. New York, The Macmillan Company, 1970.

Crozier Michael, Samuel P. Huntington, Joji Watanuki, (1975). The Crisis of Democracy, Report to the Trilateral Commission.

Zaki Ameen (2009), Living by the Point of My Spear.Lightening Source, UK Ltd.

CHAPTER 2

Aishia Bibi (2013). Blasphemy. A Memoir. Sentenced to death over a cup of water. Chicago Press.

Brancati Dawn (2016). Democracy Protests: Origins, Features and Significance. Cambridge University press.

Ibn Ishaq (d773AD), edited by Hisham (d840AD). Translated by Alfred Guillaume (1955). S

Levin Daniel (2009), Denial on Temple Mount, The Forward, Oct 23.

Mc Donald M.V. (1985), The History of Al Tabari: The Foundation of Community translated by M.V. McDonald annotated by W.Montogomery, 1987 Vol V11 p.24-25.

Mohamed A.Z. (2017), Pakistan, Blasphemy Laws, Human rights and Abuses. (on line)

Nosheen Ali (2008), Outrageous State, Sectarianized Citizens: Deconstructing the Textbook Controversy in the Northern Area, Pakistan. Multidisciplinary Academic Journal (online). Cornell University.

Marsha Pripstein Posusney & Michele Penner Angrist, editors (2005). Authoritarianism in the Middle East: Regimes and Resistance.

Schacht Joseph (1982), An Introduction to Islamic Law. Oxford University press.

Samuel P Huntington (1991). The Third Wave.Democratization in the Late Twentieth Century. Norman and London, University of Oklahoma Press.

Sirat Rasulullah, The Life of Muhammed. Oxford University press Karachi, tenth impression Samuel P Huntington (1991). The Third Wave. Democratization in the Late Twentieth Century. Norman and London, University of Oklahoma Press..

Zaki Ameen (2009), Living by the point of my spear. Lightening Source UK.

CHAPTER 3

Azam Kamguian (2005). Unveiling Islam and Multiculturalism. CDWRME.

Al- Misri (Shihabuddin Abu al-'Abbas Ahmad ibn an-Naqib al-Misri (AH 702-769 / AD 1302–1367). Reliance of the Traveller. The Classic Manual of Islamic (Sharia) Law (Umdat Al-Salik). Translated by N. Keller (2001) Amana Publications.

Ibn Ishaq (d773AD), edited by Hisham (d840AD). Translated by Alfred Guillaume (1955). S

Sirat Rasulullah, The Life of Muhammed. Oxford University press Karachi, tenth impression 1995.

Oriana Fallici, (2002) The Rage and the Pride. Universe Publishing.

CHAPTER 4

Ali Unal (2007) IN The Quran (with Annotated Interpretation in Modern English)

Al- Misri (Shihabuddin Abu al-'Abbas Ahmad ibn an-Naqib al-Misri (AH 702-769 / AD 1302–1367). Reliance of the Traveller. The Classic Manual of Islamic (Sharia) Law (Umdat Al-Salik). Translated by N. Keller (2001) Amana Publications.

Ibn Ishaq (d773AD), edited by Hisham (d840AD). Translated by Alfred Guillaume (1955). The Life of Muhammed. Oxford University press

Spencer Robert (2009). The Complete Infidel's Guide to the Quran. Regnery

CHAPTER 5

Ibn Ishaq (d773AD), edited by Hisham (d840AD). Translated by Alfred Guillaume (1955). The Life of Muhammed.

Muhammed Aashiq LLahi Bulandshaahri (2014) Illuminating Discourses on the Quran vol.1.p.502

Al- Misri (Shihabuddin Abu al-'Abbas Ahmad ibn an-Naqib al-Misri (AH 702-769 / AD 1302–1367). *Reliance of the Traveller.* The Classic Manual of Islamic (Sharia) Law (Umdat Al-Salik). Translated by N. Keller (2001) Amana Publications.

CHAPTER 6

Antonie Wessels, (1972), A Modern Arabic Biography of Muhammed,

Robert Spencer (2009), The Complete Infidel's Guide to the Quran. Regnery Publishing, Washington.

CHAPTER 7

Azam Kamguian (2005), Unveiling Islam and Multiculturalism. CDWRME.

Bousquet G.H. (1966), L'Ethique sexuelle de l-Islam. Archives of Sciences and Religions. Paris.

Fallici Oriana (2006), The Force of Reason

Ibn Ishaq (d773AD), edited by Hisham (d840AD). Translated by Alfred Guillaume (1955). The Life of Muhammed. Oxford University press

Ibn Warraq (2003), Why I am not a Muslim. Promethus books New York.

Schacht Joseph, (1982) An Introduction to Islamic Law. Oxford University press

Spencer Robert (2009), The Complete Infidel's Guide to the Quran. Regnery Publishing, Washington.

Zaki Ameen (2009), Living at the Point of my Spear,

CHAPTER 8

Santillana David (1938), Istituzioni di diritto musulmano malichita con riguardo anche al sistema sciafiita, 2 vols., Rome.

CHAPTER 9

Kamguian Azam (2001), Unveiling Islam and Multiculturalism: In Defence of Secularism & Universal Women's Rights. CDWRME Publications.

Schacht Joseph (1950), Origins of Muhammedan Jurisprudence, Clarendon Press.

CHAPTER 10

Further Reading

Bridget Gabriel (2008), They Must Be Stopped: Why We Must Defeat Radical Islam and How We Can Do It. St. Martin's Press.

Don Richardson (2008), The Secrets of the Quran. Published by Regal Books.

Emmet Scott, (2014), The Impact of Islam, paperback. Published by the New University press Review.

Francis Fukuyama (1992), The End of History and the Last Man.

Jake Neuman (2015), Killing the Quran.

M.A. Khan (2009), Islamic Jihad. A Legacy of Forced Conversion, Imperialism and Slavery. iUniverse, Inc New York.

Marsha, ed., Pripstein Posusney & Michele Penner Sngrist. (2005), Authoritarianism in the Middle east: Regimes and Resistance, Lynne Rienner Publishers.

Patricia Crone (1987), Meccan Trade and the Rise of Islam.

Robert Spencer (2014), Arab Winter Comes to America: The Truth about the War We're in.

Robert Spencer (2005), The Myth of Islamic Tolerance: How Islamic Law Treats Non-Muslims. Prometheus Books.

Robert Spencer (), Islam: Religion of Bigots.

Rebecca Bynum (2011), Allah is Dead: Why Islam is Not a Religion Perfect, Paperback

Setyn Mark, (2006), America alone. Regnery Publishing.

Susan Cartland (2017), Women, Faith and sexism – fighting HISLAM. Melbourne University Press.

Tom Haydan, (2012), Inspiring participatory democracy. Paradigm Publishers

Tony Blankly, (2006), The West's last chance:Will we win the Clash of Civilizations? Regnery Publishing.

Wafa Sultan (2011), A God who Hates Saint Martin's Griffin

WEBSITES

https:// https://edition.cnn.com/world
https://www.huffingtonpost.com
https://www.theguardian.com/world/2017
http://www.bbc.com/news/world
https://corpus.quran.com/translation
https://www.thereligionofpeace.com
https://www.answering-islam.org/responses
https://www.westminster-institute.org
https://www.centerforenquiry.net
https://www.gatestoneinstitute.org
https://www.answering-islam.org
http://www.nairaland.com/2674968/did-muhammed-curse-muslims
https://www.israelnationalnews.com/Articles/Article.aspx/1931
http://www.ahlalhdeeth.com/vbe/help

PRIMARY SOURCES:

1. The Quran, N.J. Dawood's translation;
2. The Hadith collection of Bukhari. This collection of stories / traditions is the second most important set of books in Islam. It follows the Quran.
3. The Hadith collection of Muslim, (third most important set of writings).
4. The Hadith collection of Abu Dawud.
5. The biography of Muhammad, known as "Sirat Rasulallah", written by Ibn Ishaq, and translated by A. Guillaume as "The Life of Muhammad," (the most authentic biography of Muhammed's life).
6. The biographical material found in Ibn Sa'd's "Kitab al-Tabaqat al-Kabir" (Book of the Major Classes), translated by S. Moinul Haq.
7. The History of Tabari. This 39 volume set is almost finished being translated by a collection of both Muslim and non-Muslim scholars.

Printed in the United States
By Bookmasters